My life as a Gypsy woman in Slovakia

When the Russians came, old Cibrikaňa said: "It's the end of the war, we've survived. After every darkness comes the dawn. But after every dawn also comes the darkness. Who knows what's in store for us."

In reply my mother said: "And after that darkness comes the dawn, and then another darkness, and then another dawn, it's all in God's hands, and we have to have hope."

The *Interface Collection*, coordinated and developed by the Gypsy Research Centre at the Université René Descartes, Paris, is published with the support of the European Commission.

Some Collection titles receive Council of Europe support for distribution in Central and Eastern Europe.

The views expressed in this work are the authors', and do not necesarily reflect those of the publisher nor of the Gypsy Research Centre or its research groups (historians, linguists, education specialists etc.).

Director of the *Interface Collection*: Jean-Pierre Liégeois
Text Editors: Alice Bialestowski and Astrid Thorn Hillig

Original title: *Narodila jsem se pod šťastnou hvězdou*
English translation © 1999 by Carleton Bulkin
Cover: Emmanuel Gonnet / Desartes
Photograph by Irena Stelhi: Portrait of Ilona Lacková, 1984
DTP: Frédérique Vilain - GD Infographie

© 1999
Centre de recherches tsiganes (Gypsy Research Centre) and
University of Hertfordshire Press
University of Hertfordshire
College Lane
Hatfield - Hertfordshire
AL109AB - UK
Tel. +44 1707 284654
Fax +44 1707 284666
Internet: UHPress@herts.ac.uk
Web address: http://www.herts.ac.uk/UHPress

© 1999
ISBN 1-902806-00-X

Published 2000

Printed in Great Britain by J. W. Arrowsmith Limited, Bristol

Ilona Lacková

A false dawn

My life as a Gypsy woman in Slovakia

Recorded, translated from Romani and edited
by Milena Hübschmannová

Translated from Czech by Carleton Bulkin

Centre de recherches tsiganes
University of Hertfordshire Press

In 1954 Milena Hübschmannová (b. 1933), then a student of Indian languages at Charles University, Prague, turned her attentions to researching one of these, Romani, among its speakers in the Gypsy quarters. There she met Ilona Lacková, and the two have been close friends ever since.

In 1976 Milena began tape recording Ilona's account of her fascinating life every time the two of them were able to get together, be it in Prague or Prešov (500 km apart). Eight years later, Milena began selecting passages from the hundreds and hundreds of pages transcribed from these recordings. She then translated these excerpts from Romani to Czech and put them together into a coherent narrative – a task made simple by the fact that Ilona is an excellent storyteller.

The resulting life story was ready for publication by 1986, but under the Communist regime it was impossible to find a publisher willing to take on a book presenting an authentic Gypsy viewpoint at odds with the authorities' version of reality. After 1989, it was the market economy and rising anti-Gypsy racism that put potential publishers off the project.

Ilona Lacková was born in 1921. She still goes round the schools telling children about the Roma, and she is still writing stories. Milena Hübschmannová teaches Romani language and culture at Charles University in Prague.

Contents

To Ústí nad Labem and my studies at the university

Postscript

Foreword

Milena Hübschmannová

I have begun to write a foreword to Elena Lacko's stories several times now, and each time I have come to a halt in the middle. What can I say about Roma better than the song of a lone Romani woman's life experience? I will try once more – at least so I can tell how this book came about.

I first went to visit Elena as a student of Hindi, fascinated by the similarity of the Romani language to its linguistic relatives, despite being separated by a thousand years and thousands of kilometers from its ancient Indian homeland. At that time, Romani was not taught on the hallowed grounds of any institution. Only in 1976 did it take hold in the Language School in Prague by stealth, and since 1991 it has been taught as a full-fledged university subject at the Philosophical Faculty of Charles University. I learned it from the Romani families I met on the streets of Prague, who willingly and lovingly confided their *romipen* – their cultural treasures – to me.

One of them was Ilona Lacko. (Elena is her official name, and Ilona or Ilonka is her Romani name. Her last name is pronounced LATS-ko, and its feminine form in Czech and Slovak is "Lacková".) Her name inspired the hope that she would lead the Romani people out of the closed circle of incomprehension between Roma and *gadže* (non-Roma). Lacko wrote the first Romani play and rehearsed it with her relatives in the shanties of a Gypsy settlement; she was written of with admiration in the newspapers and raised *romipen* from the mud of ignorant condescension.

I hitch-hiked to Prešov in order to see her. It was dark when I arrived. The first group of Roma whom I greeted with a request, stammered in Romani, that they show me where Lacko lived, led me right below the window of her apartment. There was light in the ground floor window of the old house. My new acquaintances knocked on the window of the old house.

"We've brought a girl to see you," they said in response to the question *K'oda?* (Who is it?) and left. A young, very dark woman who seemed indescribably beautiful to me came to open the door. She invited me in and into the kitchen. Her apartment at that time was a little kitchen and a tiny room. In the room there were four children sleeping. Her husband was not at home. On the kitchen table Ilona had various papers spread out. She did not ask me who I was, what I was, why I had come. Her first question was: *Na sal bokhaľi?* (Are you hungry?). An indispensable part of Romani welcoming rites. Without even waiting for an answer, she began to clean some potatoes. And then – I can see it as if it were today – I went with absolute confidence to the sideboard, took out a knife, and peeled potatoes with her. Ilona also remembers this time. Of that first meeting she once commented: *akorestar sam amare* (from that moment on we were fast friends).

I began to travel to see Ilona regularly, alone or with trusted friends. I am indebted to her for innumerable nights' lodging. She took me around the 'Gypsy settlements.' I later saw such material poverty only in the slums of the Indian poor on the outskirts of Bombay or Calcutta. As there, those 'of nobler birth' never deigned to set foot in a 'Gypsy settlement.' Many of the settlements were huddled in the forests, far from the towns, where the Fascist laws of the wartime Slovak state had driven them. Incredible structures of makeshift shanties made from incredible materials, in some places mere bunkers – a hole dug out of the earth, with a canopy of sod like a great doghouse, clay instead of a floor, some sackcloth instead of a door, and often the only piece of furniture was a stove.

People drank water directly from the stream; there was no electricity and no plumbing. No one who has grown up from birth in a real apartment can easily imagine that pulling a handle so it doesn't fall off, turning off the water so as not to ruin the gasket, and pulling the flush chain on a toilet so it doesn't snap in two are not 'inborn talents.' Anyone who has mastered this myriad of supposedly simple tasks associated with living in an apartment had to learn them. From a young age, day after day. How many times does a child reaching for a handle, opening or closing a door, turning off the water hear: "Don't slam the door! Don't yank the handle off! Don't turn the water tap so tight! Don't smudge that, don't dirty that, don't pull that!"

Roma have never had an actual territory from which would grow illusions, cultivated for generations, of the immutability of material values, or the idea that not folding your linens carefully in the laundry room, smudging the bathroom wallpaper and damaging the floor are greater wrongs than not giving a child a kind word or a smile for no reason and no purpose, just out of happiness that he or she is in the world.

Later, when well-paid Czech and Slovak recruiters brought the first 'Gypsies' to Bohemia as an indispensable labor force on construction sites and to dig trenches, these people from the bunkers were housed in villas abandoned by Sudeten Germans expelled after the war. As a result, in the eyes of the *gadže* all Gypsies were barbarians who tore down the wallpaper, burned the window frames and the door frames and demolished apartments.

In no settlement, of course, even in the 'worst' ones, were all 'Gypsies the same.' Everywhere, literally everywhere, there were to be found two or three families who tried with all their might to get out of the frightening material poverty of the settlements. The men earned money by the backbreaking labor of digging trenches, where no one else wanted to work, the family became better off, and they earned the money to build or buy a house. Some pulled it off but how many were there who wanted to and could have and yet were not given the opportunity? The ideological leadership of contemporary majority society has branded Roma "citizens of Gypsy origin," "a social group with a dying ethnic identity and a backward culture," people who must be uprooted from "undesirable concentrations of Gypsies and dispersed among other citizens," so they might be easily re-educated. For example, under Communism, directive number 502 from 1965 prevented Roma from building houses in Gypsy settlements because those settlements were supposed to be liquidated by 1980. (To this day there are more than 300 Gypsy settlements in Slovakia, some newly created, two or three kilometers from a town.) The same directive does not permit a town to have more than five per cent "citizens of Gypsy origin." They were allowed to move to Bohemia only within the framework of an organized dispersal, with selected families sent to selected localities. Many times Lacko – and I was present, thanks to her – had to deal with the case of a desperate family which had invested their hard-earned money into building a house in the settlement and, when it was almost finished, the structure was bulldozed to the ground and the rest of their savings went to pay a fine for "building without a permit."

Many times I was there when a Gypsy began to build in a village, with the permission of the National Committee, and what he put up by day was destroyed at night by "unknown perpetrators" for whom it was simply unimaginable that "white" people would have to put up with a Gypsy in their midst. After some time the Gypsy usually gave up, got over the loss of the money wasted and headed back to the settlement. In some cases Lacko "won." But even where she won in court, the Romani plaintiff never dared to build opposite a fortress of "white" hatred. On one hand, many Roma who wanted out of the settlements and had the money to do so were forced by a "collective solution" to persist in the material poverty of the settlement. On the other hand, many of those who did not want to and did not have the money were forcefully moved into apartment buildings, where they were completely at sea. In no time at all, all Gypsies were accused of destroying apartments.

In the settlements where Lacko took me, I not only experienced shock at the material poverty, of course. I also entered a trance, an experience that an overly technological, overly rational, institutionalized, alienated *gadžo* society cannot offer, the sense of going on a journey to "the three worlds." Leading me there were Romani tales, told in a shanty where the audience, squeezed in up against one another, experienced together the victory of good over evil, the radiance of wishes come true, gladness from harmony, unity and peace. The songs pealed from one shanty or another without interruption, with the intense reality of other worlds, the beauty and harmony of "other worlds", permeated with the respect, wisdom, and beauty of the cultured Romani word and the everyday life of this material world. Even in the boisterous arguments conducted with florid curses could the deep hinterland of reciprocity, solidarity and support in unity be sensed.

That is how I met the Roma whose life was still conducted by the law of *romipen* – Romani tradition, culture and language. Thanks to Ilona Lacko I met these Roma frequently. Forty years of harsh, assimilationist, manipulative policy have made barbaric inroads into the "three worlds" of the Roma. Above all, the loud slogans but also certain aspects of social policy opened a "historical opportunity" to "citizens of Gypsy origin" – the gate to a prestigious, promised land, to white majority society. Naturally, they were allowed to tread here only on the assumption that they would leave their language at the customs house – their "Gypsy cant", their ethnic identity, their "backward culture which holds them back from civilization", their family ties, their community solidarity, everything which in the least recalled their "Gypsy way of life." Children were forbidden to speak Romani in the schools. I personally came into contact with enterprising teachers who collected a one-crown fine for every "Gypsy" word. In one children's home I saw children shaved completely bald as a punishment for speaking the Gypsy language. The helpless, uncomprehending children then found the traditional contempt of their white fellow pupils augmented by their evident "mental retardation" and they were transferred *en masse* to special schools.

Of course, I also spoke with enlightened teachers who were learning Romani in secret and did everything to welcome their Romani pupils in accordance with the celebrated heritage of Comenius, "teacher of the nations." One of those enlightened teachers, a Mr. Šimek from Kežmarok, said: "It's just that Gypsy children feel like they're at their stepmother's when they're in school. No wonder they don't want to go!" And when Romani children didn't go to school the social workers came accompanied by the police and their Alsatians and took them out of their "backward environment" to be re-educated into "socialist man."

Until recently Romani children comprised 80 per cent of the occupants of children's homes. When the desperate parents defied authority, perhaps with a knife in their hands, they found themselves in a corrective institution for attacking a public official. So it was in the 1950s when, for all Roma who were governed by traditional *romipen,* the child was their greatest and most sacred possession, when a Romani woman who abandoned her child was spat upon and excommunicated, when a father who drank his money away confessed his shame in public in song. Of course, within two generations it was possible to subvert the Romani community, family, and personality in such a way that many mothers who have lost the Romani ethic and have not acquired the ethic of the *gadže* leave their children in orphanages without anyone forcing them to do so.

On crossing the border between the "old, backward way of life" and the "new, socialist society" Roma also had to put aside their honored, traditional crafts. This measure affected everyone, but it was a double blow to the Roma, because vocationally they were not prepared to succeed in jobs other than as completely unskilled laborers. For them, even these jobs represented a new life that was demanding, exhausting, often incomprehensible: a change in the rhythm of the day, work tempo, proficiency and values. A Romani musician who played like Paganini had to "put aside his bow and take up a pick-axe". Since he could not read music and did not know who Marx and Engels were he did not have the background to pass the state licensing exams to become even a bar-room performer. Basket-weavers and blacksmiths had to cease plying their trade if they did not want to be labelled "private entrepreneurs, remnants of capitalism." The right to work became for many an unbearable obligation, and anyone who failed to fulfil it went through the gate of socialism straight to the gate of a corrective institution. And yet a number of Roma, far more than non-Roma are able and willing to accept, "harnessed themselves to labor" and "did honest work" – to use the high-flown terminology of an earlier time. They "made it," they "integrated," they established themselves. By the showy, ostentatious material values which they had learned from the *gadže* to appreciate, even to overrate, they strove to prove that gypsies were not dirty, disorderly, ragged and smelly. Those who previously stole potatoes from the peasants' fields out of hunger ceased stealing. Many became familiar with their *gadžo* neighbors, co-workers and fellow pupils. The absurd thing is that the democratic regime which followed, which released Roma from the correctional institutions, recognising that they had been put there for not being willing or able to work, now locks them up again because yet again they have taken up the bad habit of stealing, because they have been fired from their job and getting a new one is practically impossible for them as Gypsies (today called Roma).

And if today they arrive in prison for other reasons – for burglary, fraud, acts of violence – is that not merely a natural retaliation for signs like "Death to Gypsies," "Vietnamese Go Back To Vietnam, Roma Go Back to India," "Gypsies to the Gas

Chamber," "We Don't Serve Gypsies" and so on? The worst aspect is that this retaliation – out of helplessness and powerlessness – is never inflicted on the original perpetrator but on the "opposing side" as a whole. And thus the vicious circle of mutual antagonism, misunderstanding, and incomprehension between the powerful majority and the minority continues to spin. And thus the ancient saying *Rom Romeha – gadžo gadžeha* (Rom with Rom, *gadžo* with *gadžo*) – a mild counterpart to the general *gadžo* conceptions that gypsies (today called Roma) are criminals and barbarians – gets in the way of people of good will who would be happy to work toward a mutual understanding.

None of the changes in *gadžo* society that the Roma have experienced in the last thousand years in Europe nor any change of regime, of which Ilona has personally experienced several, has meant true equality for Roma and truly equal civic opportunities. And for this reason Roma react to the promises of a better future, which every regime makes using its own terminology, with a logical and understandable schizophrenia: on the one hand, they try to take advantage of those promises as best they can – the basic need of a person, and of any living organism, not to be hungry, exhausted and downtrodden, to occupy a suitable place in a larger whole, and to realize his own individuality. On the other hand, the experience of majority *gadžo* society – in the grip of ethnocentrism's clamor and a psychological complex by which it is convinced of civilization's superiority – always turning promises of a better future against Roma, has taught Roma not to believe those promises, much less to consider them a sacred symbol of identification with the state – with which, in reality, they would so gladly identify.

This historical experience, encoded in collective memory, led Ilona Lacko to give ear to the Communist call: "Citizens of Gypsy origin, come join us!" In the 1950s many Communists meant this call sincerely. By then, they had struggled together with Roma in the Slovak National Uprising against the Nazis and hidden together with Romani partisans in the forests. Together with Roma they had endured the slights and the hardships caused by the Hlinka Guards, a paramilitary group during the wartime Slovak state. For Roma these calls were like a salve on the awful suffering they had lived through under Fascism: concentration camps where a half million European Roma had perished, the hunger, poverty, and beatings in the forced labor camps, the forced resettlements from towns, the humiliation and the mockery. Their faith in Communism was also reinforced by the fact that the soldiers of the Red Army, among whom were Georgians and Uzbeks, members of non-Russian nationalities, did not hesitate to enter the "Gypsy camps," to embrace and rejoice with Roma and to let them eat their fill from their rations. This was an unheard-of act from *gadže*. That respect evoked astonishment. Those Roma who had a broader outlook, like Ilona Lacko, then found out that in the Soviet Union there was the first, and at that time the only, Romani theater, Romen, that literature written in Romani had been published there in the 1930s. Through the journalism of Egon Erwin Kisch it came to be known that there were prosperous Romani collective farms, and Ilona corresponded with a Romani university lecturer in pedagogy from Moscow, Roman Demeter. Later when the Communist party, making use of her intelligence, abilities and unbelievable energy, helped her to complete her education, to become an example of a "model socialist citizen of Gypsy origin," the historical mistrust of any *gadžo* regime retreated to the background and Ilona began to hope that socialism would accept Roma among other human beings. In the first years of our friendship I hoped for the same. We considered the poverty of the settlements as "remnants of capitalism" (which in a way it was) due to the intransigence of functionaries, the ignorance and limitations of individuals (which in a way it was), and the ill-will of the police (an offense against socialism) would be punished in no time "by the authorities." The two of us strove to inform both individuals and society which, we were convinced, "was striving honestly to make the slogans and ideas of socialism and the equality of peoples and races a reality," yet again and again rendered Roma unequal. Ilona, who had personally experienced hunger and poverty, worked harder than anyone else so that Roma could get out of the mud and filth of the settlements.

At first I suspected rather than knew consciously that the greatest crime – which would become apparent only in later generations – was the killing of the Romani culture and language. Perhaps it was an emotional awareness, because that culture had given me something I didn't get elsewhere: a kindly personal interest, an unselfish hospitality without the expectation of a "payback", a respect that I may have gained partly by my own respect for Roma; and there were also forays into those imaginative, non-material dimensions of which I previously had no inkling. Nothing bad ever happened to me among Roma, I was never "robbed" and no one refused me help when I needed it. As I have said, at that time I suspected rather than knew that with the loss of the language, to which were linked all the verbal artistry that daily recalled these humane values, with the disintegration of the community which was careful to preserve respect and ethical standards, Roma would be driven into a cultural and ethical vacuum from which there was no way out except into corrective institutions. The taking away of one set of values does not mean the automatic acceptance of another, as the ideologues of socialism imagined.

As time progressed, both Ilona and I began to see and understand that the ignorance of *gadže* about Romani culture was not a question of individuals lacking information but the basic beliefs of the system, the program of socialism, a planned ethnocide regulated by guidelines both public and secret. Nonetheless, we continued to strive to discredit this ethnocidal program. It brought us both the label of "bourgeois Gypsy nationalist." What was funny was that Lacko was not "bourgeois" and I was not a "Gypsy." On the other hand, I would distort the truth greatly if I did not mention that in spite of this official label there were always brave individuals to be found, both among Communists and functionaries, who carried out some small ethical or ethnic justice: they intervened in the removal of children to institutions and released them to their families, they struggled through courses in the Romani language for teachers who could not communicate with their Romani pupils, they gave permission for Romani musical ensembles. Despite the fact that this was during the time of the toughest assimilation policy, they permitted an "ideologically harmful" action which drew attention to the irreplaceable social function of the Romani culture and language. They semi-illegally put out a small bi-lingual collection of Romani poetry, punished an employee who acted unjustly and brutally against Roma, and similar actions. These were drops of rain falling on the desert, but even these collossally strengthened the hope that humanity would someday progress not only technologically but also ethically.

After several years of intensive meetings, Ilona and I gradually stopped seeing each other. Not because we had become estranged. I never felt that there was a racial or ethnic barrier between us. It is true that certain of Ilona's statements were alien to me, and that it took time for me to come to know her well enough to understand her. It sometimes seemed funny to me that she would apply a cream to herself so she wouldn't be so black – while in the meantime I would spend hours lying out in the sun so I could become a little bit blacker. It seemed unbelievable to me that, contrary to her lifelong efforts and activity, she would sometimes deny that she was a Rom. Of course, from my side it was simply an unbelievable lack of comprehension, an inability to empathize with the situation of a Rom who did not steal, did not burn the floors, did not change money on the black market, who sent her children to school, worked, and yet read in the newspapers day after day that Gypsies or Roma stole, robbed, changed money illegally, destroyed flats, and did not go to work; of a Rom who, at every step on the street, felt the disdainful glances of "white" people, who on every street corner read "Death to Gypsies." Of course, Ilona is one of those Roma for whom the protective mimicry of *gadžo* ways was momentary. She always came back home to her Romani ways and to her efforts to ensure them their place in the sun.

If Ilona and I stopped seeing each other, it was because I was busy with a family and with work and couldn't make the trip to Prešov as I could during my student years. She was in the same position. Sometimes she stopped by when she was enrolled in culture and journalism correspondence courses through the university in Prague. Then we didn't see each other again for years, although distances of space and time did not divide us.

I began going to see Ilona again in 1976 when I was forced (but also chose) to strike out on my own. I found that Ilona was a widow. She was also on her own – in other words, retired. She was doing piece work for the Dopleta company which, in addition to filling knitting orders, also did photographic enlargements and colorizing: wedding photos, graduation photos, photographs of sons in the army and daughters in ballroom dancing classes. Marvelous pieces of kitsch. Ilona traveled around different villages by bus with portfolios of samples and collected orders. I started travelling with her as before when I was younger, not hitch-hiking this time but in a faithful, dilapidated old car. And Ilona told stories. She told stories about things she didn't talk about when her husband was alive. Nothing bad – just a more objective evaluation of her own life. It was fantastic and I began to record it all. We recorded for whole, long evenings, a week, ten days; for the entire time I lived – understandably – at her place.

When I first put a microphone in front of Ilona, she had a tendency to speak in Slovak. She speaks excellent, cultivated Slovak, without the least "Gypsy" accent, has a large vocabulary, and yet it wasn't quite right. When she spoke Romani, every word, every turn of phrase, every sentence reflected the way her being was saturated with the reality of which she told. Not the least little word, no note in her intonation was superfluous, empty, or out of place. And her Slovak, whether spoken or written – Ilonka, don't be angry with me, this was occasionally true – is sometimes too rich, too expressive. It was sometimes touching how those political phrases of which she had not quite got the hang, or the feeling for, mingled with the language of the popular literature that accompanied the years of Ilonka's girlhood. It had its magic, yet it was an unintended one which might have amused intellectuals but would distort Ilona's image.

As time goes on, I become more and more convinced that language – whether *gadžo* speech or Romani – also works for Roma as a trigger-signal which opens the door to the *gadžo* or the Romani part of their bi-cultural personality. This is probably the way it is – not only for Roma but for any bi-lingual population. The Romani part has been developed for hundreds or thousands of years. That ordered, harmonious, beautiful *romipen* is preserved within it. In the *gadžo* part, there are inferiority complexes exorcised with self-aggrandizement and a number of received values, not yet mastered and not yet clearly grasped, all jumbled together into chaos.

A Czech who has not had the opportunity to appreciate the Romani mode of expression, to be astonished at its respectfulness, its propriety, its harmony, at the naturalness of its images and metaphors, can unfortunately judge a Rom only by his disharmonious Czech. Only a few Roma I have met know how to express themselves in a Czech that is as pleasing as their grandfathers', and perhaps their fathers', Romani once was. It may be possible to acquire the grammar and vocabulary of a language in one generation, but to acquire the cultural dimension of a foreign language is a process that takes many generations. My feeling is that those Roma who no longer know Romani (the assimilationist pressures were enormous) and still do not know Czech or Slovak are worst off of all. And, as I began to suspect earlier, linguistic impoverishment is both a cultural and an ethical impoverishment as well. The old, traditional Romani stories are not told in Czech. Songs with lyrics in Romani are sung, but their texts are not what they once were: an automatic self-analysis, the synthetic confirmation of a *raison d'être*, an insistent communication which finds resonance within the community and thereby echoes its interdependence.

The mastery of another culture in its deepest dimensions is even more complex than the mastery of another language. Usually the easiest part to master is the most superficial part, the trappings. Moreover, much depends on the channels through which Roma receive *gadžo* culture. Besides mass media, particularly television, it is imparted by people who are willing to communicate with Roma – and they always were and are either people who are exceptionally enlightened (the minority) or people at the edge of *gadžo* society who do not typically convey the most cultivated of what the Czech language and culture have to offer. Naturally, what I say here does not apply equally to all Roma or to all Czech *gadže*. As soon as we begin to speak collectively of any population, nation, or group, it always leads to distorted generalizations. On the other hand, a certain general model does exist and to a lesser or greater extent, in the most varied specific forms, it flickers through in reality itself. Such a general model of a bi-cultural, bi-lingual Romani personality was also apparent when I spoke with Ilona. I always felt better, more at ease, and more inspired when she spoke Romani. (I naturally never asked her how my ability to express myself in Romani affected her and whether she felt its cultural flatness to be unpleasant.)

I recorded Ilona's autobiographical, and, at the same time, ethnographically enormously interesting, narrative, several times a year over a period of eight years. During that time, as I transcribed it all from the tape recorder, the number of pages and eventually sheaves of Romani texts grew. In transcribing them I again experienced the state of trance I fell into as Ilona told her stories. At the same time, as the project progressed, I felt more and more strongly that I would be doing Ilona, Roma, and also non-Roma a great disservice were I not to pass her testimony along to others. From selected passages I put together an hour-long radio program. The part of Ilona was read by the actress Miss Dana Medřická. Although the program was broadcast late at night on FM radio, it received widespread favourable response from listeners. At the urging of the editor Mirka Präusová, I resolved to rework the stories into a book. It was not a simple task since it was difficult for me to leave anything out at all. Everything seemed to me important not only for understanding Ilona but, above all, Roma, their culture, customs, way of life, feelings and outlook. It was not easy to transfer the radiant simplicity of the Romani into Czech and at the same time to preserve Ilona Lacko's unusual ability to handle her native language in such a way that the unexpressed and inexpressible behind the words could be felt. Finally, I was afraid of what Ilona would say when she read the manuscript. Would she have reservations about making public certain facts she had confided to me in private? My heart lightened when Ilona gave her consent to the manuscript.

The book was completed in 1986.

Mi del o Del bacht sasťipen,
o jilo phundrado achaľipnaske the kamibnaske.

May God grant you happiness and health,
and a heart open to empathy and love.

Milena Hübschmannová and Ilona Lacková during a recording session, 1984.
Ilona's university diploma can be seen on the wall behind her.

Translator's Note

In her narrative, Ms. Lacko makes occasional reference to people, events, and institutions which are intimately familiar to Czechs and Slovaks but which will mean little to most readers in English; to ease the way, I offer the following historical notes.

Most of Ms. Lacko's story is set in Slovakia, which was dominated by Hungary for a thousand years prior to 1918. High concentrations of Roma have lived in eastern Slovakia for centuries, and during that time they developed their own, distinctive dialect of the Romani language. Over the same period, the Czech lands had relatively fewer Roma, and though they tended to be better integrated into society than in Slovakia, most remained outside the mainstream.

Czechoslovakia declared its independence from Austria-Hungary in 1918. Social and cultural differences between the Czech and Slovak nations remained significant throughout the interwar period, despite the similarity of their two languages. Shortly after 1938, when Nazi Germany annexed the western border regions from the Czech lands, Bohemia and Moravia were organized into a Nazi protectorate. Slovak politicians seized the opportunity to form a nominally independent state with Hitler's blessing.

Foremost among these politicians were the members of the Slovak People's Party, an opposition party in prewar Czechoslovakia but one which gave the wartime Slovak state its nationalist and Fascist orientation. The party's paramilitary wing was known as the Hlinka Guards, named after the party leader Andrej Hlinka, a Catholic priest and advocate of Slovak independence who died before the war began. Many Hlinka Guards were prominent members of the gendarmerie, or national police force, and were active proponents of the Nazi policy of Aryanization. Older Slovak Roma remember the cruelty of these gendarmes with bitterness. Meanwhile, the vast majority of the prewar Czech Romani population was herded into Czech-run labor camps and then exterminated in Nazi concentration camps at Auschwitz, Auschwitz-Birkenau, and elsewhere.

Toward the end of the Second World War, Slovak partisans staged a valiant uprising against their Nazi occupiers, and the Czechs moved to expel from their reclaimed borderlands some two million ethnic Germans, many of whom had supported the Nazi party, and many of whose families had lived there for centuries. After the armistice, Slovakia and the Czech lands were reunited in a common state. Many Slovak and Romani laborers were recruited to work in the Czech lands, drawn by promises of jobs and cheap housing, especially in those areas vacated by Germans.

This labor migration trend continued even after a Communist coup in Prague subverted the democratic order in February 1948. The Party sought to bring the economy under the control of the state, and the agricultural sector was forcibly collectivized. Large private landowners ("kulaks," from the Russian word for "fist") were forbidden to hire laborers, leaving many Slovak Roma without any means of earning a livelihood. When Lacko writes of the "old money" and the "new money" in this period, she is referring to an unpopular monetary reform in 1953 that rendered the currency non-convertible and set off worker's riots.

The Communist Party also sought to exert its control over the political life of the country. It staffed the existing post-war system of "national committees" on the district, regional, and national levels with loyal party cadres and other politically reliable officials. Lacko herself was given political training by the Communist Party and hired by the Prešov regional "national committee" in Slovakia. From this position, she worked diligently to improve the lot of Roma: promoting better community hygiene through the Red Cross, organizing literacy classes, and serving as a liaison between Roma and local authorities. While sympathetic to the party's aims, she sometimes butted up against the limits of the its tolerance and understanding for her efforts and chafed against the constraints of both party doctrine and state policy – not for political reasons or, as is so often the case, because of thwarted personal ambitions, but because she was unable to reconcile party teachings and practice with her experience and knowledge of people as human beings.

During the period of Communist rule, policy toward the Romani minority was overtly assimilationist. In the early 1980's, over 300 Romani settlements were liquidated in eastern Slovakia, and this process has continued to the present day, albeit at a much slower rate.

Note on terminology

Rendering the terms *Rom* and *cikán (cigán)* in English present particular challenges in English. Roughly, *Rom* may be translated directly into English as "Rom" (plural form "Roma"), and the pejorative *cikan* as "Gypsy."

However, *cikán* is usually more insulting than the English "Gypsy." Although it is, loosely speaking, an ethnonym, it is not capitalized. In Czech orthography, as in English, nouns referring to members of national or ethnic groups are capitalized as a rule. The tendency not to capitalize *cikán* in Czech, unlike all other ethnonyms, certainly reflects the age-old ignorance of most Europeans about the identity of Roma. That ignorance is perhaps being gradually and slowly dispelled in the Czech lands, yet *cikán* persists in the contemporary language as both an ethnic slur and as an alternative to the more "highfalutin" *Rom*. In contrast to the Czech *cikán* as used today, "Gypsy" is not consistently pejorative in English (although the uncapitalized "gypsy" should be understood as such). (While some Czech writers such as Dr. Ctibor Necas, the accomplished and sympathetic scholar of the Romani Holocaust, have sought to rehabilitate the word and so have used the capitalized form *cikán* in their published studies, *Rom* is by and large the preferred usage in written Czech today.)

In this volume, the editors decided to use "Gypsy" consistently for *cikán*, instead of the possibly more accurate "gypsy." I believe they hope to avoid offending some readers and misleading others. Hopefully all readers will observe how often in this text the word "Gypsy" *cikán* is used condescendingly, mockingly, or dismissively, and draw the appropriate conclusions about the position of Roma within the larger cultural context of Ms. Lackova's life story.

As for the term *Rom*, unfortunately, English has not settled on a respectful way of referring to Roma (Gypsies). Many English speakers, particularly in Great Britain, use "Romany" as both adjective and noun (with the resulting plural form "Romanies"). Other terms in use include "Travellers," "Roma and Sinti," "Manus," and "Rroma." Still others denote distinct subgroups of Roma. In this translation, where the Czech text uses *Rom* and its related forms, I have used "Rom" (singular noun), "Roma" (plural noun), and "Romani" (both adjective and name of the language of Roma). This usage corresponds to the way many Roma – and in particular, the speakers of the eastern Slovak dialect of Romani who are the subjects of this book – refer to themselves and their language. It is also the standard usage recently adopted by the U.S. State Department in its annual country human rights reports.

All place names and most personal names in this book retain their original spelling, except for those place names that are well-established in English usage (e.g., Prague).

Nearly all Romani-language quotations and individual words and saying in this book are in the dialect native to the Roma of eastern Slovakia. They are almost always translated in the text. A glossary of key Romani words appears at the back of the book.

This translation of Ilona Lacko's book *A false dawn: my life as a Gypsy woman in Slovakia* is based on the Czech-language text of *Narodila jsem se pod šťastnou hvězdou* (Prague: Triáda, 1997), lovingly prepared by Dr. Milena Hübschmannová from extensive, audiotaped personal interviews with the author. The original interviews were conducted in Romani. I am indebted to Dr. Hübschmannová, Pavla Boučková, and Marta Miklušáková for graciously reading parts of the draft English translation; any errors that remain are entirely my own doing.

Carleton Bulkin
Prague, April 1998

Ilona Lacková advertising her photo-colorizing service, 1984.

My relatives

Bachtalo manuš, so les hin lačhi famiľija
Happy the man who has a good family

I had a very good family

My grandpa was named Andrej and my grandma, Bora. Papa was named Mikuláš and Mama, Marie. They gave me the name Ilona, because it was popular at the time. There were five girls born the same year as I in our settlement and three were named Ilona.

My father couldn't read. Grandma put him in school because Grandpa used to be a count's servant as a child, but Papa came to the first grade and had to learn a little poem by heart. In Hungarian, because at that time there were Hungarian schools in Slovakia. He didn't learn the poem, so the teacher bent him over his knee and thrashed him with a switch. Papa ran away from school and never went back.

Papa was an outstanding musician. He played first violin and could also play the viola, the bass, and the dulcimer. From the age of fourteen he played with Grandpa in a band.

There were nine of us children. The oldest, Južka, was born in Russia, and he died when he was seventeen years old. Ďulka died at seven months. Then me, Maruša, Tono, Haňuša, Adámek, and Vilma. And there were two other daughters from Papa's first marriage, Ema and Marga.

When I was born, my Mama was frightened at how black I was. She thought it was dirt, so she took some lye and scrubbed my face until I was completely bloody. I screamed so loud the whole settlement heard me. My grandma came running, my father's mother: "For goodness' sake, what are you doing?" She grabbed me and carried me away to her little closet of a room.

"But the child is so awfully dark!" my mother lamented.

"And what did you think she would be? She's a Romani creature!"

My mama was white-skinned, because she came from Polish stock. An orphan from Warsaw. Her mother had died during childbirth and her father two years afterwards. Her uncle took her in. When the war broke out, her uncle was called up. Mama was fourteen years old at the time, since she was born in 1900. Her beloved uncle sewed her birth certificate and a few florins into a sachet, hung the sachet around her neck, and said: "Maybe we'll see each other again, but maybe not." He kissed her, walked away, and they never saw each other again.

17

Warsaw was bombed and the orphanage where Mother was living was evacuated to Moscow. The children sewed gloves and khaki for the front. On an electric machine. Even then, there were electric sewing machines! At first the girls would sleep in the factory, and then they put them with various Russian families. Mama went to live with a Russian woman who was all alone in a small wooden house on the edge of Moscow.

In the meantime, Papa was fighting on the front line. Actually, he wasn't fighting, because he didn't feel like fighting. He was a musician, not a killer! During one attack a lot of soldiers fell. Nothing happened to Papa, he wasn't even scratched, but he rolled to the ground and pretended he had been killed. Those who really had been killed fell on top of him, and he lay buried alive under the corpses. The Austro-Hungarian soldiers retreated and the Russians occupied the area. They cleared away the corpses. Papa, as he was lying underneath them, was also more dead than alive, but he was breathing. Some Russian caught him by the jacket and asked: *"Bolnyj?"* Papa just nodded his head. They took him prisoner and that was exactly was Papa wanted.

The *avstrijaki* – that's what they called the Austro-Hungarian prisoners – worked on the same estate, near Moscow. They worked in the fields and took care of the livestock. Papa would tell how there were an awful lot of snakes in the fields. The snake is *džungalo*. A loathsome thing, something that Roma are terribly afraid of and shun. It is an Unclean Force. So Papa was also afraid, of course.

"Nikolaj," the Russian overseer asked him, "are you afraid of snakes?" He had his hand behind his back, in it he was holding a big, black snake, and he was about to put it right on Papa's neck.

"Me afraid of snakes?" Papa started to say. "I used to buy and sell them. In our parts the counts and princes eat snakes, and I would catch them for them!" The truth was that as a little boy my grandpa caught frogs for Count Pálffy. That's where Papa got the story about the counts' food from. "But your snakes – they're a joke next to ours! In our parts the snakes are so big, four ensigns couldn't carry one away! And when they bake one – do you think it fits in one pan? That's a mistake! You have to cook our snakes in the kind of kiln you use to fire bricks. Then when you eat a bite, you gain a kilo!"

The Russian overseer just goggled his eyes and was so ashamed of the paltriness of their snakes that he dropped the miserable creature from his hand and let him get away. Papa signed up to work in the barn with the cows to make sure he wasn't attacked in the field by a snake, the kind four ensigns couldn't carry away.

Of course, Papa was a musician, not a miserable cowhand. He wanted to play. And because he really did want to, in a few days some kind of itinerant accordion player, a Russian, happened onto the estate, Papa took up with him, disappeared from the estate, and then together they roamed the countryside, playing in the taverns.

Papa had an enormously valuable violin. He used to say he would have gotten ten thousand rubles for it if he'd sold it. I don't remember any more how he got it, but he remembered it his whole life long.

One time Mama's girlfriend was getting married. She invited that Russian accordion player and my father to the wedding so they would play for her. My future mother was the bridesmaid in the wedding. As soon as Papa saw Mama for the first time, he went plain crazy. He was crazy about her because my mother was immensely beautiful. White, radiant, she had long, thick, fair hair, a slim figure, about my size. Papa knew right away that she was the one and only woman he would live with till the end of his days.

18

Papa already had a wife and two daughters in Šariš. He had married a poor Slovak woman. But as soon as he left for the war, his first wife gave both little girls to our grandma and began to live with another man. Grandma had word sent to Papa at the front, and he was devastated. But then when he saw my mother, he was glad that his first wife wasn't waiting for him.

My mother's girlfriend's wedding ended and my mother took off for home, to the little wooden house. Papa came after her at a distance. She went in the house, locked the door behind her – and Papa knew where she lived.

The next day he came there before the women came back from the factory. He brought a bottle of vodka, gave it to the landlady, and told her he would kill her with his violin if she didn't let him into the golden-haired Polish woman's sitting-room. The landlady took the bottle of vodka and let Papa in. She hid him under the bed, locked the door behind him, and went off somewhere.

Mother came back from the factory. She was going on fifteen years old. She was religious, because she had been raised by the nuns in the orphanage. She had a bed with a canopy, knelt by the bed, and began to pray. When she had finished, Papa crawled out from under the bed and said, "Máňa, from this moment on you are my faithful wife and I your faithful husband." And then he did with her what he wanted. Mother was afraid, she cried, but Papa said: "Never in my life will I let you out of my arms." And that's how it happened. The two of them grew old in their love, and when Mama died, Papa died six weeks afterwards, because he could not exist without her.

As is right and proper, my oldest brother Jožka was born to them nine months later. Except that all of a sudden Mama ran away from Papa. Why she ran away, neither he nor she ever told me. Papa looked for her like a madman. He wandered all over Moscow for a month, day and night, from house to house. For a month he didn't sleep or eat, he only walked from one place to another and looked for Mama.

One evening he came to a small, run-down little house, peeped in the window and what did he see but Mother, warming up a little tea for my brother. Papa took his professional violin, which cost ten thousand rubles, broke the window to pieces with it, glass was flying on all sides, the violin shattered, but Papa didn't care, he jumped through the window and said: "Máňa, you're coming with me to Šariš!"

How Mother came to Šariš

The Great October Revolution broke out. Papa and Mama and other people from our parts took off for home. They went on foot. They had nothing to eat and they cooked up the horses that'd died. But Papa said he'd rather die than eat horse meat. A Rom who ate horse meat was *degeš*, unclean, the last of the last. Every *žužo* Rom, clean Rom, shunned him and not even a beggar, if he was decent, would drink water in his house. Much less take food from him.

Finally they loaded our soldiers into cattle wagons and in May they reached Prešov. Grandma, Papa's mother, thought that Papa wasn't alive. She cried for him terribly, because he was her only son. Her only child. I don't know how it's possible – our Roma at that time were having twelve, fifteen, and more children, and Papa was an only child. Grandma had cried for him for five years, until she'd gone deaf because of it. Only when she saw Papa at the train station in Prešov did her hearing return to her.

Great crowds of people were thronging at the train station. Everyone came to greet the returned soldiers. Mother stood next to Papa, seventeen years old, and wearing an outfit made of white rep – a long skirt, a close-fitting jacket, and on her head a white scarf of her mother's, which she cherished her whole life like the eyes in her head. She was carrying my brother in her arms. She looked like the Virgin Mary. People made way and looked at her.

Grandma had a lot of feather-blankets, piled up to the ceiling. When they brought Mama to the settlement, Grandma sat her on the blankets. The Roma in the settlement crammed themselves into Grandma's house, sat on the floor, and looked at my mother, how she was sitting up on the blankets and radiant white.

And Mother looked at them. She was dumb with horror. The whole time she hadn't had any idea that Papa was a Gypsy. He told her he was a Doctor. And he really was a Doktor, because that was his name. Mikuláš Doktor. Mother thought she would be coming into a doctor's elegance – and she found herself in a Gypsy Camp. She was afraid the Gypsies would eat her. All kinds of terrible rumors about Roma were going around: that they stole children, that they were cannibals, and who knows what else. Mama cried and told my two-year-old brother: "What are we going to do? The gypsies will kill us. They'll eat you!" And my young brother said: "If those Gypsies want to eat me up, I'll run away from them!" And he said it in Romani! They say that in a month he was speaking Romani like every other child from the settlement. It took Mama longer before she learned our language. From what I remember, she spoke Romani fluently, but until her death she had a Polish accent.

Papa's first wife also came to look at Mother. She spoke with her nicely and asked her if she wouldn't like to raise her two daughters. That, she said, she had gotten unused to them since Grandma had had them at her place. Mother nodded without even knowing what at. She had no idea that Papa had already had a wife and two daughters before. He had forgotten to tell her from love itself. Both my half-sisters stayed with us, Mama treated them as if they were her own, and we all grew up in an atmosphere of love. Even today we treat each other like siblings. Papa's first wife lived with her husband in a village near Prešov, and they didn't have any children. We didn't see her much, but people in our house didn't say bad things about her.

Grandma and Mama respected one another, but they didn't love each other. When Mama was out of earshot, Grandma said of her: that crazy Polish woman! She didn't like Mama mostly because of how she went nuts with the washing. One day Mama would soak the laundry in the evening, the second day she would boil it and scour it, then rinse it in several tubfuls, and on the third day, when the laundry had dried, she would iron it. That was how the nuns had taught her to do it. The rest of the women from the settlement did their laundry at the creek with lye. They beat the clothes against smooth boulders and to tell the truth, their laundry was just as clean as Mother's. And they had it done one-two-three. Of course, Mother claimed that laundry could be clean only when it was washed the way she did it. So be it. The truth is that her laundry just shone.

Mama did the laundry in the little room where Grandpa and Grandma took refuge when our family began to grow. They left us the larger room and they themselves retreated into the small one. During the laundry she shuffled Grandma and Grandpa into the sitting-room, where they didn't have any peace with all the children there. Grandma would swear: "May the Lord God cut off her hands so she can't carry on with the laundry like that! May those lordly manners rot in her brain! Crazy Polish woman!" Grandma probably didn't mean these curses seriously, because Mother never had a hand cut off in her life, and her particularity about cleanliness didn't rot out of her until her death.

When I was small, I had one great goal: to be able to do laundry like Mama. To have laundry just as clean and white. I also wished I could sew like her. The Roma in the settlement were very poor. They all wore old clothes given them by the peasant farmers. And when they had worn them out completely, the womenfolk begged some more hand-me-downs. They bought new clothes only for weddings and for the fair. No one knew what a needle and thread were. And our mother was a trained seamstress, having spent the entire war sewing in a factory that made soldiers' khaki. The women in the settlement would come to her and say: Máňa, fix my skirt, pretty pretty please! Máňa, sew me a blouse!"

Mother would get angry: "Get a needle and sew it yourself!"

"Oh now, Máňa, how could we come up with a needle in our house?" A needle cost money and at that time Roma had no money. For working at the peasants' they got potatoes, milk, a little flour, curd cheese, once in a while an egg. But never money! And when they did have a spare crown, they would buy salt, kerosene, tobacco, things you used every day. What good was a needle? Mama would lend the women needles, teach them to thread them and to sew. Of course, when there was going to be a fair somewhere, they would get the money come what may – in exchange for scrap metal, for medicinal herbs, for raspberries or mushrooms, or for what grew right in the forest. The women would buy a little fabric and go to Mother again: "Oh now, Máňa, sew me some clothes!" And Mother would sew them. She would spread out the new clothes on Grandma's feather-beds. Three or four made out of gleaming satin. I liked them terribly and imagined that when I was big, I would also have satin clothes that I had sewed for the women in the settlement, spread out on the feather-beds piled high. So that was my greatest life goal: to be able to do laundry and sew like my mother with the white-skinned face and the long, blond hair.

Once Mama ran away from Papa. It was like this: two or three of the peasant girls in the village had a sewing machine. Mama would go to their place to sew. They would let her use the sewing machine in exchange for her sewing for them for free. Sometimes she had so much sewing that she stayed at their place overnight. She brought my oldest brother Jožka with her, the one who was born in Russia. My grandma took care of me. I slept in the little room and she wouldn't let me out of her sight in case it occurred to my mother to scrub me with lye again to make me lighter. One time my mother said that she was going to the peasant girl's to sew and that she would stay overnight. She took my brother with her as usual. Papa was sitting by the window on a bench and fixing his violin. All at once he got up quick as lightning and ran outside. He dashed to the gendarmes' station and told them: "Quick, telephone the revenue officers on the Polish border, my wife's run away from me!"

"What's gotten into you, Mikluš," the gendarme said, "how do you know that? Who would your wife go running off to when she's got no one there! And anyway, she wouldn't leave the little dark girl here!" By this he meant me.

"For goodness' sake, call there! I can feel it in my bones, she's run away!"

So the gendarme called the revenue officers – and what do you know! They caught Mama three steps from the Polish border.

I was about four years old then and I had no idea what Mother wanted to do. But when she told me about it later, I cried terribly: "And would you have left me all alone?" I

21

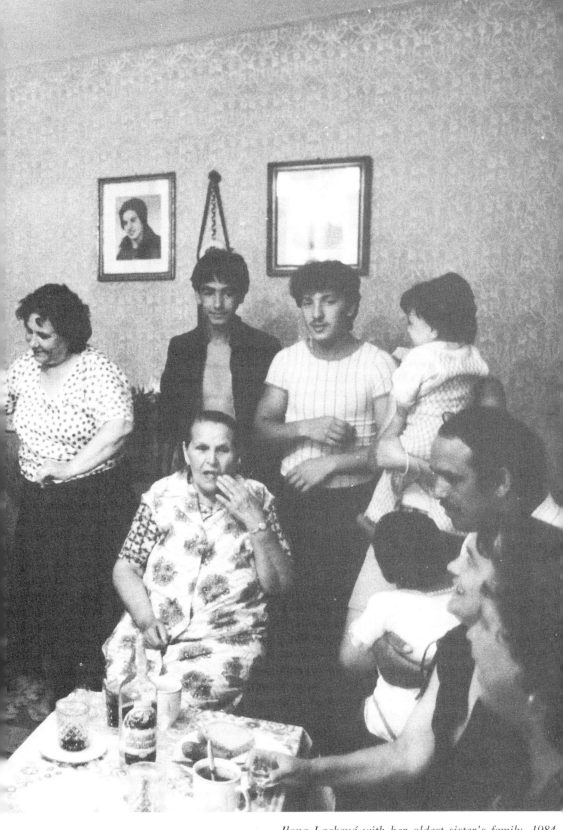

Ilona Lacková with her oldest sister's family, 1984.

sobbed. Mother opened up her little prayer book, and she had a lock of black hair tucked inside. "Your hair," she said, "I cut it off and took it with me to remember you by. I would have come back for you." Even now it makes me cry whenever I remember how Mama wanted to run away from us.

Mama really loved our oldest brother, Jožka. He was very smart, he was a good student, and he was beautifully white. He finished the eighth grade and Mama had him enrolled at the high school. That was something people hadn't seen. A Gypsy boy – and the high school! That was just completely out of the custom then. And also, few Roma had the money to send their child to study. As far as money, we were a little better off than the other people from the settlement. Papa would go to Prešov to play in the pubs – every day, on foot, seven kilometers there, seven kilometers back. So he would bring back a crown or two. Mama worked at the peasant's, I would help her, and in the evenings she would sew and knit sweaters in a Norwegian pattern for the villagers – and that's how she saved the money for my brother's studies.

Only it never happened! My brother's godfather was the landowner. Roma took rich peasants for godfathers because the *kirvo*, the godfather, was obligated to give his godchild at least a job, if not some kind of present. Jožka's godfather went into the forest once for wood in the winter. My brother went with him, of course, to help him load the wood. The forest was situated on a steep slope. And the way the oxen were struggling to pull the cart up the hill, one of their harnesses broke. The godfather sent Jožka to the estate for another harness. "See that you're back one-two-three!" he ordered him. My brother ran down the hill, grabbed the harness, put it on his neck, and dashed up the hill. When he had tramped up the hill, he was terribly hot and out of breath. He wanted to cool off a bit, so he started eating snow. He got a severe inflammation of the lungs and died in three days. His dying was not easy. He lay in agony and could not die.

"He hasn't settled his accounts with somebody," said Grandma, "that's why he can't go. He would have to come back to earth and his soul would have no rest." We all knew who had to answer for his death. Mother went to call on the godfather. He resisted, he didn't want to go. But his wife was a God-fearing woman, and so she finally went with my mother to the dying Jožka. She came and asked his forgiveness, my brother looked at her, and he expired.

Mother cried for him terribly. She cried for him her whole life.

What exactly is a *čedona*?

When I was little, I loved my grandpa most of all. Grandpa was an exalted person. As a boy he served the count. His cousin – the son of Grandpa's mother's brother – would go to catch crayfish and bring them to the chateau to the nobles. He brought Grandpa with him. Grandpa was a black little boy, very black, and that was just what the countess liked about him. They made him a page boy. He waited on them at table and learned Hungarian from them. Then when he went back to the settlement, all the Roma would come running all around him and he would have to tell how they went riding in the carriage, what kind of food the counts ate, what a fork looked like, what kind of clothes the countess wore, how they arched their eyebrows, how they breathed, and how they wrinkled their noses – in short, everything that went on at the chateau. He always spent only two or three months at the chateau, in the summer, because the rest of the time the aristocracy lived in Vienna. For Roma, life at the chateau was something exotic – and for the nobles at the chateau our Roma were something exotic. The blacker they were, the more interesting. The countess also wanted me as a servant girl. She told Mother that she would take me to Vienna and that I would have great luck there. But Mama wouldn't hear a word of it.

When Grandpa was eighteen years old, he got married to Grandma and began to work in the mill. Besides that, he had a band and went to play at weddings and at village entertainments.

Grandpa really loved Grandma. Never in his life did he beat her, although there were times when she deserved it. Grandma drank. Grandpa didn't drink – and he was a guy, but Grandma was a woman – and she drank! Every day she drank a shot of rum on credit. She would go to a Jewish woman who sold cheap booze, the Jewish woman would write every shot into her little book, and when Grandpa got paid at the mill, he went and paid for what Grandma had drunk her way through during the month.

When Grandma made Grandpa angry he didn't beat her, but he said: "You're one big *čedona*!" What that means, no one knows. Neither Grandpa nor Grandma knew, but it always upset Grandma terribly. Once she had done something bad again and Grandpa told her: "You're one big *čedona*!"

First thing the next morning, when Grandpa had just left for the mill, Grandma woke me up: "Get up, little girl, your Grandpa called me a *čedona* and I'm going to run away from him! We'll go to Chmiňany." The daughter of Grandma's sister lived in Chmiňany – she's still alive, she could be ninety years old. "We'll never go back to Grandpa's!"

I cried, because I didn't want to go, Grandpa was very good to me, bought me candies, I'd always hold out my skirt and he'd pour them in. "I want to stay at Grandpa's!" I wailed. But Grandma grabbed me by the hand and I had to go. We went on foot, of course. Chmiňany's about ten kilometers from our place.

We walked and walked until the first houses in Chmiňany were visible, and I started crying that my feet hurt.

"That's no matter," said Grandma, "we'll sit down for a little and have a bite." We sat ourselves in the grass, and Grandma pulled out a fifth of rum from her apron, some bread and started looking for the bacon. "Where did I put the bacon!" she fumed. "I must have gone and left it at home! Ilona, we've got to go back for the bacon!"

"Granny, we can't really go back all that way for bacon! The bread will be enough for us. My feet hurt."

"You'll make it! You think I'd leave the bacon there so your grandpa could eat it all up? That because he called me a *čedona* I'd go leaving him any bacon? I'd eat it myself even if I had to choke to death!" Grandma grabbed me by the hand and we tramped back to Šariš. At home she picked up the bacon and yanked me off to Chmiňany once again. I went because there was nothing else I could do.

In Chmiňany, Grandma ceremoniously presented herself to the daughter of her sister, saying that she had left Grandpa's because he always called her a *čedona*, and that she would never go back to him. Then she said she would bake some *langoše*, because she was hungry for them. *Langoše* are pies filled with curd cheese. I had forgotten that my feet hurt and went to play with the children. I had my dress-up clothes on, white with red polka dots, with a frilly skirt. Mama sewed our clothes herself, and compared with other Romani children we went around dressed like princesses. And so the children ran up to me and pawed at my clothes, wanting to peel off a polka dot, touched my frills or just looked at them with wonder. When they got tired of the clothes we began to play tag. The fact that it was raining didn't bother us in the least. But as we were chasing each other, I slipped and fell into a great big mud puddle. My beautiful, polka-dot, frilly clothes were hanging like a rag on a scarecrow. I came inside to Grandma in tears.

"What have you done to yourself, you big *čedona*!" cried Grandma. "Your mother will kill me!" Then she pulled the clothes off of me, washed them, and put them up to dry. Then she baked some more *langoše* and was happy.

That evening the door opened and there in the doorway stood – Grandpa! He had come to get us. "Why did you run away, now?" he said, gently. "Do I beat you, wife of mine?"

"You called me a *čedona*, and as long as you call me a *čedona* I won't come back to you."

Grandpa promised not to call Grandma a *čedona* any more, but he didn't swear to it. Besides, Grandma knew that she couldn't even ask him for such an oath.

We couldn't go home that evening because I still didn't have dry clothes. We slept over in Chmiňany and first thing in the morning, before daybreak, we left so Grandpa could make it to work on time. He carried me the whole way. He was sorry for me because I was little and my feet hurt.

Grandpa was the *čhibala*, the Romani mayor, in the settlement. Later my father inherited this job from him. When times were bad and the Roma had nothing to eat, they would go to the fields and steal potatoes, corn, and cucumbers from the peasants. The peasants sent gendarmes into the settlement, and Grandpa would go with them from one shanty to the next, saying: "Just take a good look around! Can you find one single potato here?" The gendarmes really couldn't find anything, because the potatoes had long been eaten, often even with the peels. They only took enough from the peasants' fields so the family could eat at least once a day. "Look at how wretchedly our people are living – and look at those peasants with their bellies hanging out!" Papa would tell the gendarmes.

The gendarmes weren't from our parts, they stationed them here from somewhere in Bohemia, so they didn't have any relatives in the village and didn't have to defend anyone. They'd say: "You're right, Mikluš, but next time gather the potatoes so no one catches you doing it."

Some of the peasants were terribly stingy. Once a peasant woman invited me to help her with a big cleaning job; they were planning a wedding. I scrubbed the floors, washed the windows, and beat the rugs. I was about ten years old. Then the peasant went with his wife to buy a horse and his wife said: "Finish up here and then you can sleep over at our place; we'll come back tomorrow. But don't even think about taking anything from the pantry! Don't you touch anything, or else the Lord God will punish you and you'll be even blacker than you are!" She didn't leave me any food and I was afraid to go into the pantry because the Lord God would punish me. When they came back the next day, I was as hungry as a blind dog. And what did they give me? A plate of soup and a slice of dry bread.

We ate sparingly at home, twice a day at most but, thank God, we didn't go hungry. Only Grandpa spoiled me and brought me little morsels. My grandfather died young. I was six years old then. When he was dying, he called me to come and kiss him. I kissed him on the lips, and to this day I remember how cold he was. I kissed him, he closed his eyes, and he died. The people broke out in tears. They loved my grandpa and respected him, because he was a noble, exalted, and kind person. A person like him deserved a big sendoff, and that's what he got. For the longest time the Roma throughout the whole area would tell the story of how beautifully Grandpa left for the other world and what a superb burial he had. They took me to the coffin to beat it with my childish fists and call: "Grandpa, wake up, Grandpa, wake up!" I believed that he would really wake up from the coffin alive, and so I beat and called with all my strength. I had to stop every so often and rest, and when I started to beat the coffin all over again, brand new waves of wailing and lamentation would fan out over the settlement.

When they buried Grandpa on the third day, that night Mother strewed ashes on the ground in the sitting-room. We didn't have a floor, only the compacted earth. Every Saturday we mopped it with yellow loam, and it shone like the sun. No one in the settlement had a floor. "We'll be able to tell if Grandpa will come," said Mama, "by the footprints in the ashes." You see, a dead person can turn into a cat, a dog, a bird, a nightmare, into anything he wants. Depending on what it is, he leaves the footprints of a cat, dog, or a bird. Or a human being. He can even come back to earth in his own form, only you can't see his face. All Roma believe this.

Well, and Mama said that in the morning she found two footprints in the ashes. Human ones! Grandpa had come to see us in his own form. That meant that he was a good person, worthy, and that he didn't have to turn into a dog.

Of course, afterwards Mama smoked the house out, because the dead person belongs to the other world and no longer has any business among the living. She put pieces of dead twigs and fruit into a pot, set them alight, and a marvelous scent spread through the whole house.

Grandma cried for Grandpa for the longest time. She was young when he died. Young and beautiful. She had long, thick, black hair. When she sat down, she had to be careful not to sit on it. A lot of men from near and far courted Grandma, but she didn't want to hear a word about any of them. She remained faithful to Grandpa to her death. And she would say to me with sadness: "You see, little girl, now there's no one to call me a *čedona*."

I wanted to live in love, like them

In our family – and among Roma in general – no one talked about love, but we were happy being with each other, happy to spend time with one another. We were all bound by some kind of warm vibration which streamed constantly from one person to another. Our heart also linked us with the animals that lived with us in the settlement.

One member of our family was Cita. A little, itty-bitty she-dog. She would go running around with us and always stay close by. She played hide-and-seek with us, and when we were it, we always won, because Cita would sniff out everyone in the willows or between the shanties.

But rabies came to the area, and the town crier announced that all the Gypsies' dogs would be destroyed. We had to give Cita up to the knacker. We each kissed her on the forehead in turn, one after another. When she walked out of sight, we cried for her for a long time.

We were happy children. We were always dashing outside. In winter and in summer. We were brought up by the whole settlement, not just our mother and father. As soon as any adult heard a child say a bad word, he would rebuke him: "What did you say? Aren't you ashamed of yourself? Don't you know what *pat'iv* is?" *Pat'iv* is respect, honor, decency – it was a magic spell. If anyone ever didn't know what *pat'iv* was, he was *pre ladž* – to be shamed, and the others began to shun him as a *degeš*, a carrion crow. That kind of rebuke was enough for us to be ashamed and walk off to some quiet corner with our eyes cast down.

Were we left to run around wherever we wanted? Yes and no. Because from the age of five or six we would go with the women to gather mushrooms, strawberries, or medicinal herbs. The boys played music from the time they were little. A little squirt who couldn't even walk right would already be dragging a violin around.

Our parents never beat us. Romani parents did not punish their children with beatings. At least they didn't use to. Something really extraordinary had to happen for a child to get a thrashing. Here's a kind of joke they tell: the teacher says to a Romani father: "Why don't you give your boy a hiding when he's been bad?" And the father says: "Why would I give him a hiding? Even without that he knows that I'm stronger than he is!"

I remember only one hiding in our family. My brother Toňa got it, and it happened like this: when I was a child there were hardly any cars, but still every once in a while a motor car came chugging through Šariš. Toňa and some other boys thought up this stupid game: that they would lie down on the bridge and wait for a car to come. Whoever didn't get up and run away would win.

Mama was working in the field and the women from the settlement came running up to her: "Máňa, your boy is lying on the bridge and waiting for a car to run over him!" And they immediately began to wail and pull their hair out as if Toňa had already been run over.

Mother went into the willows, cut herself a nice, thin switch, grabbed the boy, and whupped him on his backside. "You going to get yourself run over?" "No?" "You going to get yourself run over?" "Noooo!" – And that was the only hiding ever in our family.

When I was bad, they threatened me with the butcher's dog. I really loved eating fatty meat, probably because we had it so rarely.

One time Mama made *gomboda* – you mix boiled potatoes with flour, make little dollops out of it and cook them in soup. I hated this food from the time I was little and to this day I will not take *gomboda* into my mouth.

Mother gave me a full plate and said: "Eat!"

"I won't, I don't like it!" I yelled. I was about four years old. "Eat!" said Mother, getting angry. And so I put my bare foot in the soup. "Shame on you!" yelled Mother. And I broke out in tears. I bawled for two hours and just wouldn't stop. Papa took me in his arms, carried me around the sitting-room, tried to calm me down, and I kept bawling.

Then Mama said: "Fine, if you're going to eat only meat, you'll marry the butcher's dog!"

I was so frightened that I stopped bawling. The butcher had an enormous dog, a sheepdog. It was much bigger than me. I was scared that he would really come to take me for his wife – but sometimes I said to myself: but what if he turns into a prince? I'll live with him in a castle and never have to eat *gomboda* again.

Grandma would threaten me differently. "If you're bad, a *gadžo* will snatch you up!"

(The other day I was walking in town, past the bank. There was a lady standing outside with a child, and the child was bawling. The lady was saying: "If you don't stop right away, the Gypsies' ll snatch you up and eat you!" I went up to her and asked: "And will they make a Gypsy roast or Gypsy schnitzel out of him, or will they eat him raw?" The lady was ashamed, grabbed the child, and disappeared from the bank's door. If I'm going to be fair, I have to admit that our women threaten their children the same way – only the other direction. "If you're bad, a *gadžo* will snatch you up!")

I was never beaten by my mother, but I feared her. She was strict. All she had to do was look at me and I'd be bawling somewhere off in a corner. What Mother said was law. She had the kind of personality that everyone obeyed her. Even Papa. He would have given his life for her, he loved her so much, and still she was hard on him. Papa would ask, say: "Máňa, would you make me some beef broth today?" "We're having cabbage soup today!" said Mother, and Papa would only laugh: "All right, Máňa, if you want cabbage soup, have it your way."

For example, I wanted to put on some clothes I liked. And Mama said: "No! Today you'll wear this and this!" Even if I crawled on my knees, I still had to put on what she wanted. Or once a new haircut came into style, called a little Antoinette: you rolled the hair into little ringlets and pinned them up on your head. That was how both the peasants' daughters and the Romani girls in our settlement were doing their hair, there probably wasn't a single young girl who didn't have a little Antoinette. I wanted a little Antoinette too, so I wouldn't be different from the others, but Mama said no! I didn't dare disobey her.

Why was she like that? I don't know. She just was. Different strokes for different folks. But it's also true that I'm grateful to her more than anyone else for what I've accomplished in life.

Of course, Mama knew how to pull a prank once in a while, too. There was a guy in the settlement whose name was Pekár, and he was really scared of mice. He already had a wife and children, but when he saw a mouse, he acted like a little boy. Once Mama caught a mouse, held it by the tail and ran after Pekár. Pekár shrieked as if it were the devil himself who was chasing him. He flew inside a shanty, Mama going after him, he jumped on the stove, and the stove collapsed under him! Then Mama had to have a new one built for them.

Pekár was the son of the Cibrikans, who were experts on medicinal herbs and knew how to interpret dreams.

Mama had a little cash-box walled up behind the stove. None of us knew about it. She'd toss a kreutzer into the box now and then. When we had to move out of the village during the war, she gathered up the cash-box so no one saw her, and walled it up again in the new place, down the hill from the forest. She told me about it only shortly before her death.

I never heard Mother sing. It occurred to me that she had some secret trouble that she kept with her always. Maybe she was troubled by the fact that she didn't have any relatives. Sometimes she would say: "I'm heading off for Poland, where I'll definitely find someone from my family." But it never came to pass.

I never heard Mother sing, and yet they say she sang so beautifully! Not long ago my sister Ema came to see us, the one Papa had from his first wife. We had two glasses of wine together, I turned on the gramophone for her, and I was in such a good little mood, I began to sing along with the record. My sister said: "You sing nice, girl, but if you

29

could've heard your mother! You would have felt your body run hot and cold when she sang!" And I had never heard her sing even once!

No one ever photographed Mother in her life. The only photograph of her is from her state identity card. It was between the pages of her prayer book. But my sister Maruša took the book and her children stashed it away somewhere. So we don't have any pictures of Mama at all.

So, I tell you, Mama never thrashed me in her life and Papa thrashed me once. And this is how it happened: our settlement was a great big one, so there were always plenty of marriageable girls. Meaning fourteen-, fifteen-year-old girls. If a girl turned sixteen or seventeen and still wasn't living with a husband, the family began to be afraid that they would be stuck with her *po purano ciral*, like "curd cheese gone bad."

The *čhaja* – the marriageable girls – would gather every evening at Helena's place. Helena had no children and at night her husband would go to catch crayfish for the castle gentry, so there was room in her shanty for gatherings. Helena couldn't have gotten along without us, because she was happy by nature, and until her death she liked having a good time, singing, dancing, and acting like a young girl. We used to play *kuchně* at her place. Meaning that one would bring a little flour from home, another some potatoes, a third some fat, and we'd make pancakes and drink herb tea with it. Of course, some young men from the settlement would come too. They brought musical instruments: one picked up his father's violin, another a viola, a bass, they'd play for us and we'd sing and take long looks at one another, thinking who'd be right for who. People formed couples and every so often one would disappear in the willows outside the settlement.

In the morning that led to an uproar. The girl told her mother – it wasn't the custom among Roma to keep a secret to yourself – and the mother pulled her guilty daughter by the hair through the whole settlement *pre vatra* – to the central area of the community. *Pre vatra* is where roundtables, debates, discussions, and dramas were played out, matters that affected everyone. "Your boy has dishonored my daughter!" screamed the mother so the whole settlement could hear. "I will bear this shame on my head! The engagement feast will take place this very day!" The boy's mother howled: "You've raised your daughter to be a whore, and she's turned the head of my virtuous son!" The brothers, whose job was to look after the honor of their sisters and thus of the whole family, thrashed the girl so every eye could see that they did not approve of her shameful act. People came pouring out of the shanties and stood all around the whole scene, sometimes set on edge with the absorption of a theater audience, sometimes shouting and egging on one side or the other like fans at a sports match. The representatives of both families, egged on by the audience's enthusiasm, made a real spectacle out of the argument. Unbelievable insults and curses were brought forth: may a pear tree grow up out of your heart, from this day may you never speak again but only bark like a dog, may your children be born with little piggy tails, and the like. That neither of the actresses was serious was proven by the fact that not a single child was born in our settlement with a little piggy tail, nor did anyone grow a pear tree up out of their heart. And when words were no longer enough, the women tucked up their skirts and bared their privates at each other. The peasants had stopped on the bridge overlooking our settlement, enjoying the Gypsy spectacle ... Well, and that evening there was an engagement feast. In the morning the adversaries got hitched, and in the evening there was a grand celebration of eternal kinship.

My Papa was a great guy and enjoyed the respect of both the Roma and the peasants. He said: "Girls, if any of you bring that kind of shame on my head, I'll kill myself." And I loved my Papa more than anything else in the world, so I never brought him that kind of shame.

Sometimes I went to fun-loving Helena's with the *čhaja*, the girls, but mostly I read at home. I was the only one from the settlement who read books.

There were also boys from other parts who came courting. One time three young men came from Kapušany, spent the whole night having fun at Helena's, and in the morning when they were getting ready to go to the train, someone said: "There's also girls in the house here where the leader's family lives. Let's go take a look there too." They meant me, Maruša, and Haňuša. I was going on sixteen. And so the young men knocked on our door. I was still reading. I threw on a patchy old robe that Mama had made me out of old skirts from the peasant's wife. I opened the door. On the other side were some guys I didn't know.

I don't know what got into me, I said: "Come in and have a seat. We don't have any chickens, but if you don't have a seat, our chickens will stop laying." I don't know why I was in such a good mood. I didn't even ask where they were from. And the guys said they were in a hurry to catch the train home to Kapušany, and could I come see them off. It was early in the morning, summer, harvest time, I was getting ready to put scarecrows up in the field. I said I had to go to the field, I'd promised our peasant's wife.

"Just come with us, cutie!" laughed a good-looking, fair-haired boy my way. You couldn't even tell he was a Rom. On the table there was a little vase with flowers from the meadow. He took a violet and stuck it in his lapel. I got dressed and so did Maruša and we went with them to the train.

We had two small rooms and the closet. We children slept in the front room, Mama and Papa in the back one, and Grandma in the closet. Mama overheard something going on up front. She shook Papa awake: "Get up, Mikluš, get up, your daughters are going off with some youngsters. Run after them!" And she drove Papa after us. He hadn't even managed to get his shoes on, and he was running with just one shoe on, his other foot bare. We had already clambered up the slope to the bridge.

"Come home this instant!" Papa yelled. "What kind of trollops are you, running around with strange boys!" Papa took off his one shoe and threw it at me. Maybe he didn't mean to hit me, only to show me that he was coming after me. But all the same he got me in the back. I barely felt it. I picked up the shoe and went back. And Papa was standing there with tears running down his cheeks. Because he'd thrown his shoe at me and because it must have hurt. We went home and Papa's tears were still flowing. "Do you see," he told Mama, "because of you, I've hurt the girl! What's wrong with her taking a young man to the train? Our daughter won't bring any shame upon us."

I took this so terribly to heart, that if a count made of pure gold had come after me I wouldn't have gone with him. I loved my father very much.

And in three years that good-looking, fair-haired boy who picked the violet from our vase picked me for his wife.

Mother died in 1957. She was fifty-seven years old. She didn't suffer and didn't have any kind of serious illness – she'd drudged herself to death. She worked her whole life long, never stopping for a moment. She ate little. When there wasn't anything to eat, she said: "I'm not hungry," and divided everything among us children. And also, she never got over the death of my brother Josef that was born in Russia and was so beautifully white.

When Mama died, Papa stopped talking. He sat and looked in the same direction. He didn't say another word until the day of his death. He died six weeks after Mother.

Childhood and youth in Šariš

Bachtalo manuš, so barol giľenca pherasenca
Happy the man who grows up with a song and knows how to be happy

The Roma of Šariš

Kaj but Roma, odoj giľi šundʼol
Where there are many Roma, there is song

Barvaľipen lovenca, čoripen giľenca pherasenca
Wealth is money, poverty songs and jokes

Rom nane ňigda korkoro
A Rom is never alone

Te man nane, joj man dela, te la nane, me la dava
If I have nothing, she will gime me some, if she has nothing, I will give her some

Rom Romeske te merel na dela
A Rom does not leave another Rom to die

Čalo vodʼi feder sar čale goja
A satisfied soul is better than a satisfied gut

Every day, all around me, I heard words of wisdom that were our mainstay in poverty and squalor, taught us to take life as it came, to live through each moment, and to be content. Poverty led us to help each other and respect one another. And because these sayings or old saws were used in other settlements as well, Roma used to think, no matter how poor they were, that their settlement was the best and happiest one, and they would not let themselves be shaken even by the opinion of the whole wide region. Every settlement had a nickname according to how the Roma there lived, how they made their livelihood, what they ate, or how they behaved. Our settlement had the proud title of *lavutariko vatra* – the musicians' settlement, even though half of our

33

Roma made their living as day laborers. Like all Roma, with the exception of two or three settlements where they dealt in pigs, we lived from hand to mouth, but all the same we thought there was nothing better than the Šariš Roma.

Šariš was a large village and it was grandly called *varošis* – a small city. Our Gypsy settlement was under the bridge on the edge of the village. Not even one Romani family lived in town. It never used to be true that a Rom would live among *gadže*. We lived in the settlement, all by ourselves.

The peasants' children didn't play with us. They used to shout at us, in Slovak: *Cigán more lapsa, predal koňa za psa!* – catch a Gypsy *more*, sold a horse for a dog! They would throw rocks at us and we'd throw rocks at them. Of course it never got as far as brawls between their parents and ours. God help the Gypsy who dared to lay a hand on a peasant! They would have burned down our village. And so we were better off keeping our distance.

No *gadžo* ever entered our settlement in my whole life. Only the gendarmes. Or the town crier, when he came to read out some decree. Once in a while, if someone got a letter, the fellow with the mail bag would come as far as the bridge over the settlement and call out: "Heyyy! Mikluš' girl has a letter here!" And we went clambering up the slope to get it. Our *gadžo* godparents would yell for us from the bridge the same way when they called us to come and dig potatoes.

Before the war there were Czech gendarmes in Šariš. Once they came into the settlement to our house to investigate something. Just then Papa was playing and I was singing. I really liked these times. The gendarmes stayed standing underneath the window and listened. Papa saw them and invited them in. They knocked, came in, and raised their caps. What did you know! They'd raised their caps in a Gypsy house! Papa knew a few Czech songs, he'd taught me "Strahováček" and "Teče potůček bublavý,"

Ilona Lacková on the site where the old Gypsy hamlet once stood, Veľký Šariš, 1984.

so we had a little concert for them. The gendarmes just melted. (They didn't have any relatives in Šariš, the poor guys!) Afterwards Papa was saying: "Take a look at these Gypsy children, how their ribs are sticking out and their stomachs are bloated with hunger! And you want to lock up their parents?" – "You're right, Mikluš," said the gendarmes.

Near the gendarmes' station there was a plum orchard. The gendarmes wanted to make a little extra money, and so they thought they'd sell the plums to the wholesalers. They came into the settlement for us so we'd pick them. They didn't give us money for doing it, but they let us eat as many plums as we could stuff ourselves with. The *gadže* would yell at the gendarmes: "Just you wait 'til that insatiable Gypsy scum eats up all your plums, along with the leaves and the branches!" They were jealous of how the gendarmes were doing us a favor.

When the Slovak state came into being, the Czech gendarmes had to leave. Papa cried for them. He went to walk them to the station and on the way he played for them. Because of that the peasants cursed him. After the gendarmes came the troopers, and they hated us Roma.

There were fifty or sixty shacks in the settlement, and six hundred souls lived in them. We built our shacks from unbaked bricks, from *valki*. The forests belonged to the wealthy peasants, so we couldn't use wood for building, it was expensive. There was plenty of clay everywhere, and we could have as many *valki* as we wanted. There was one Romani family that specialized in the making of *valki*. Of course, they weren't *amare Roma* – our Roma – and we didn't consider them *žuže* Roma – clean Roma. They lived at the other end of the community, called pod Bikošem, and they ate carrion. We shunned them. They got a shack in the community and produced unbaked bricks for the entire town. At that time, many peasants also used *valki* for building. Of course, it took about ten thousand *valki* to make any kind of peasant's building. A thousand was enough for us: one large room and a smaller one. A thousand unbaked bricks cost fifty crowns.

Our settlement – like most settlements – grew over several generations from a single family. That's why there were only a couple of last names that recurred constantly: Dužda, Horváth, Čonka, Cibrik, Bandy, Eštočak, Kaleja. Kaleja was the most frequent one – in translation it means Hey, Black One! Only our grandfather was a Doktor. And our father after him. Where did someone get that kind of last name? Not even among the *gadže* did you find the name Doktor. Now, of course, in Prešov there are about thirty Doktors, because my brother Toňu had a lot of boys and they also have Doktor boys. People say your fate is bound with your name. That hasn't been true of them yet. But me, when I graduated from the School of Culture and Journalism at Charles University in Prague, in my heart I told myself: I wonder if my name, Doktor, didn't give me good luck here?

We didn't go by last name among ourselves, we went mostly by our nicknames. All the Roma in the settlement had a nickname, a so-called *romano nav* – Romani name. They would give themselves the names of rich peasants or Jews from the town, believing it would bring them riches and luck. And so Malinek, who named himself after the big landowner Malinovský, was killed by electricity when he was fixing the peasant's lamp; Cajzler, named after a Jew who bought medicinal herbs in bulk, died young and left behind four children. However, Khamoro – Little Sun – was always smiling and happy, and čhonoro – Little Moon – stuck out because he'd be thin for a while and then he'd be fat for a while. Many settlements had their *dilino* – crazy person. We didn't have any crazy people. Actually, I knew only one crazy woman and she came from Ostrovany. She used to walk around the region, singing and tying her clothes to the trees. Then she died.

Nor was there a single old bachelor among us. All the men had wives.

No one from the settlement was blind, but on the other hand we had two deaf-mutes: a brother and sister. They were born that way. But the little girl was sweet and wise, understood everything, and everyone loved her. She married happily. And then, of course, there was a one-legged man in our settlement. He lost his leg in the war.

All the females in the settlement were thin, only Moškaňa was fat, even though she was the poorest person in the whole area. She hardly ever ate, because she didn't have anything to eat, and yet she got fat. People would rack their brains over how it was possible, and couldn't understand it.

No female smoked. When I was young that never happened! The only person who'd sneak a few puffs was Lájoš' mother-in-law. Lájoš brought his wife from Chmiňany. His wife died and Lájoš inherited the mother-in-law. She was tiny, teeny, and smoked an enormous pipe. Obviously in secret, otherwise the children would have spat at her and thrown rocks. She used to go to the shrubs underneath the bridge to smoke. One time my friend Papiňori and I caught her there, but we didn't tell on her.

Papa's first wife was a *gadži*, a Slovak woman. She came from a terribly poor family – she had four sisters and one brother. They lived with the Roma in the settlement because they were so poor that the peasants didn't want them among themselves. All four sisters married Roma and their brother, a small, poor little kind of *gadžo*, also took a Romani girl for his wife. In fact, it was my grandmother's sister. Only the little *gadžo* died shortly afterwards, his wife shortly after him, and there were five orphan children left behind. The orphans would go knocking at Roma's doors, one time this person would give them something to eat, another time that one, so they didn't go hungry. The Roma wouldn't have allowed the orphans to go hungry. They used to say: *miro čhavo, tiro čhavo, te chal kamen so duj* – my child, your child, both need to eat.

Later a young man from Sabinov married one of the orphan girls. He was an outstanding musician, perfect in every way, so much so that they called him *Ľimalo* – Little Snot. That was because he would go playing with a band from the time he was six years old. His father put him on a table, otherwise you couldn't see him, and he played with the grown-ups. The name *Ľimalo* stuck with him until he died. And the girl didn't want to marry him because of the name. Finally he persuaded her, they got married, and she began to have children. One after another, they were all girls. Fifteen girls! But Little Snot wanted a boy. Only on the sixteenth try did they have a boy. All the girls were as beautiful as princesses, but they had to sleep on the floor, because they couldn't get so many beds in the room.

How we made a living

Our family was the best off in the settlement. Papa would go to play, he had his own band. In the evening they set off on foot for Prešov, played in the pubs, sometimes in various houses too, and came back late at night or in the morning. Their earnings in their pocket – two to three crowns. The young bucks in the village also hired them for village entertainments and weddings.

There was great competition among the musicians. Eastern Slovakia was just brimming with Romani bands. People would say *Rom pes pal o bašaviben murdarel. Ko na džanel te bešavel, na chal.* – Every Rom would give his right arm to be able to play. He who can't play won't eat. – That was the truth. Anyone who couldn't play was left to day laboring for the peasants. At that time there wasn't any other work. But later, when every Rom had learned to fiddle, another saying started going around: *The le lavutarenge o lavutara bašaven.* – Even in musicians' guts the musicians play. – If Mama hadn't slaved from morning to night, we would have gone hungry like the others. Mother sewed for the peasants' wives, crocheted, wove, and in addition to that she rented a piece of the field from our peasant woman and we planted potatoes there. In exchange she had to work thirty days on the peasant's field. I ran away from school, picked up a hoe, and went straight to Mother in the field. Mama said: "Child, how come you aren't in school? You won't learn anything that way!" But I think she was glad that I was helping her. I couldn't have been more than ten years old, because our youngest, Vilma, still wasn't in the world yet, and Vilma is eleven years younger than me. I worked with Mother on the field the whole day, but the peasant woman only counted it for half a day because I couldn't do as much as a grown-up. When we had worked off our rent for the little field, we got money, Mama got five crowns and I got two fifty. And we'd slaved from sunup to sundown. I don't remember as a child ever seeing Mother sleep. She got into bed when we children had already long been asleep, and in the morning we were still dead to the world and Mother was already weaving or crocheting.

During the day my sister Maruša took care of the children. As the oldest daughter, I should really have been the one to take care of them – that was the custom in Romani families – except I was either helping Mama in the field or going to school. Not Maruša, studying wasn't any fun for her.

The guys didn't go to the fields, that was women's work. They learned to play from the time they were little. First Papa started teaching my brother Toňa to play the hammer dulcimer, but then he took him to a famous dulcimer-player for lessons.

There was playing in the settlement every day, actually the musicians practicing. And the people were fine with it. I liked it very much, and I would have liked to learn to play the violin, but Papa said: "What have you got under your skirt? There you are! A violin doesn't belong in a girl's hands! The violin is our bread, not some fun little toy. You want to go playing in the pubs like some slut?" I don't remember in my youth any Romani girl playing on a musical instrument.

People in the settlement made their living any way they could. The whole family contributed. The children – when they were barely four years old – would go with the adults to pick raspberries, strawberries, mushrooms. Mama also took me with her. She gave me a tiny basket and I would gather mushrooms in it. I was bite-sized, and I crawled into the bushes and always found a lot of mushrooms. Except I would say: "Mama, if you don't buy me some bread, I won't go anywhere with you!" Bread was a bigger treat than cake is today. And so every time we went mushroom-picking, Mother would buy me off with a piece of bread.

No one in the settlement had a watch, and we measured time by the sun and the moon. One time there was a beautiful full moon right over our shack – meaning it was midnight. Mother woke me up: "Get up, we're going mushroom-picking!" We went late at night so the count who owned the forest wouldn't catch us.

I was terribly sleepy. "I'm not going anywhere!" I whimpered.

"Come on, you'll help me wake people up!" Mama said. She knew how to deal with me. Waking people up was an important job: she took two pans, walked through the settlement, took two milk cans and banged them against each other and called out: "Get up! Get up!" She gave me two small tin cups, I banged them like her and also called out: "Get up! Get up!" The people, completely alarmed, came running out of their doors: "What is it? What's going on?"

"We're going mushroom-picking, you stinking loafers!" Mother laughed.

After a while all the females were outside, every one with a basket or a sack in hand, and a blanket over herself, and the whole crew headed into the forest, which was called Giráš. It was so light that we could gather pine needles. We came into the forest and the very first thing we did was put together a fire. We stuck potatoes in the ashes and then in the light of the full moon and our campfire we began to look for mushrooms. In those days the mushrooms were so big you tripped over them. No sprinkling any powders, no chemicals, nature would give people good, healthy food.

But then what happened! Someone from the village noticed the fire, and the peasants thought something was burning. On top of everything else, that night the count who owned the forest went out for a ride under the full moon. The count came trotting up, the peasants came streaming in, and again the usual curses came falling down on us: "You Gypsy scum, you vermin, you Pharaonic tribe, you want to burn down the forest?"

The count ordered the women to empty their mushrooms into one pile. "This is my forest! These are my mushrooms!" he shouted. I held my little basket with both arms and pressed it to my belly.

"You empty out your basket too, you black little Gypsy!" he shouted at me.

I began to shriek terribly: "They're my mushrooms! They're my mushrooms! I picked them!" The count's horse got frightened, became alarmed, and I kept screeching and screeching until the leaves started falling from the trees. "Take her away!" said the count and he tried to bring his horse under control.

We took off running. I ran and ran and in my arms I clutched the little basket with the mushrooms. I was the only one who brought my mushrooms home.

We waited a couple of days for the count to forget and went to get more mushrooms. But we didn't make any more fires in the woods.

There was a Jew in town, and he bought medicinal herbs. It was mostly us Roma who gathered them. If a peasant went gathering chamomile, agrimony, or linden blossoms, they'd say he was as poor as a Gypsy. And no peasant could bear that kind of disgrace.

The most beautiful outings were for linden blossoms. The linden trees grew up on the hill. When they were in bloom, fifty or sixty of us would get together and tramp uphill. And because we wanted to get a lot, the women cut off branches with their axes, bound them up into *zajdi*, into kerchiefs on their backs, and we went back. We unloaded the linden branches in front of the shacks and we would pick the blossoms until late at night, while Feriãko would tell us fairy tales. Then we fell asleep on the linden branches and slept until morning underneath the stars in the marvelous linden scent. We were in a swoon from it. The whole settlement slept outside, and we had barely gotten up when we started picking off more of the blossoms.

Then someone told the gamekeeper that the Gypsies were cutting the branches off the linden trees. He came and started shooting. Into the air, of course, but we thought he meant it seriously, and we all dropped down like lightning. We went around on our behinds, and the women had their skirts all in shreds and their behinds scraped raw.

The gamekeeper went to see Papa: "Mikluš, straighten this out!"

"The gamekeeper's going to call in the troopers against us all the way from Hungary, and they'll lock us all up!" said Papa, to persuade the Roma. We were afraid, so we didn't trim any more branches off the linden trees.

We used to carry medicinal herbs to the castle. The castle was large, no one lived in it, the aristocracy gathered there only for the summer, and so they allowed the Jew Cajzler to dry herbs in one room. We carried them in sacks, and he paid forty hellers for a kilo. But what did we go and do! We stuck a rock in the sack so it weighed more. Sometimes the Jew figured it out and then there was an uproar, sometimes he didn't and we made more money. The one whose sack had already been weighed took the rock out carefully and put it in the next one, so the same rock was weighed about ten times. The Jew wasn't any worse off because of that, because he had a badly adjusted scale. Besides, no Rom knew how to add, so he swindled us on the total. This was evened out with our rock.

Once – I might have been ten years old – I went with my friend Papiňori to gather wormwood. Each of us had a *zajda* on her back, both of us were barefoot, Papiňori ahead of me, me following her. All of a sudden Papiňori screamed and something smelly and disgusting went squirting into my eyes. I started howling too. Papiňori had stepped on a toad. Only it wasn't an ordinary toad but a shocking apparition as big as a suckling pig. It goggled its eyes at us. We howled as if we'd gone mad. The peasants who worked on the neighboring fields came running. "What is it? What's going on?" We were incapable of speaking. In our horror we only pointed at the phantom.

"As long as Šariš has been Šariš, a devilish creature like that has never turned up here," said one peasant. "These innocent girls had reason to be frightened."

For two days Papiňori raved in her sleep. Both among the Roma and among the *gadže* throughout the whole area, people talked about the toad for the longest time, and Papiňori and I became famous because we'd found it.

When I began to study at the university, we also had psychology. It was my favorite subject. We learned how various percepts and experiences are embedded in a person's subconscious and affect him for his whole life. Often I recall impressions from my childhood. For example the intoxicating scent of the linden blossoms that we slept on in summer, the noiseless light that fell on our eyes from the stars, the rustling of the branches in the little willow trees, the lightning-bugs that got caught in the women's hair and shone like the most priceless gems. I recall scenes from Romani families: a mother wiping a child's messy face, she's smiling, and the child smiles at her; a woman cooking by the fence, her husband standing beside her and their sometimes leaning toward each other like two leaves on a single tree. Sometimes it seems to me that the stars beneath which we used to fall asleep shine from the eyes of our people, and their quiet breath is like the gusts of wind that blew in the willows. I have never experienced such peace, harmony, and oneness with the universe as in the settlement among our people.

A Rom is his own doctor

We didn't know what a doctor was. Partly because there wasn't money for a doctor, also because people didn't get sick as much as today, and finally, as the saying went: *phuri Romňi feder sar doktoris* – an old Romani woman is better than a doctor (even the peasants said that). Or: *o Rom peske doktoris korkoro* – a Rom is his own doctor.

I must admit that as a little girl I had pneumonia a couple of times. And that was because our mother bundled us up an awful lot. She wove us clothes, caps, and gloves. No Romani child ever had a scarf on his neck or gloves on his hands in his life! Only us. The women would try to persuade Mama: "Máňa, don't bundle the children up that way! Look at our kids! They run around naked and they stay healthy all year long." But Mama wouldn't hear of it and almost every year I had pneumonia. They used to treat me with a solution of manure. They'd squeeze a fresh cow patty or horse patty into some milk, cook it up, and three times a day I had to drink it. It was disgusting, but it helped.

In Prague I met with a professor from India and found out from him that they used the same treatment in Indian villages. Another thing they did if someone's eyes were infected was wash them out with mother's milk. Just like we did in the settlement! The children often had *phumbale jakha* – eye infections (most likely it was conjunctivitis) – the women would let some mother's milk out from their breast into the children's eyes and in a while the infection went away.

If someone had a headache, they would apply leeches. Even the peasants treated themselves with leeches. In Ubrež they had some fresh waters where leeches lived, and so the Roma in those parts would catch them and sell them. They must have known which leeches were all right and which were "crazy." A "crazy" leech could do more harm than good.

As a little girl I never broke anything, because I was scared to. The other children would climb walls, trees, over fences, but not me. One time we went with Mama and Papa to gather mushrooms. In the forest there was an abandoned gamekeeper's lodge with a cherry tree next to it. The cherries were turning ripe just then, so Papa said: "Come on, little girl of mine, I'll put you up in the tree and you toss the cherries into my hat." I might have been six or seven years old. He hoisted me up and seated me on a strong branch that was pretty low. I was picking the cherries – and started to slide off. I said no, no, howled, and was scared. "Don't be scared, child, let go with your little legs! Papa'll catch you in his arms," said Mama, showing me how to slide off. But I said no. Finally Mama had to climb up and get me.

In our house they said: *God'aver manuš džanel te daral, kana kampel* – a wise man knows how to be scared when necessary. I comforted myself with this, and that's why I never broke either a rib, an arm, or a leg. But one time I burned myself badly. I wasn't even going to school yet. Grandma was making *pišota*, little pies filled with potatoes, and I was standing next to her and messing in the dough. "Here you go," said Grandma to get rid of me, "here's a piece of dough, make yourself a *marikľi*, a patty-cake." I was happy, kneaded it into a little ball, rolled it out flat with the rolling pin, and was going to the stove. Except I missed my step on the stool and fell on the stove-top with my forearm. Did that ever hurt! A piece of my skin was stuck there. Grandma ran over and sprinkled salt on the burn. I thought I'd go out of my mind! But the salt cleaned out the wound and I didn't even get a blister. Than Grandma ran outside quickly, picked some kind of leaves, and made me a bandage out of them. Unfortunately, I don't know what kind they were. My burn didn't ooze any pus and healed quickly.

When a child was crying and couldn't be comforted, the Roma believed that someone had given it the evil eye. And they believe it to this day. You can give the evil eye to an adult too, and even to dough! That's why Romani housewives carefully covered their dough with a cloth, so nobody gave it the evil eye and the people who ate it afterwards wouldn't get sick.

When my Máňa was two years old, someone gave her the evil eye on me so bad that it's a wonder she didn't die from it. We were staying in Kapušany at my mother-in-law's. Máňa was playing on the ground, and she had long, golden hair after my mother. She was so beautiful that I said to myself many times: is this really my child? Her grandma had given her two spoons – we never had toys – and Máňa was clinking them together and was happy. My husband's uncle Franc came to see us. He said: "Dear, sweet God, how can there be a child that beautiful on this earth?" He sat for a little while looking at Máňa and then he left. After a while Máňa started to cry. She cried and cried and couldn't be comforted. I took her in my arms, carried her around the parlor, sang to her, but the girl just kept on bawling and pressing her little head to my neck. My nerves were shot, I had work to do, and I started to scold her. "Don't yell at her," my mother-in-law rebuked me, "she's probably been given the evil eye. Do you know she can die from that?" Then she took a cup with water, plucked nine glowing coals out of the stove onto the burner and tossed them into the water by turning them over with a knife. Máňa bawled until she began to choke, and soon she was completely blue. The coals started to sink to the bottom, one by one.

"You see," said my mother-in-law, "she's been given the evil eye in a bad way. The number of coals that sink to the bottom shows how many times she's been given the evil eye." Then she washed Máňa with the *jagalo paňi*, fire water, the water she'd tossed the coals in. She washed her little eyes, her mouth, her temples, under her arms, and her legs. She splashed the rest of the water on the door hinges and into the corners of the parlor. At the same time she said something to drive the spirits away. In two minutes Máňa had fallen asleep, sleeping like the dead, and when she woke up, she was fine.

It was Franc who'd given her the evil eye. Not on purpose, Franc was a good person. As he was enjoying watching her, he fixed his eyes on her in such a way that it made her ill. Then my mother-in-law tied an *indral'ori*, a little red piece of cloth, around Máňa's wrist to ward off the evil eye.

Some social workers think that Romani children grow up like wild weeds and no one takes care of them. But that's not true. The kind of care every mother lavishes on her infant! I saw it every day with my own eyes. Two or three times a days the mother would let out some milk from her breast onto the child and wipe his little legs, his arms, his behind, his tummy. So he would grow up nice and strong. When the child screamed, the older women would call to the young mother: "Exercise him, he's *prephaglo*" – all racked and rent. Every knolted up experienced mother knew from the child's crying what it needed: whether it had been given the evil eye, if it was all turned around from being carried wrong – *prephaglo* – if it had an upset stomach or gas. When it was *prephaglo*, the mother put it on a flat table – and then: right elbow to the left knee, left elbow to the right knee, for maybe half an hour, until the child calmed down.

But what good were all the doctor's knowledge and attention good for against hunger! How many children had their tummies sticking out and legs rickety from hunger! At home we washed them in water that had been used to make *haluški*, in the summer mothers buried them up to their little necks in warm sand. The children grew up, but for many of them their crooked legs never straightened out.

In our parts, more Roma died from tuberculosis than from anything else. No medicine was strong enough for that. Besides, not even the *gadže* knew how to treat it then.

When someone got sick, the first thing to do was to look for the *keriben*, the magic that brought on the sickness. The Roma recognized three main causes of disease: a punishment for bad deeds – *o Del les mard'a*, God had punished him, it was said. Then they said: *arakhl'a les e vera*, his broken oath had caught up with him. And finally *pokerde les*, a spell had been cast on him.

It was believed of some women that they knew how to cast spells. They would get a *kotor*, a piece of clothing from the person they wanted to do away with, sew the *kotor* into a frog's mouth, bury the frog down in the hearth or pack it in clay and put it in the oven – and as the frog dried out, the one with the spell on him wasted away and died. As soon as anyone got sick, the entire family began to dig around the hearth and took the stove apart in case they found a *keriben* somewhere.

The entire settlement took care of the child even before it was born. The older women made sure the pregnant woman observed "the rules for pregnant women." She couldn't, for example, took at a frog, a snake, a slug, or at any kind of foul animal. If ever she put her hand out toward a dog or a cat, the rest would call out at her: "Don't touch that, you'll give birth to a freak of nature!" They would do it in such a way that she didn't get frightened – and if she'd already gotten frightened, God forbid she should put her hand on her body, because then the child would have a *jag*, a fire, a scarlet blemish, on the same spot. And if a pregnant woman got hungry for some kind of food, they would give her as much of it as she wanted, even if she belonged to an enemy family. She was walking past a shanty where they were making, let's say, cabbage pancakes, she got a whiff of it and got hungry for them – since our shanties' doors were always open – and right away the woman of the house would call to her: "*Av te chal!*" – come and eat! – and that even if they weren't on speaking terms. But the woman had caught sight of her, seen that she was hungry for pancakes, and invited her to have some food, and they didn't say more to each other than that. If a pregnant woman didn't get what she was hungry for, she could lose the baby.

Otherwise pregnant women were always being reminded to sing, so the child would be a happy one and become a musician, and not to curse anyone or use bad language, not to get angry and try to think only of nice things. The husbands and mothers-in-law of a pregnant woman would tell everyone else: "Be nice to her, so a nice person will be born." Of course, that meant the men and the mothers-in-law had to be nice all the time, because the females were almost always pregnant. And that's probably why the pregnant women were urged: "Learn to forgive."

The castle nobles

On a hill that lay below Šariš there was a castle. It belonged to the counts. The aristocracy came to Šariš only in the summer and spent the winter in Vienna. The castle was administered for them by a man named Pulský, the biggest landowner in Šariš. During the war the roof on the castle burned and after the war the peasants took apart the bricks and stones for building new houses.

The aristocracy also had a small castle in Malý Šariš. The countess was as black as a Romani woman and liked to go horseback riding. They used to hire us to do work for them, and we dug potatoes for them. The whole settlement always went to the fields together. The black countess' son liked us enormously and followed us around, and the peasants' daughters were jealous of us. In the evening he would walk us home from the fields and we had to sing for him. Pekar – that poor guy's gone, too – took a hoe and made like he was conducting. We tied some flowers from the field to the hoe and the count laughed.

One time we wanted to frighten him. Our womenfolk pretended to be having a fight. We were pulling each other by the hair, punching each other, cursing each other, throwing potato stalks at each other. But he wasn't that stupid; he could tell that we weren't doing it for real, wasn't frightened, on the contrary, he laughed so hard he was rolling in the potatoes.

In the afternoon his mother received us to check on us. He told her something in Hungarian and then she wanted us to repeat the fight. So we went at it all over again and she laughed so hard she got the hiccups, and she gave each of us ten crowns.

Our menfolk never fought. We were *lavutariko vatra*, a musicians' settlement. It's said: "A musician can allow himself to do things that a *degeš* may not do – and a *degeš* can allow himself to do things that a musician may not do." A *degeš* could never presume to wear black clothes and a white shirt – and a musician would not allow himself to get mixed up in a fight, because it would not have been in keeping with his dignity. And also – how would he play if, say, he lost his fingers!

But the women! There were constant arguments in the settlement – but mostly just to have a little excitement. One time two sisters-in-law were brawling so fiercely that one bit the other's finger. It almost made her choke with anger, and they had to catch her by the legs and hang her upside down. Some of the womenfolk would have such angry fits that they would thrash around as if they were having an epileptic seizure. Another woman then had to sit on her face with her bare bottom so she could get over it. But *romaňi choľi sar balvaj - avel, džal*, Romani anger is like the wind – it comes and it goes. In the morning the women argued, at noon they still weren't speaking, but one would already be sending for the other's child to come taste what she'd cooked. And in the evening they were best friends again.

Every summer at the castle they would have May festivals. And my father played at the May festivals with his band. He took us with him so we could see what kind of things there were in the world. The landowners from the whole region would gather there. They traveled in carriages with white horses in harness, and we would have been happy never to have seen anything else ever again! And we also turned the countesses' heads. We had long, thick, black hair, and one after another the countesses would take it into their hands and say: *schööön, schööön* – meaning it was pretty.

Of course, the aristocrats would dance. They danced the Hungarian czardas and waltzes. Nothing else. One time Papa asked them if I, his daughter, could perform a foreign dance for the lords and ladies. At that time the charleston had come into fashion and we learned it right away. We learned it from each other. Someone had been in the movie theater, become familiar with the steps, others became familiar with them from him, and after a while the whole settlement was dancing the charleston.

The aristocrats assented. The parted to form a circle, Papa started playing, and I and one other boy from the settlement started to dance. We danced like madmen, in a while we couldn't feel the ground under our feet, and only when the band stopped playing did we slowly begin to come to.

The counts and countesses applauded so forcefully it's a wonder we didn't go deaf. Papa said in Romani: "Hold out your skirt!" I held out my skirt and tens and twenties began to fall into it. For the first time in my life I had made money. At that time I could have been seven or eight years old. I ran through the whole town with the change in my skirt, the boy running with me and yelling: "I danced too! I danced too!" I reached home completely out of breath and poured the money out on the table. Mama counted it up, gave half to me and half to him.

One time Papa took us to another of the counts' May festivals. We were there all day without anything to eat, just watching how the countesses were dressed, how they spun during the czardas, and during that exhilarating spectacle we also completely forgot we had a stomach.

In the meantime, down in the settlement our grandmother had cooked a whole pot of *pišota*. On the one hand she was sorry for us that we'd had nothing to eat, and on the other hand she wanted to show the aristocrats that we weren't beggars. The *pišota* were swimming in butter as if in soup. She covered the pot with the lid, tied it up in her *zajda*, and trudged up the enormous hill to the castle. "Children, I'm bringing *pišota*," she said. We all came running up to her. Grandma untied her *zajda*, took off the lid – and what a smell! We were brought up not to throw ourselves on our food, even if we were dying of hunger. We had to wait until the grown-ups told us we could eat. Grandma said nothing. We waited and waited, the *pišota* giving off their scent, we were salivating – and Grandma began to wail, "Aaai, aaai! I forgot the spoons at home! We can't pick up the *pišota* with our hands in front of the nobles!" The scent of the *pišota* and Grandma's wailing dirge carried high over the May festival. Slowly the lords and ladies, the director of the school, the castle keeper, the counts, and the countesses, gathered around the pot. The director pulled a little knife out from his pocket and cut little sticks out of switches from a hazelnut tree. We also did it that way at home, but Grandma was acting like we never ate with anything other than silverware and like she was seeing sticks from a hazelnut tree for the first time in her life. Then she said: "If it please the lords and ladies, they may taste our Gypsy *pišota*." The counts and countesses rushed toward the pot as if they hadn't eaten anything for a week, picking up the *pišota* from the butter with the hazelnut sticks, abandoning all their etiquette, smacking their lips, slurping, and gobbling their food down – and in the end there wasn't a single *pišot* left for us. But we were all satiated with pride that the aristocrats didn't scruple to eat Gypsy *pišota*. We would have shunned their food, because they fed on all kinds of filth such as frogs and crayfish. Fortunately they forgot to offer us some then. If you think about it, the castle aristocrats were in fact *degeše*.

How we ate and what we ate

It wasn't a given that you had a spoon. In our settlement there could be found plenty of families whose belongings didn't include a spoon. Where a household had a capable guy around, he carved a spoon out of wood, but there were also those who didn't know how or were too lazy to. An orderly household kept three or four spoons, and the whole family ate with them in turn. And in the doorway there would be children from the neighbors' houses: "Auntie, Mama sent me to ask you to send a spoon." If someone bought a baking pan or a frying pan, he really acquired it for the whole settlement. Few families had matches. What for? The housewife would take her pot lid and go to a neighbor who was cooking just then: "Haňa, give me a light!" She took a few cinders on her pot lid and at home she used them to light the leaves in the stove. Whichever woman in the settlement was the first to cook something, she put some in a bowl from the pot and sent one of her children: "Take this to Zuzka or Haňa, they're always hungry there." There was great solidarity among Roma.

Our Sunday dish was *haluški*. Every Sunday we had a special meal with *haluški* and curd cheese.

There was no breakfast in the morning, we waited for the *haluški*. The peasants' wives from Medzany went to sell curd cheese and butter on Sunday, and I would run over to them first thing in the morning, buy two lumps of curd cheese for two crowns and a quarter-kilo lump of butter. Grandma and my oldest sister Ema cooked. On ordinary days Grandma would also stand me by the stove – from the time I was six or seven years old – put a chopping board and a spoon in my hand, and say: "You've got to cut nice, thin little noodles, learn how, you're a female!" On Sunday, of course, my practice *haluški* didn't pass muster – and besides, *haluški* for ten to twelve people, that was something only Grandma and Ema could manage.

In the afternoon Grandma placed a huge bowl of *haluški* on the table. We stood around the table and ate standing up from the same bowl. Where would we have found chairs for so many people? They wouldn't even have fit in our parlor! And so when we had those special *haluški* we stood up as at a reception. Only Papa ate separately and sat down while doing it. What's more, Mother would be so nice to him that she'd stir his *haluški* around the pot with the butter in it.

Haluški were such a filling dish that afterwards on Sunday we didn't have dinner.

The end of winter was the worst time for Roma. There was no work in the field, and though we helped the peasants cut wood and clear snow, it wasn't tempting work. People left weddings for the summer, and the few village entertainments there were didn't bring in much money for the musicians. In most families, their supply of potatoes ran out – if people had managed to put together a supply at all. And so people would go to gather *kirňavki*. *Kirno* means rotten. *Kirňavki* were the frozen potatoes that remained on the field through the winter. We went and dug them out from under the snow. The peel was completely black and the inside white, and it was crumbled into a flour. It smelled terrible. The women mixed this smelly substance with water and baked flatcakes out of it. Even the flatcakes smelled and were rubbery as shoe leather. We ate it and were glad that we had something to put in our mouths.

*K*alemardo

Kalemardo is a word that maybe can't even be translated. It means "punished by blackness." The color black was a curse. Every taunt and every insult of the peasants at our expense was smeared with the color black. For them we were "black Pharaohs." When they wanted to make fun of us, they asked us: "You know why a Gypsy has white palms? Because when his mama smoked him in the chimney, that's how he held onto the stick." The worst thing was that among ourselves we separated each other into castes, black and white. If someone was a little lighter, he would jeer at us black ones: "You crow! You shoe polish! You're like something they pulled up out of the ground! Hey look, her mama gave birth to a sack of coal!" Though we yelled "Curd cheese! Dough-girl!" at them, we still felt inferior. But at Christmas time Roma concluded their best wishes for the coming year with a beautiful sentence: *Kaj te dživas jekhe avreha sar odi kaľi phuv le kale mareha.* – May we live with one another like black earth and black bread. – This wish reminded us that we should stick together and not pay attention to whether someone was white or black.

My best friend was called Papiňori, or Little Goose. Because she was a beautiful white girl. Goose isn't an insult in Romani at all, on the contrary, it expresses admiration for the fact that someone is white. The nickname Papin was very exalted.

One time we had an adventure that completely amazed me. In the summer a soldier's garrison came to our town and was quartered in the school. The word got out that the soldiers gave the leftovers from their lunch to the poor. A whole horde of us Romani children set off for there and they told us we should get into line and wait. And so we got into line and we waited. I let Maruša from my family in ahead of me because she was white, I let Papiňori in front of me because she was a beautiful, white girl, and in the end I stayed completely in the back, because I was ashamed that I was black.

The officers ate in the garden in front of the school and we – each of us with a little milk-can in our hand – waited and waited for them to finish eating. All of a sudden someone called out: "Gypsies to the kitchen! Hurry, hurry, and keep in a nice line!" I went in last, the cook looked at us and looked at us and then said: "Come here, you pretty little girl!" Everyone looked to see who he meant. I thought it meant Maruša from our family or Papiňori, but he was looking at me. Except that I didn't dare go, because I thought that I was terribly ugly from being so black. And the cook said: "Yes, you, you! You there in the back, you pretty little black Gypsy baby!" So he really did mean me. I went up and he filled my milk-can full of food.

The whole way home I thought about how he called me the "pretty black one," and I just couldn't figure it out.

One girl in our settlement was a beautiful white girl, except that she went around unwashed and ungroomed. One time her mother was arguing with our mama and our mama said: "What good is it that your girl is pretty, when she smells like garbage and her hair's like feathers!" And her mother yelled: "What good is it parading your girl around and her wearing clothes that are all ribbons and bows when she's as black as a crow!"

It hurt me terribly. I stopped enjoying my clothes with the ribbons and bows. I even stopped enjoying the fact that I was the only girl from the settlement who wore underpants. I was enormously proud of that, because at that time Roma had no idea what underwear was! Only our mother dressed like the city girls. When we went on the merry-go-round, all the girls held on to their skirts so the wind wouldn't expose their nakedness. I, on the contrary, let my skirt billow all around me, so the whole world could see that I had underpants.

Later when I got married and my husband wanted to take me away to Kapušany, I said: "I'm not going anywhere! I don't want to make you ashamed in front of people because I'm so black!" He laughed: "You crazy woman! You've got a beautiful figure.

After you come to live with us you'll see that you'll have the nicest legs in all of Kapušany!"

Christmas giving

I could have been eight or ten years old. The town organized the distribution of Christmas presents for the poor. No one was as poor as we Roma. And then, not even the poorest *gadžo* would have stooped so low as to go to a distribution together with the Gypsies, so in fact the distribution was only for us.

A couple of days before Christmas Eve, the town crier walked around and called out: "Old clothes for the gypsies! Old clothes for the Gypsies!" Then he went from house to house collecting hand-me-down blouses, skirts, trousers, and coats.

The distribution took place the day before Christmas Eve. The town crier came into the settlement: "Move it, you Gypsy scum! There's going to be a distribution!"

Our people thronged into the municipal building. In the main hall was a stage where from time to time there were amateur theater productions. On the stage was a pile of clothing for the gypsies. The children, women, and men crowded on the floor. The parish priest, the mayor, the butcher, a soldiers' representative, a couple of peasants, and the town crier were on the podium. The parish priest gave a talk about how we should be grateful, humble, honest, and hard-working. The children fidgeted. One infant broke out bawling in his mother's arms and godfather Čanda told him loudly not to disturb the priest. Godfather Čanda caught crayfish for the castle aristocrats, thought he knew how the aristocrats did things, and sometimes arrogated to himself the right to bring us into line. Then the mayor spoke about discipline, order, industriousness, and civic responsibility. Finally the town crier was supposed to give out the presents. He held a pair of men's trousers up high: "Who gets these?" "Me! Me! My boy! Just my brother's size! Give them to our grandfather, he doesn't have anything to wear, the poor man has to lie in bed all day long naked ...!" The people shouted over one another and pressed forward to the stage.

"Here you go, since your grandpa doesn't have any trousers!" the mayor decided. "Naked rear ends are prohibited in our town!" Loud guffaws both in the hall and on the stage. The gentlemen were having an excellent time. The trousers sailed through the air for godfather Čangora's grandpa. People turned their heads toward them hungrily. The town crier held an old loden coat in his hands. Again a hullabaloo broke out. My father's voice drowned it all out: "Our bass player needs that coat. In the wintertime he has nothing to go out playing in." The hall fell silent. My father's word was law. The little, thin, black bass player made his way to the podium. He took the loden coat from the town crier.

Next came a wide, pleated skirt, the kind the peasants' wives used to wear. A murmur went through the hall, but the people waited to hear what Father would say, and whom he would assign the skirt to. It looked like discipline would be maintained and the gentlemen's fun would be over. Just then the butcher leaned toward the town crier and whispered something to him. In a moment the light went out and the crier shouted: "Grab it!"

The people began howling and clamoring. "Let go, I grabbed it first! ... Let go, you, I got it!"

"Shoes! Who needs shoes?" the town crier called out, and the shoes swooshed over our heads. One piece of clothing went flying after another. In the dark. There was indescribable shouting, shrieking, insults, curses, and weeping in the hall. People fumbled for the rags flying by. One caught one trouser leg, someone else the other, neither wanted to give up his booty, rip! and the trousers were in two pieces. It went the same way with the coats, the skirts, and the blouses. "I've only got one shoe! I've only got one shoe!" wailed no-nose Lina. The gentlemen on the podium were choking with laughter. I was bawling and terribly ashamed.

Finally the light went on. The women had become disheveled and their clothes torn as they were fighting over the gifts. Under their feet rolled crumpled skirts, jackets with torn sleeves, and trousers with the seams ripped apart. The people were silent. They were exhausted, and without a word we left for the settlement.

Afterwards the peasants said the Gypsies didn't know how to appreciate anything.

The butcher

There didn't use to be any television and few people had a radio – and so people had to find their own entertainment. The peasants had a good time making fun of us as best they could. They'd get up their schemes, start an argument – and boom, they had a show like out of the Wild West. They stood on the bridge and watched the women tearing each other's hair and flashing their bare privates at each other. There were even those who brought little chairs to the bridge.

The most vicious one of all was the butcher. He had a little shop not far from our settlement. He learned to speak perfect Romani, and that's why we loved him at first. When we came into the shop or when he ran into us in town, he'd come right to a stop and speak our language. It made us feel awfully good and we believed everything he told us.

For example he'd say to Gejza: "Ay, mister, haven't you heard?"

"And what should I have heard, sir?"

"Haven't you heard that Andriš slept with your wife?"

"What a thing to say, sir, my wife is a respectable woman!"

"Respectable! Every woman is respectable, but only with her words!"

So Gejza went running to the settlement, beat his wife, argued with Andriš, and then dragged his wife to the church, where with her hair all undone she had to swear she hadn't had anything to do with Andriš. This all took place in public, *pre vatra*, and the *gadže* had something else to have fun with.

On Easter Monday in Slovakia in our parts there was a custom where the men would douse the women with water. The Torysa flowed near the settlement and everything that passed for a man went running from morning til night with a bucket, and as soon as some female showed herself outside, she got a pail of water over her head. The butcher stood on the bridge and goaded the guy on: "Throw her in all the way! Throw her in the water!" The guys, who by now were all raring to go, started catching the women and one after another threw them in the icy Torysa. The women shrieked and yelled and choked on the water.

"Hold her head underwater! Dunk her good! For real, as long as she holds out!" bellowed the butcher. "If she drowns on you, you'll find another one, a young one!" The men went completely wild, as if they'd lost their minds. They held the bucking women's heads under the water. The peasants were going to church for mass, but they didn't get there. They stayed standing on the bridge and applauded the circus show that was going on.

At the beginning my Papa also chased us with a bucket of water, but when he saw what the butcher was doing, he threw the bucket away and shouted: "Stop! Can't you see the *gadže* are making a laughing stock out of you?!"

On the bridge the butcher hooted: "Hey you womenfolk, throw him in the water!" The women who'd managed to crawl out of the Torysa and who by this point were staggering around, spitting out water, and were barely conscious, were turned upside down by the butcher's shouting, hurled themselves on Papa in a frenzy and threw him into the Torysa. They may not have even known what they were doing.

Papa then came home, wet and blue to the bone, his teeth chattering. He got a cold and lay sick for a long time with a fever. The worst thing was that for a time he lost his authority among the Roma.

The peasants didn't like it when a *čhibalo* had any authority over his people. They wanted to be able to manipulate us. They tried to plant the kind of mayors in the settlement that would do what they wanted and not what the Roma wanted. Papa always stuck with our people, but sometimes he was in a very difficult position.

After a while the Roma recognized that the butcher wasn't any friend of ours, even if he spoke Romani. We were mortified by his ridicule and his malice. And so we girls and women agreed that we would get even with him. One time he called about thirty of us to come dig potatoes for him. He was rich and had plenty of farm land. We came first thing in the morning and said: "Look here, we're going to work on the field and meanwhile the children are hungry! At least give us some bread and bacon for the children." The butcher gave us some bread, bacon, and soup bones. "Go take it home, but make sure you're back quickly!" We brought it home all right, but we never came back. We went to work for a different peasant.

In the evening the infuriated butcher came tearing in as far as the edge of the settlement. We ran up to him from all sides. The men stood at a distance and looked menacing. The wisest one among us, the old woman Cibrikaňa, said civilly: "Just so you know, we did not come to pull a fast one on you for no reason! It was to get even for how our men beat us unjustly because of your lying slander. And also because the devil has taken root in you." Then one after another the women let fly with: "You lied about me when you said this … You made up this and this kind of story about me ...!" Naturally obscenities also started flying. And the butcher disappeared from the settlement as quick as he could.

The grocer

There were also *gadže* in the town who sympathized with us. It cost one of them plenty. The grocer. He had a little store not far from our settlement. The Roma bought candles, kerosene, salt, and tobacco from him – and because they mostly didn't have money, they pawned him their skirts, blouses, and clothes. "Hold it for us until the peasant pays us for working on the field."

The grocer waited and waited – one person came to pick up her skirt, another one didn't because the few crowns the peasant farmer paid were spent on other things. And so the Gypsy rags grew moldy in a little closet behind the store. They grew moldier and moldier, until a truck came and the grocer had them loaded on the truck and they hauled them off to a trash heap somewhere. The store had to close down because he went bust. And yet he neither insulted us nor cursed us.

The prewar Communists

In Šariš there was a big mill, in the mill there were workers and they founded a Communist party. On May Day they went to Prešov to demonstrate. They went with banners and slogans. And we Romani children went running after them as far as Prešov. We didn't have the foggiest idea about politics, but we were happy that something was going on, and we wanted to be there.

In the church the parish priest preached that Communists were godless and that they had made horses' stables out of the churches in Russia. "May the Lord God punish you!" the peasants shouted at the departing workers.

Mother prayed for the Communists and used to say that Lenin was a good man, we picked it up from her, and Pudlajner from the mill could only be astonished: "Look, my man, a Gypsy child and she knows who Lenin is."

In Prešov the Communists from the whole region gathered. The soldiers came and dispersed the procession with water, spraying from the firemen's hoses. And we came home completely soaked.

Furniture polish

Čanda and his wife Helena were the only ones in the settlement who didn't have children. Childless women were mocked cruelly by the other women: a tree that bore no fruit should be put to the fire they said. But Helena knew how to reply so obscenely that everyone became ashamed and stopped.

Čanda was a funny little man. He used to go catch crayfish for the aristocrats and the peasants made fun of him: "Here, goose! Here, goose!" I don't know why. He always got awful mad, dropped his pants, stuck his bare bottom out at the peasant, and slapped it. And the peasant laughed still more.

In spite of the fact that Čanda was no he-man and everyone made him out to be a loony, Helena loved him. He never reproached her for not having children, he never left her, although he could have easily without anyone judging him for it. After Čanda's death Helena cried for a long time. And poor Čanda died a terrible death. With seven other people in a mass poisoning. They even wrote about it in the newspapers!

They brought a train car to the station with some barrels, and since the peasants made use of every opportunity to have some fun at our expense, they sent this clod of a fellow off to the settlement: "Tell the Gypsies they've brought some booze. Let them get their bottles and come down to the station."

Naturally, our people grabbed their bottles, milk cans, and pots right away – anything that came to hand – and off they went to the station. My future husband, Jožka, was visiting just then. Along with Běla, a magnificent lead violinist. Jožka also got a bottle somewhere and was getting ready to go to the station so he could have a drink with my father and with Běla. Papa never did drink very much, he'd have just a token glass with them. Jožka was a big, strong guy, and he'd already eaten his fill and never drank on an empty stomach. But Běla drank on an empty stomach.

Two hours hadn't gone by when Běla's eyes glazed over, he went into convulsions, his face became distorted – and he was dead! And Helena was running around the settlement and wailing: " Čanda's dying, ay, dear mother, my Čanda is dying!"

"Run for the doctor! Quick, go get the doctor! People are dropping like flies!" Someone ran to the village, soon the rack wagons came, and they couldn't get those who'd drunk the booze to the hospital in Prešov in time. That very day two *gadžo* beggars from Lipenný had come to the settlement, two little girls like flower-buds. They both died, because they'd also drunk the stuff. Seven people died in all. Among them was a seven-year-old boy. Four people went blind. It was furniture polish. No one could be bothered to investigate who gave it to the Roma to drink. In the newspapers there was a short item:

"Seven Gypsies died in Velký Šariš from poisoning by furniture polish."

Our girl Vilma – she might have been seven years old – was playing outside then and someone also gave her some to drink. I was watching, the child turned completely black, went into convulsions – I grabbed her in my arms and ran off to Prešov with her. I ran almost the whole way. I dashed into the hospital, but they left us sitting in the waiting room. Only when I began beating on the door and shouting: "You're killing my child!" did the doctor come out and they immediately pumped out Vilma's stomach. They kept her there for a day. I stayed with her. They put her in a room with the two dead beggar girls. Their mother was sitting by them and crying.

Helena, Čanda's widow, didn't sing with us for a long time after that, because she was in mourning. But everything passes, both good and bad, and so she began to sing with us again, invited the young people to her place, and was in good spirits with us. But she never forgot her Čanda.

Holidays

The Roma were always poor, but at Christmas and Easter everyone wanted to show how much they could afford. They saved the whole year long from what little they earned. From kreutzer to kreutzer. And on the holidays they bought meat. For Easter it was ham or sausage. People put them in the window so everyone could see what they had. They baked buns and put them in the window as well.

On Ash Wednesday the Roma buried a double bass. On Tuesday there was also a ball, and there was dancing right from noon on until the next day. And on Wednesday at noon they buried the double bass. Our menfolk dressed in their holiday best – black clothes, white shirt, and they'd go to the ale house. The double bass lay on the table like a corpse and the men would lament, cry, and wail over it. The peasants had fun just watching.

When the show was at its best, the innkeeper would come and hurl a bucket of water on our menfolk. Soaking wet, they ran home. With that, Shrovetide ended and the seven weeks of Lent began. Throughout that time there was no music anywhere and life was hard.

During Whitsuntide the *gadže* decorated their windows with linden twigs. While the peasants put two or three sprays in their window, we put whole triumphal arches.

It was beautiful, fresh, and green. Our menfolk went from house to house and played for the peasants. The peasants' wives would throw them a kreutzer. When they had gone round the whole town, they came back to the settlement and played for us. They stopped at every shanty and played everyone their song. Naturally they played for free for us Roma. Grandma would say: "Hurry up, little girl, run, open the window, let in the fresh air and the beautiful music!" All the windows in the settlement were open and we all had a good time.

We had a beautiful custom when there was a new moon. The men went out and bowed to the new moon with their heads uncovered. They brought a bucket of water with them and in the bucket there was small change. They believed that as the moon waxed, so would their riches grow.

In some settlements, as I heard, they kept a similar custom at New Year's and elsewhere for Christmas Day.

Later we stopped bowing to the moon, but I don't know when and how. But to this day the old, upright Roma admonish their children not to curse and not to speak obscenely in front of the Moon, the Sun, the Wind, and the Stars, because they are living beings and they radiate great strength. If a person is disrespectful toward them, they might destroy him. It was also true that if someone became paralyzed, they said: a cursed wind went round him.

Our grandmother respected the Fires most. She'd say: "Child, child, how would we Roma survive if we didn't have fire!" And before she began to make dough, she always threw a little flour into the fire.

The fairs

A couple of times a year we went to the fair. To Viťaz, to Sabinov, to Chmiňany, to Solivar, as far as Stará Lubovňa, even to Košice. A fair was a magnificent event. Thousands of Roma gathered at the fairs from the entire surrounding area. The peasants celebrated the fairs for two or three days, but we came a whole week ahead of time – at least to those places where we had relatives. We stayed with them.

The first two days the relations would hug each other, cry in each other's arms, drink to their meeting again after such a long time – they hadn't seen each other for two months! – but the third day the calumnies started, the intrigues, the bickering, the arguing. "Your girl is uppity, she's got a tongue like this! ... Your boy is pretty flashy, but what you boy's got in his head, my boy's got in his backside! ... Your girl thinks she's a beauty, but green leaves dry up and fall away – you'll see what'll become of her in two years" ... You think the Šariš gypsies know how to make *haluški*? What do you take me for? I'd rather eat frog shit than their *haluški*! ... Think those Gypsies know how to play music? They play like a guy with TB pissing on a hot stove ..." Every exchange of opinions was accompanied by illustrative gestures that sometimes crossed over into dance figures or acrobatic movements – and again, it was all for show. The most ingenious actresses were Marča and no-nose Pipka from Sabinov. They were an indispensable part of every fair and people always waited until they appeared and played out their duel of word-images and dance figures such as not even the best poet and the most inventive choreographer in the world could think up.

When we parted a week later to go home, we'd cried in each other's arms again, kissed each other, and assured one another that we were the most devoted relatives. And as long as two Roma weren't related, if they found sweethearts in each other, it was agreed that "my boy will marry your girl and we'll be a family!" And it really happened. Sometimes children got hitched that way who'd made mud *haluški* together, their little behinds bare, and sometimes children who hadn't even been born yet.

The *gadže* went to church during the fairs, but not the Roma. An old story explains why not: the peasants built a new church in the village. On Sunday the Rom wanted to go look at the church, but the peasant stopped him at the gate, "Where do you think you're going, Gypsy? You think we built ourselves a church so you gypsies could go stink it up for us?" And the Roma said: "Just you wait, you old hayseed, until we Roma build our own church, we won't even let your God in!"

The fairs drew the Roma mainly because it was a place you could get together. Not only with relatives, but with other Roma who'd come from far away, up from Poland, from Hungary, from Russia. We learned about each other, how we lived, how we spoke, how we cooked, what we ate, how we made our living: in one place they cooked *haluški* in such and such a way, in another place some other way, in one settlement near Košice they were said to eat gophers, somewhere else they caught badgers and sold badger fat to the pharmacies, in Spiše the Roma were rich and their young men went out courting on bicycles, around Svidník the Roma talked through their nose, near Humenný they called shoes *bagančata*, and when a girl said "I bought some *bagančata* with high heels," you could have split your sides laughing! We found out at the fairs who was born, who died, who'd married whom, who was walking the earth as a spirit after their death, where the phantoms appeared at nighttime, where there was work to be found, that the blind guy from Michalovce had two wives, each sleeping on one side of him and they never argued, and the like. The fair was a marketplace of sensations, information, a congress, a convention, a conference, a festival.

At the fair the guys bought us girls gingerbread hearts. One time a guy from Sabinov wanted to buy me a heart, but by that time Jožka was already coming to call at our place, so I said: "Don't make bad blood, don't summon misfortune on our heads, and don't buy me a heart!" He was sad and bought me at least the biggest gingerbread doll there was at the fair. When the other young men saw that, they started to buy me, Maruša, and Hanuš gingerbread too, so we came home with our skirts full of gingerbread. Mother had a great big basket she kept her clean laundry in. She took out the laundry and we poured the gingerbread into the basket. By evening the basket was empty, because the children from the settlement had eaten up all the gingerbread. Except the big gingerbread doll, which Papa hung on the wall where it stayed until during the war when the Fascists made us move to Korpáš.

When the fair came to our town, Šariš was flooded with swarms of Roma from the whole area. Our womenfolk went to the fair asking: "Where are you from, girl? Where are you from, boy?" "From Sabinov ... From Chmiňany ... From Vranov ..." "Myyyy goodness, that's a long ways away! You must be hungry, come and eat!" And they were already turning out *haluški* and hosting Romani strangers.

People would come on foot to the fairs from as far as fifty or sixty kilometers away. Our whole *kumpaňija* would set out on the road. At night we stayed with someone's relatives who lived in settlements along the way, and when it was nice we slept outside and in the morning traveled some more.

One time Jožka, my future husband, came with us, and also Moškaňa and her husband. Moškaňa weighed at least one hundred and twenty kilos. She didn't have to eat a mouthful all week long, but still she wouldn't lose even a tenth of a kilo. I don't know what kind of *natura* she must have had!

Jožka came from a family that dealt in pigs. He started to pretend he was buying that fat creature. He rattled off at her husband: "How about if you sell me your fat, black pig?"

Moškaňa's husband stammered: "H-h-h-ow much will you give me for her?" My husband didn't stutter, but he aped the other man: "H-h-h-ow much do you want?" We were falling on the ground with laughter. The fat, black woman couldn't even breathe, she was laughing so hard. It didn't bother her in the least that we were having fun at her expense, since she knew no one wanted to offend her. She was glad she could make people enjoy themselves. And enjoy ourselves we did, the whole night long. In the morning we continued on our trip. We walked through a forest and came upon a fountain. Papa collected some water in his hat – it was utterly ice-cold – and we all had a good long drink.

We walked past a settlement where the Roma lived in holes in the ground. A pit was dug a half-meter into the earth, three by three meters, and over it a little roof made of branches covered with turned-over sod, with an opening in the middle where the smoke came out. A piece of sackcloth hung in the entryway. Those Roma ate dogs! They sat around the fire wrapped up in sackcloth and warmed themselves. Papa was frightened. They were hairy, wild people, and all kinds of rumors went round about them. They blocked our way. Papa offered each of them a little tobacco: "Here you go, good boy." "Thanks, uncle," they said with kind faces and did nothing to harm us. "I see that you are people blessed by God," said one. "May God rain riches and many sons down on you," they blessed us.

But all the same afterwards we told the story of how dog-eaters had attacked us. So we'd create a sensation! Of course, we also praised them as kind-hearted and true Roma.

During the war Roma were not allowed to leave the settlement. Anyone they caught somewhere he didn't have his official place of residence, they'd chuck him in a work camp. And that's how we stopped going to fairs.

Fun and jokes

We were tormented by poverty and often didn't know what we were going to eat tomorrow, especially in winter when there was no work on the field, but even in our poverty people knew how to think up all kinds of fun and a joke for every one of life's moments.

In the winter we went sledding. At night when the peasants were sleeping, our guys would borrow their sleds from them. Understandably, the peasants didn't know about it, but they couldn't tell a thing, because in the morning they had their sleds back in place. We would clamber with the sleds up the hill below the castle. We had *ududa* with us, little lights made out of potatoes. You hollow out a potato, put some tallow inside, a wick in the tallow, light it, and it burns beautifully – most Roma used little potato lamps even at home. Then three big guys would huddle on one tiny sled, and they'd fly off, down the steep hillside, *ududa* in their hands. The little lights looked spectral as they retreated. The peasants used to say the area below the castle was haunted. Someone claimed it was the spirits of engineers, doing a crooked job of surveying the plots of land.

My papa went sledding too. But can you believe what happened next? The sled was really a couple of boards slapped together that couldn't hold three big guys, so they fell apart in the middle of the hill and Papa went down on one board with a nail in his backside. And, begging your pardon, this was the father of seven children!

In the summer we went diving in the Torysa and held each other's heads underwater to see who could hold out the longest. We splashed each other, chased each other, yelled, and laughed. The peasants watched us from the bridge and I think they envied our happiness, which they couldn't permit themselves because it would have diminished their peasant dignity.

No one in our settlement stole. *Rom Romestar na čorla*, it was said, one Rom does not steal from another. We would have driven the thief out of the settlement – and what would he have done in the world by himself? The *gadže* weren't going to allow a Rom in among themselves, and other Roma wouldn't have had any pity for a thief. Our people didn't even steal from the peasant farmers, because we relied on their giving us work and inviting our musicians to play at weddings. At most we went at night for some potatoes or corn.

But in the settlement there was one orphan and that one really did steal. Not from Roma, from *gadže*. One time he brought a watch from somewhere, another time money. We held it against him because we were afraid the peasants' wrath would then fall on all of us. Finally the gendarmes sent him to the reformatory. He came back when he was eighteen years old.

It happened in the summer when we were gathering linden blossoms. The orphan was gathering them with us. All of a sudden he said: "Where are Gabi and Mujoro?" He spoke Czech, because he'd been in a reformatory somewhere in Bohemia. Gabi and Mujoro were two little boys who'd dozed off at our feet while gathering the blossoms. Panic took hold. "Where are Gabi and Mujoro?" "I saw a boy I didn't know walking over there!" said the orphan and pointed toward the little town. Some men were grabbing sticks and rope from the well and running toward town. It looked like they were stirring up both the peasants and the gendarmes. And that made the orphan scared. He called out: "Come here!" and took the people inside his shanty. Gabi and Mujoro were sleeping next to each other on his bed, breathing peacefully and blissfully.

At first the people wanted to beat the orphan up, but when they saw that the boys were all right, they were able to laugh. Only we admired how the boys could steal right under all of our noses! He was a master at his craft, but he finally went crazy.

The mask

One time Papiňori and I created a diversion in the settlement. Papiňori used to go clean the peasants' yards and somewhere in a woodshed among the old junk she found a mask. It was such a terrifying mask that anyone who looked at it went dumb with horror. Papiňori came to get me and saiy: "Ilon, come on, let's go scare people!"

I say: "How are we going to do that?"

She showed me the mask and my knees gave way beneath me, she had to revive me.

"That's excellent!" I said. "Who are we going to scare first?"

"Šudaňa."

Šudaňa was a big beast. She made money off the Roma. She worked in the slaughterhouse and would bring home stolen pig's ears, pig's feet, and intestines, wrap it all up in her underskirt, come waddling into the settlement and wring the Roma's last money out of them for those delicacies. But when she saw that someone really didn't have anything to eat, she wouldn't take anything for it. She couldn't look at starving children, in that respect she was like other Roma. Šudaňa died at the age of eighty-five and drudged away at the slaughterhouse until her death. She was a tall, stout female, strong as a horse.

Šudaňa lived at her son's place. We went up to her shanty. It was dark and no one was outside. Šudaňa lit the kerosene lamp. Through the window we saw how everyone was sitting around the table and stuffing themselves with pigs' ears. Papiňori put the mask on her face, pressed it to the window, and knocked. Šudaňa lifted her head and looked out the window. She was so terrified that at that moment she looked worse than the mask. She wasn't able to get a word out, and only after a little while did she start to shriek: "Aiii, Feriček, aiii!"

Her little Feriček was about fifty years old. "What's the matter, Mama, what's the matter?"

"A devil! *Bižužo*! The Unclean One! The Unclean One is coming for me already!"

Feriček turned toward the window and started to faint. "Get the ax!" said Šudaňa, but Feriček sat as still as if he were frozen and let his teeth chatter.

Papiňori took the mask off her face and hid it under her skirt.

"Who are we going to frighten now?" I said.

"Old One-Leg."

We went to One-Leg's shanty. As usual his wife was off having fun with the neighbors and wasn't home. One-Leg was lying on his bed and looking at the ceiling. "Now you put on the mask," said Papiňori. "So it's fair."

I put on the mask and stepped up to the window right opposite the bed where One-Leg was. I scratched at the door with my nails. He saw me. "Aiiii! Get away, you unclean force! I don't want to die! Go haunt the marshes and the swamps! I don't want to die!" he said and then crawled out of bed, stood up on his one leg, lost his balance, fell, crawled along the ground to the floor and moaned: "I don't want to die!" And we were so stupid that we laughed at him.

In the meantime Feriček had run out of his shanty, rustled up his ax, and was shouting: "The devil, people, the devil!" At that moment everyone was up on their feet and wanted to know what was going on. Feriček was describing the devil, and our mask was a hundred and twenty times more horrible in his description than in reality. We ran home to our house in the meantime, I quickly wrapped the mask in Mother's skirt and hid it in the bottom of the trunk. Then we went outside and I was so impudent that I said: "What's the matter, uncle, what's happened to you?"

"Don't you know, Ilonka?" and all over again Feriček started describing the devil that was becoming more and more monstrous and by now had an extra hoof. Meanwhile One-Leg had hobbled out stark naked and was shouting that he wanted to get the *bižužo*.

For several days people talked of nothing but the devil. They were afraid to go outside at night, and when someone went to pee in the willows, his entire family went with him.

But what about the mask? Mother might open the trunk any moment to look for her old skirt. We started to be afraid of mask ourselves. And so there was nothing to do but tell our secret to Mother. She didn't get upset and only said: "Girls, the best thing would be if that mask were gone as soon as possible! Hide it under your skirt and take it away back where you took it from." And that's what we did. Papiňori buried it in the junk in the peasant's wife's woodshed.

The three-meter-tall bandit who wanted to steal our grandmother

The fear we caused Šudaňa, Feriček, One-Leg, and the other Roma in the settlement came back at us. The old Roma believe that what goes around comes around, whether good or bad.

In the settlement there was a Polish woman. She was called Špacajka. Her husband was a Slovak, a master mason. He drank through everything he earned and ran after women, so they never managed to have enough for their own little house. They came for shelter to the Roma. One Rom from our settlement built a shanty for his son, but his son went to live somewhere else, so they rented the shanty to Špacajka and her husband the mason for twenty crowns a month.

Mama and Špacajka were the only two Polish women out of six hundred Roma, so they were drawn to each other. It upset Špacajka that my grandmother berated my mother and she decided she would give Grandma a good scare. She got together some men's clothes from somewhere, a Moravian shepherd's hatchet-stick, and a pouch like people used when traveling, and then she smeared her face with soot and broke into our place when only Grandma and Maruša were home. Špacajka was tall, and in that get-up, which our grandma described to us in detail afterwards, she must have looked a fright. She stood in front of Grandma and started to threaten her with the hatchet-stick. She emitted shrieks – she didn't want to speak, so Grandma wouldn't recognize her. Grandma went black with horror. "Go get some people!" she whispered in Maruša's direction, but Špacajka started stamping the ground and waving her hatchet-stick and Maruša was so scared she couldn't move. Then Špacajka quickly left so she wasn't caught in the act and given a thrashing.

There was pandemonium in the settlement! Some bandit – three meters tall! – wanted to steal our Bora (that was Grandma's name) and Maruša! I was so scared a three-meter-tall bandit would steal our grandma I couldn't sleep!

But can you believe what happened next? Some Roma in our house were playing blackjack, which was forbidden. Somehow the gendarmes found out and all four of the card sharps were locked up in the clink. The village prison was a room at the gendarmes' station, they slept on plank-beds there, and when the prisoners had cut wood for the gendarmes for the winter and washed their floors, they were released. As our boys were sitting in jail, they stuck some kind of tramp in there with them. He was tall, had a hatchet-stick and a pouch across his shoulder. The guys pounced on him: "So it was you who wanted to steal our Bora and Maruša from us!" They beat him up so badly the poor man could hardly move and he vainly swore that he had never been in Šariš before in his life.

Then when the card sharps came back home we made big heroes out of them, because they told how they'd punished the three-meter-tall bandit for wanting to steal our grandmother. Only some years later did Špacajka confide to our mother that the bandit was she.

What the womenfolk pulled on the smugglers

Not far from us there was a wood belonging to a nobleman, and seven Jews who were smuggling Hoffmann's tincture used to walk through this forest in secret. It was forbidden, but like everything that is forbidden it was done. The Roma didn't dope themselves up since they didn't have the money to do so, and only after the war did it unfortunately start up in some parts.

Our womenfolk figured out what time the Jews came through the forest. Late at night, of course. The women agreed they would lie in wait for them in the bushes and when they came round, they would stick out their bare backsides at them. All the older women had to go, they enlisted Grandma too, although she was afraid it would make Mother upset with her yet again.

And so some thirty females crawled into the bushes and waited and waited, and when the Jews came round with their suitcases full of Hoffmann's tincture, the women stuck their bare behinds out at them. The one who came up first was a tiny little Jew pulling a suitcase bigger than he was. He shrieked so loud the whole forest could hear him and started running away. Our womenfolk could have split their sides laughing. When the Jews saw what was going on, they spat and marched bravely on. And once again there was something to talk about in the settlement.

The Jews in our own Šariš

There were twelve Jewish families in town. When Jewish merchants came to our parts from another area, they stayed with the Jewish families. But when they came to a town where there were no Jews, they stayed with the Roma.

Our Jews had pubs and stores, and only Cajzler bought up medicinal herbs. Jews didn't have agricultural land. When I got married and went to Kapušany, I stared like a madwoman at the Jews there with their own fields. That was something unusual.

There was also a synagogue in Šariš. When I was in the third grade or so, we had a friendship with the Jews: we Christians would go watch their worship services and they ours. We had a really kindhearted Jewish teacher – the ale house keeper's wife – and it was she who suggested it. Then she really did take us to the synagogue and we stood up above in the balcony. The cantor had a little cap on his head and sang beautifully, *ayvayvayvay*. But they didn't come to see us in our Catholic church.

I used to walk home from school with a little Jewish girl named Olga, and she was the ale house keeper's daughter. From her I found out that they called us Catholics *goyim*. I could have cracked up laughing, because in our language the word meant intestine.

On Saturday the Jews observed the Sabbath and they couldn't do anything, not even make a fire in their stoves. They'd call us Roma: "Ilonka, come light a fire for us." They let us taste their matzoh bread, but I didn't eat any. The *gadže* said they mixed the blood of Christian girls into it. Olga swore to me that it wasn't true. I believed her – because the peasants also made up impossible things about us Roma – but all the same I didn't eat the matzoh bread.

The Jews were as picky and choosy about their food as we were. We sold them mushrooms, and as soon as there was a single little hole from a worm they wouldn't take it. The peasants, though, ate whatever they got, worms or no worms, it could have already started to smell bad, the main thing was not to throw it away! The *gadže* were like oinkers when it came to food. Probably because of their stinginess.

We had a number of adages like *sako peskero kamel* – everyone wants their own thing, *sako peskero rodel* – everyone's looking for his own thing, *sako peskero pat'al* – everyone believes his own thing, *sako peskero džanel* – everyone knows his own thing, *sako peskere dromeha* – everyone walks his own road. To this you could also add: *sako peskero chal* – everyone eats his own food. Everyone shuns food that's different. Everyone considers different things to be clean and unclean. Everyone is somehow different from the next person. Sometimes it's hard to understand that the next person might be just as good as I. But until people understand that, the world will never be free of suffering.

One day they collected all our Jews and took them away. They perished in the concentration camp. Only Šaňa survived, she lives in Israel. Olga, who used to walk with me to school, wanted to escape to Hungary, but they caught her at the border and shot her.

They Aryanized the Jews' houses and shops. That means they distributed them among the peasants who'd joined the Hlinka Guards. The store where Grandma drank on credit was Aryanized by some guy named Vajda. Before the war he was a Communist and during the war, for tactical reasons, he joined Hlinka's party. After the war he hanged himself.

The *mulo*

Our people are terribly afraid of *mule*. All the Roma in the world believe that the souls of the dead, the *mule*, return to earth and wreak horror on the living. They return for various reasons. They want to take revenge against someone who hurt them or owed them something, or if something is tormenting them, some wish of theirs didn't come true, or if they miss their relatives. The avenging *mule* wreak such horror on a person that he loses the ability to speak and can even get sick, they'll give him bruises, take him from this world, throw dishes, rattle chains in the attic, and make all kinds of cadaverous mischief. The souls of good relatives come to give warnings and call attention to things. But it isn't pleasant to be together even with that kind of dead people. A dead person should stay where he belongs and not get mixed up with the living. The *mule* who come back to earth are suffering. And someone who's suffering causes difficulties for others. That's why we ask God on behalf of these wandering souls to take them, forgive their sins, and grant peace both to them and to us.

Every Rom has some experience with *mule*. Take my mother-in-law, the stories she could tell! My mother-in-law's mother worked with the bricklayers from the time she was a little girl. When she was fourteen years old, the foreman made her have a child. Then a second one and finally a third. Of course, he didn't marry her, because she was a Gypsy girl. They married her off to a Rom and he beat her terribly over those three illegitimate children. Her whole life he reproached her because he had to feed three bastards. Purely from her sorrow, my mother-in-law's mother became a burglar. Not that she would go stealing, but she was fearless, told everyone what she thought, and took what she needed, in public. One time she needed some cabbage, and so she set out for the nearest cabbage field. She took my future mother-in-law with her, she must have been about ten years old. The came to the field and all of a sudden some *gadžo* turned up behind them. In normal circumstances it wouldn't have even occurred to the burglar woman to be frightened, on the contrary, she would have made it clear to him somehow that she needed the cabbage and that she'd give him a run for his money even if he were the very commander of the gendarmes. But of course that time my mother-in-law's mother was petrified and was incapable of stirring from the spot. That was how she recognized that it wasn't a *gadžo* but a *mulo*. Just then he also came at them from in front of them. He looked awful, except for the fact that you couldn't see his face, because *mule* never show their faces. By his clothing and his movements my mother-in-law's mother recognized that he was the deceased landowner whose cabbage field it was. He had come to protect his cabbage. When the initial horror left the burglar woman, she grabbed her daughter by the hand and scram, went home as fast as their legs could carry them. They had to make do with "naked *haluški*" without cabbage.

I also had an experience with a *mulo*. I might have been twelve years old. I wanted to go the movie theater very badly. They were showing some kind of cowboy movie. In our little town they never screened anything but cowboy movies. The thing was, they didn't let anyone in for nothing and a ticket cost a crown. I told our girl Maruš: "Maruš, let's go caroling and we'll earn the money for the ticket." It was Christmastime and a whole horde of Romani children was always going caroling through the village. We stopped in every courtyard, sang "The Baby Jesus is Born" and the peasants' wives would give us *šinga* – big rolls – or a five-heller piece. I figured that caroling would get us the money for a ticket to the movies.

We set out from home in the morning when it was still dark so we could be there before the other children. But there was no one anywhere in the village, it was dark everywhere, and not a single window was lit up. I said: "Well, all right, it must still be night time!" What did we know what time it was? "What are we going to do? Come on, let's go home." And we went home. As we were coming down the slope from the bridge to the settlement, I saw how someone was standing in front of our house. Some female. You could tell she was a *gadži* by her dress, skirt down to the ground and a kerchief with fringes.

"Look, there's some peasant woman standing over there," said Maruša at the same time I wanted to say it. We came up closer to her: "Praise be to the Lord Jesus Christ, auntie, where are you going?" She, nothing. She didn't say anything. Just stood there without moving. Her face couldn't be seen. I was seized with horror, went numb, and I couldn't even turn my eyes away – and as I was looking at her I saw that she was like some kind of air, the kerchief, the skirt, and she were all just flickering, quivering, black air. She made us so scared that were more dead than alive. Then the apparition dispersed. Maruša saw it just as clearly as I did, the long skirt and the kerchief with the fringes. To this day I don't know what it could have been.

Musicians saw the *mule* most of all, when they came home late at night from their playing. One time our father was coming home from Prešov with his band, taking a shortcut as usual across a meadow. All at once he saw an apparition standing in front of him in the tall grass. It was rising and sinking, rising and sinking. And the musicians were already feeling queasy. As the lead violinist, like it or not, Papa had to go forward. "Good evening to you, and may Jesus Christ be praised." The creature did nothing. It bowed its head and raised it again. A *mulo!* The musicians stood as if rooted to the spot, and they couldn't move. They kept standing until finally Papa said: "We can't stand here all night, we've got to get home." He plucked up his courage and one little step after another he approached the phantom. He looked – and it was a horse! It lowered its head, snatched some grass, lifted its head and chewed it thoroughly. Over and over again. The musicians took off running and didn't stop until they got home. Father rushed in the door and rolled onto the bench.

"What's the matter, Mikluš, what's the matter?" asked Mama, frightened.

"A *mulo!* He took on a horse's shape!" No one could talk Papa out of believing that the horse was a mulo. But in the village there lived a ninety-year-old *gadžo* and he had horses. He always let them out at night so they could graze on someone else's pasture. And that's probably what the *mulo* was.

Dreams

Our people believed in dreams. Every day they discussed who had dreamed what, especially if it was some kind of unusual dream. They sat outside *pre vatra* and all of a sudden one girl started saying: "I had a dream about a fish." And the older womenfolk, like Pavlina and Cibrikaňa, immediately started asking: "What did you dream about the fish?"

"It was swimming and all of a sudden it turned its belly upward."

Pavlina didn't move a muscle in her face, but she gave such a look that we all knew: *aiai*, that's not good! "A fish stands for a child. A child will be born in your family, but don't count on it living." And really, the girl's sister gave birth and the child died.

I was also filled with dreams. Whenever I dreamed about raw meat, someone in our house had a quarrel. As soon as I dreamed about the meat, I tried hard to keep from getting angry so I could avoid the quarrel. It didn't do any good, because it always came to some kind of dispute all the same. But at least I was ready for it and I told myself: it has to be, there's nothing to be done about it. Yet it will pass and everything will be fine again.

Of course, a lot of my dreams didn't come true, but three events in my life are tied to dreams, and I will never forget them.

One time early in the morning I went to the stream to do laundry – I was already married – and my girlfriend who was doing her laundry next to me said: "*Ai*, Ilon, do you know what? I dreamed that you would have twins, two little girls." It was a year before the end of the war, and at that time we were living downhill from the forest, where the Hlinka Guards had driven us from the town. There was hunger and poverty and we didn't know what would become of us from one moment to the next. I became angry and said: "You're crazy! I should bring children into this misery? I don't want children!" I was so upset that I didn't speak with the girl afterwards. Who gave her the right to have such stupid dreams about me?!

In three weeks I found out that I was expecting. I went to her to apologize. "You were right, but it's not going to be twins, because I don't want that." "Whatever you think. If I were in your shoes I'd do better to prepare twice the diapers and twice the bedcovers." I cut her short by saying she had a lot of ideas in her head. Well, and during the birth the old midwife said: "Girl, do you know, there are going to be two of them? There's another one scrambling into the world after the first one!" And I only had one bedcover and one set of baby clothes, because I didn't want to believe my girlfriend's dream.

Many, many years later a dream betrayed to me that my husband would die. He was having an operation because his intestines had gotten twisted up. The operation came out well and the doctors told me that I didn't need to be the least bit afraid, and that they would release him from the hospital in a week. But that night my dead mother came to me in a dream and said: "Don't cry, little girl, everyone's time must come eventually. In two days something big will happen." In two days my husband died. He was fifty-seven years old.

The most tragic event happened four years ago. It was terrible. Maybe I could have prevented it, I don't know. I dreamed about pure, ghostly water...a lake...on the bottom of the lake lay our little Román, our Máňa's youngest son. A magnificent little boy with curly hair, impudent, sharp-witted, and twelve years old. In the dream he laughed as the dead laugh, and he was angelically white. I woke up in a sweat from horror. Some people we knew had taken Románek to the Šírava Lake and my son-in-law was supposed to go pick him up at noon. I had an urge to call my son-in-law to tell him to go right away, but my son-in-law is a Czech and I was afraid he would laugh at my Gypsy superstitions. I didn't phone, but all morning long my heart was twinging. At eleven o'clock the boy fell from a boat in the middle of the lake, and before they could fish him out, he had drowned.

I went through all kinds of Marxist schooling and I reoriented myself to materialism because I didn't want them to say I was backward. But our Romani reality – or suprareality – always reminded me that there was something else out there

Stories

The Roma used to tell each other folk stories, and in some places they still tell them today. Not the *gadže*, as far as I remember. I used to go into the village to pluck feathers, but no one told stories then, only real-life ones. In our settlement there were two renowned storytellers: Dida's grandfather and Květa's grandfather. Romani folk stories were very difficult, complicated, and long. Dida's grandfather would start to tell one in the afternoon and he still wouldn't have reached the end by midnight.

There was storytelling two or three times a week. The whole settlement crowded into the storyteller's shanty, and everyone gave a heller for the kerosene and tobacco. Anyone who didn't have any money brought a small log or cut the storyteller's wood.

Mama didn't like to let us go to storytelling, because we always brought home fleas. Mother was terribly harsh when it came to fleas! She pulled off our clothes, threw them in a pot, boiled them, threw the straw mattresses out, set the straw on fire, and made Papa go out to godmother Nograd's: "Mikluš, hurry over to the Nograds' for some straw! These children of yours have brought home fleas!" But it didn't do any good, because in the evening we ran off again to hear more!

In the town there was a movie theater, but what good was the most thrilling cowboy movie next to a Romani story? Even though I must admit that we also liked going to the movies. As long as we had the money for the tickets. My brother Jožka, who died so young, liked going to the movies most of all. He caught fish, sold them to the *gadže* – we shunned fish – and with what he got he bought a ticket to the movies for himself and for me.

School

I started going to the first grade and didn't learn a thing. The teacher put us Romani kids on the bench in the back of the room. The bench was for four children and there would be seven of us sitting there. The teacher paid no attention to us and we didn't pay any to her either. We shredded little pieces of paper and pretended we were making *haluški*: shredded *haluški*, minced *haluški*, steamed *haluški*, all the kinds of *haluški* our mother made. The soup was made out of ink.

After some time my Mama figured out that although I was going to school, I didn't know anything at all. She got angry and went to the principal to get him to straighten things out. The next day the teacher noticed me for the first time. "So you want to learn something!" she asked me, astonished.

It was my mother that wanted it, not me! But I said yes, I wanted to learn. The teacher lent me a primer and started to work with me. She put me on the front bench and I started learning. The teacher said I had a good head for school.

In the second and third grades the Romani children started dropping out, one after another, and by the fourth grade I was all by myself. I went to school only in the winter, because in the spring and summer I worked on the peasants' fields.

When I was thirteen we got a Jewish teacher. She was very kind, and she liked me because Papa played in their ale house. Every day he brought me two rolls to school. The Slovak children had a little snack from home, but I never had anything. May I be struck ill on this very spot if I'm lying, I never touched those rolls, I brought them home – Maruša, Haňuša, Tono, and Vilma were at home – and together we divided them up.

I didn't have any books, but I went to school early and borrowed them from the Slovak children. At first they kept their distance from me, but then the teacher started to read the whole class my compositions as the best ones, and the children came to like me. During geography and history I would even help them with the answers. I wasn't so good at arithmetic, but then my Slovak fellow pupils would help me.

One time a boy tripped me, I fell and cried, and he made fun of me, saying "crybaby Gypsy girl!" But the Jewish teacher gave him such a good slap in the face, in front of the whole class, that no one dared do anything to me ever again.

Starting in the fourth grade I sat with a little Slovak boy because, as I said, there were no other Romani children going to school with me any more. His name was Edi Orgoňaš. I sat by the window, and when I leaned out I could see the clock on the church. Edi always whispered: "Look and see what time it is!" But I didn't know how to tell time, so I made something up: a quarter to nine, nine-thirty, five after eleven. Edi was satisfied... He's also no longer living. The day before his death I ran into him in Prešov. We embraced – we both already had grandchildren – and I said: "Remember, Edi, how you always used to ask me what time it was? I pretended I was looking at the church, but I couldn't tell time at all. I made it up."

"And you tell me this after fifty years!" Edi laughed. Then he grew sad and said, "Ilonka, we probably won't see each other again."

"Why wouldn't we see each other again?" I said. "We've still got plenty of life in us." Then we said goodbye. And the next day he hung himself. He came from a poor family, studied to become a teacher, taught at a vocational school, married a woman from a fancy background and his wife was unfaithful to him. He couldn't get over that.

The Lady of Čachtice and the babbling brook

From the time I was little I loved to read. I borrowed books from the town library. And then when I was working at the peasant's I saved up for the Magazine for Women and Girls. They carried installments from novels like *The Count of Monte Cristo, The Lady of Čachtice*, and the whole popular reading library: *Steps in the Fog, Eyes under a Veil, The Red-Headed Girl from the Fifth Floor*. They really got to me! I read everything I could get my hands on.

My favorite was *The Lady of Čachtice*. She killed young girls and bathed in their blood and generally oppressed the people. But then some fellows named Drozd and Kalina stood up to her and, risking their lives, they put an end to her and her bloodthirsty appetites! Drozd and Kalina became idols of fearlessness for me and I told myself that like them, I would battle against the injustice of all the ladies of Čachtice in the world!

One boy in our parts was hired by the circus. When he came back from being out in the world, he brought a suitcase full of worn-out cowboy novels. I was entranced by them. After work I sat with the books and would read all night long. Mama would get upset that I was using up so much kerosene. When it was a clear night, I read by the light of the moon.

Every night before going to sleep I had to tell my husband a story. I told him about the contents of the books I had read. And when I had gone through all the cowboy books and young girls' novels, I didn't know what to tell about next. "I'll throw you out of the bed, Black Woman, if you don't tell me a story! Get on with it and hurry up!" he threatened. And that's how I started to think up my own tales: of the beautiful Romani dancer Džajáně, with whom a cruel nobleman fell in love and wanted to burn alive when she didn't return his love, but who himself ultimately went up in flames in his castle; of a Romani *vajda* who succumbed to a disastrous passion for his stepdaughter and as punishment was turned into a goat; of a Romani boy who led Roma beyond the sun to a land of plenty and justice, and the like. My husband praised it all enormously and said: "That's a cowboy story for you! No one would even believe they wrote about us, about Roma in this world! The things people come up with!" Only many, many years later did I tell him that I made up the stories by myself.

When I was about fourteen years old, I tried to write by myself, in secret. I wrote little poems, love poems of course, brooks babbled in them, little birds twittered, and little hearts wept or laughed, sometimes according to how my heart was actually feeling and sometimes so the rhyme fit. I wrote in Slovak, and it never occurred to me that you could write in Romani as well. The peasants made fun of us for speaking cant, gibberish, Pharaoh talk, Romani had no place in school, I had never seen a printed word in Romani in my life, and I thought that Slovak was the only language appropriate for literature. I also wrote in Slovak because I wanted to show off how well I knew the *gadžo* language. Most Roma spoke Slovak badly. Among ourselves not a single Slovak sentence was uttered, and we didn't socialize with Slovaks – or rather it was they who didn't socialize with us – we would haggle with them in their language only when they needed us for some work or when we went to ask them for a little food. They made fun of us for speaking "backwards" and "brokenly" – and imitating Gypsy Slovak also figured among their pastimes. And I wanted to show them that we knew their Slovak language just as well as they, and that's why I wrote my poems in Slovak.

When I had a few little poems written out, I set out to see the teacher who taught me in the council school. In the village, that teacher organized an amateur theater, for which he himself had written a play. He read my poems and was enthusiastic. Perhaps not so much by the poems themselves as by the fact that "a poor Gypsy girl from a ramshackle settlement sits in the evening by the moonlight and writes poems." At any rate, that's how he wrote about me in the program he prepared for the radio. It was called *London-Paris-Velký Šariš*. He recited two of my poems there. I got a couple of letters, from Ružomberk, from Košice, and even from Bratislava. And all of a sudden a reporter from the *Magazine for Ladies and Girls* came to see my teacher. What's more, he wanted my photo. I didn't have any photographs, I had never been to a photographer in my life, and no one had ever photographed me. For the coverage in the *Magazine for Ladies and Girls* I let them take the first photograph I had ever had in my life. I went with Papiňori to Prešov, and I had on a little suit made of English material. I asked the photographer to make me up all nice and white for the photograph. I sent the photograph off to the magazine. But in the meantime the Slovak state had been created and Gypsies were placed outside the law. They didn't print the article about me and sent me back the photograph.

Suitors, a wedding, at my mother-in-law's in Kapušany

Džuvľi bijo murš sar e lavuta bijo vonos
murš bijo džuvľi sar o tover bijo destos

A woman without a man is like a violin without a bow,
a man without a woman like an axe without a handle

Čhaja – the girls

Among the family's most important tasks was finding suitable husbands for its daughters and worthy girls for daughters-in-law. Young people's marriages served to form advantageous links between two sets of relatives and so to increase their power and prestige. Not much attention was paid to whether the young girls liked the partner their parents had chosen for them. From the time a *chajori*, a little girl, became a *chaj*, a big one, the mother, father, older brothers and sisters, aunts, uncles, brothers-in-law, cousins, and every last one of the relatives thought constantly about who would make her the most suitable husband. Naturally, the girls also dreamed of having husbands and did everything to make themselves likable to one of the boys who went round the settlements in groups of five or six, looking for brides for themselves. We all believed that our *pirano*, our sweetie whom we loved in secret, would marry us and that we would be happy with him till the day we died. Then we married the one our parents had picked out for us – few girls dared *te denašel* – to run away with the *pirano* against their parents' will. But in the end the couples grew old together happily, though it was not love that brought them together but the wise choice of the parents. I don't remember anyone in our settlement leaving their wife and children before the war. And for a mother to desert her children – that was absolutely unheard of. That kind of *paťiv*, respectability, stopped being the norm only after the war.

A little girl became a big one, a *chajori* became a *chaj*, when she had her first period.

67

The first woman in the family who found out about it had to give her a great big slap. A slap so hard her face was red for a whole day afterwards. People believed that then the girl would be pretty, stay young, and above all would be toughened for the life ahead of her. And that she would bear without grumbling her lifelong *zajda*, just as she had borne the slap without a word. That she would expect the unexpected. Something unexpected was always happening to us Roma. There was no way we could plan our own fate, when others were constantly deciding for us.

Well, and one day I also became a big girl. It was my mother who found out about it first. I was coming into the kitchen like this, Papa was sitting at the table, and Mama was cooking. She saw me, jumped away from the stove and lay into me with a slap so hard I went reeling.

Papa jumped up: "Why are you hitting her? Have you gone crazy? What did she do?" Mama just laughed: "She knows why, all right!" Papa didn't understand any of it, and Mama couldn't explain it to him because that would have been shameful.

Little girls could go running around the settlement as much as they wanted, but a *čhaj* couldn't take a single step outside the house by herself. Any time she moved, someone from the family automatically went with her. At least a child or someone. The whole settlement was careful that none of "their" *čhaja* compromised her reputation. If she so much as smiled at some boy, someone went to her house to accuse her of having a *pirano*.

The girls would naturally doll themselves up. We painted our cheeks and lips with red crepe paper. Everyone had to have a bow in her hair. She could have a head that was nothing but feathers and straw – but that crow's nest would be decorated with a bow. It was extremely fashionable to have gold teeth. The peasants' daughters had real gold teeth. They ate a lot of sugar and bacon, their teeth went rotten, the doctor wouldn't waste time putting in a filling, he just pulled the tooth out and put in a gold one. We had beautiful, white teeth, healthy ones, but we would wrap them up in tinfoil so we didn't look like we couldn't afford a gold one. We'd get a little bag of sweets in tinfoil for a tenner – and then our kissers would be all shiny.

Those of us that were really black would powder ourselves with white flour. When I think about how "white" women today go to the seaside to sun themselves so they get black, it makes me laugh.

Sunday with the girls

We had free time only on Sundays, otherwise we were working at the peasants' from spring until fall, sunup to sundown.

On Sunday we got together, the whole bunch of us girls, we held hands under each other's arms, round each other's shoulders, and went to Šariš to the train station, looking to see who was coming and who was going, and then we'd kick around the reasons they were probably leaving, where they were going, where they were coming from, and what they were doing there. It was all very thrilling for us.

Even more interesting were the trips to Prešov. We got dressed in the morning and went to Prešov to go shopping – which meant that we went looking for shoes we would buy if we had the money. Or our family would entrust us with some and we could actually buy the shoes. A *čhaj* had to have shoes, otherwise they made fun of her with

68

a little rhyme: *nane la ča papuči, bo na kerel oj buťi* – she's only got *papuči* because she doesn't do any work. *Papuči* were wrappings stuffed with straw and tied to the foot with string. People wore them in winter, otherwise Roma went around barefoot. With the exception of the musicians and the *čhaja*. If a *čhaj* wanted a better sort of husband, she had to have shoes.

Understandably, we went to Prešov on foot, seven kilometers there and seven kilometers back. We came back for lunch, because on Sundays the whole family had a special meal together. After lunch we rounded ourselves up and went off to Prešov again. The whole bunch of us and on foot. In Prešov we took a promenade on the corso. If we'd saved up fifty hellers, we stopped in the sweets shop for a cream puff, if not, we just walked and let the Romani fellows look us over. They gathered here from nearby villages to look for brides.

From the time I was little I went everywhere with Papiňori. She made fun of every boy, no one was good enough for her, and she was probably proud because she was so white. One time we were walking in the town with this fat kind of young fellow following behind us, with a feather in his hat. As soon as Papiňori saw him, she burst out laughing. We stepped up to a display case and pretended we were having a look at various materials. He came up to us and said: "How are you, you pretty girls, could I take a bit of a stroll with you?"

I never wanted to offend anybody, so I said: "Why not." But Papiňori started to guffaw. "We'll go for a stroll with you, but first tell us what this is: a black roller that rolls on the highway and wears a hat with a feather on its head." The young fellow turned crimson and left without a word.

Another time a clarinet player from Drienov made friends with us. He was only seventeen, but he had a reputation all over the whole region as an excellent musician. He was always carrying his clarinet under his arm in order to impress the girls. He spoke to us: "You're from Šariš, girls, aren't you?"

"Yeeees," I said, politely, drawing out the words nicely like the Hungarians did and like the Roma from Košice who got it from the Hungarians.

"Well then, we could have a bit of conversation, what do you say?" said he in response. Except Papiňori turned to me and said: "Ilon, have you seen that black cow with a clarinet under its arm?" Because he was awfully black. The boy took offense and left.

That was how Papiňori behaved toward all suitors. Finally no-nose Lina married her off to her brother's wife's sister's son. Their life together wasn't a happy one. Then her husband died and Papiňori has been a widow for a long time now, much longer than I have. She never remarried. Before it didn't use to be the custom in our parts that a widow would get married again right away. For the most part they remained faithful to their husbands even after their deaths.

One time we went to Fintice to some count's estate to gather potatoes. The estate manager was from Šariš, so the work went well for us. As usual, our whole *kumpaňija* went to Fintice together. All Roma. There were a lot of Roma there from the whole region, from as far away as Svidník and Snina. They gave us lodging in a building thrown together out of boards and people slept on plank-beds, except those of us from Šariš slept on straw mattresses because the estate manager was from Šariš. Jozef had already begun courting me then.

Papiňori and I had our places next to each other. This good-looking sort of boy from

Svidník kept looking at us. Finally he worked up the courage to address us: "Ha, gurlies, if'n yew c'd only see m'oonkle! What a mewzishun he be!" We had never heard anyone in our whole lives who spoke like that. Svidník is far from Prešov and people didn't go there for fairs, so we didn't know the Roma there. The girls started to squeal and aped him: m'oonkle! m'oonkle!

"Why's yew leffin' a' me?" asked the young fellow, angered.

I wanted to make peace with him, so I said in a serious tone: "We not leffin' a' yew, we leffin' a' y'oonkle!" And the girls howled still more.

Then that boy started to court me. With a basket in his hand. He gathered the potatoes I had dug up. He sang to me beautifully and I liked him, he was nice-looking and gentle and I got used to his way of speaking. He said: "Ilon, will you love me?" And I said: "You see the Kapušany castle on the hill over there? My fiancé lives just below that castle. If he sees that you're courting me, he'll kill you, me, and then himself. He won't hesitate to go to the clink for ten years for that. That's the kind of masher he is. The Roma in Kapušany are brawlers." He made no reply, walked away, and since that time I've never seen M'Oonkle. I don't even know who he got married to.

My *pirano*

Romani girls used to be decent. It was unheard of that a girl would make love with a boy just like that. If they had something together, it was a big public scandal, and they either had to live together or the girl was discredited sometimes for her whole life.

Of course, we fell in love with the boys and the boys with us. Whoever I was thinking of was my *pirano*, and whoever looked at me longer than at the other girls at a fair or a party started tongues wagging that he had chosen me for his *piraňi*.

I also took a liking to one boy. He was a great musician and played the violin marvelously. I didn't tell anyone about my love because I didn't want them to give me a hard time about it. I would have been consumed with shame if he had found out that I liked him, because I could not believe that he could like someone as black as me. I was probably fifteen years old. He was going on seventeen.

One day in Chmiňany there was a wedding. Roma gathered at weddings from far and wide, since it was another opportunity to exchange tidbits of news, to have fun together, to laugh, cry, sing, and dance. And naturally the boys looked over the girls and the girls the boys – and the parents chose their sons-in-law and daughters-in-law. A wedding was a beautiful event, perhaps still more beautiful for the guests than for the bride and groom. The whole gang of young people from Šariš went to Chmiňany that time, and Mama sewed us girls beautiful. long dresses, so we would be as radiant as the most beautiful bridesmaids.

We had fun, danced, looked around, sang at the wedding, and though it was noon they still hadn't offered us a single morsel of food. It was almost evening – and still no food. The Roma who had thrown the wedding were very poor. They invited only the grown-ups inside, and there was nothing left for us young folk. What now? We didn't feel like going home, but to stay here hungry? We hadn't had anything to eat since noon the day before, since we'd told ourselves: we'll eat our fill at the wedding. Then finally some woman noticed that we were dizzy with hunger and cooked us up some *haluški* with curd cheese. She invited all us bridesmaids inside. We threw ourselves on the bowl with the *haluški*. But the boys were right behind us, without being invited. In my young years there was a custom among Roma that the girls were bashful about eating in front of the boys and the boys in front of the girls. They would rather have died of hunger than take food into their mouths in front of one another and chew it over. They keep this custom in upright Romani families even today. Our juices were running, but we sat still and looked blankly at the full bowl. The girls elbowed me: "Ilona, say something to them!" I said: "Boys, you can see that we're too bashful to eat in front of you. Neither you nor we will eat our fill." They became ashamed and went outside. The lady had put the pot with the water she'd boiled the *haluški* in out in the hall. And the young men were so hungry they drank it up. But then the nice lady cooked them up some more *haluški*.

We ate our fill and went to dance some more. And the lady who had treated us to *haluški* shouted at the musicians: "Quiet! Stop playing!" The music stopped and the lady said: "Girls on this side, boys on that side! Now everyone go to the girl he thinks about all the time! Let everyone see who's whose *piraňi*!

The music started up and I was waiting to see who would come get me. All of a sudden I saw that while we were eating *haluški*, the musician I'd fallen in love with had shown up at the wedding. My *pirano*! I'd never dreamed that he could come for me. He stepped forward from the line of boys. My heart was beating wildly. Who would he go to? He headed toward me. I can't tell you how happy I was. Then he took me away from the circle and sang to me: "There's nothing between us, we're just looking at each other, but our looking is better than others' lovemaking." He'd composed that song himself. That's how it is among Roma: when someone wants to express something he's bashful of saying publicly, he'll sing it in a song. A song is sacred and untouchable. If someone says something in a song, no one can get offended or angry or mock it. Nor is it necessary to reply to something in a song. You can if you feel like it, but you don't have to. When he sang to me, I thought I would burn up with happiness and embarrassment. I was completely beside myself and hadn't the least idea what I ought to say. At other times I was very outspoken, I had an answer for everything and knew how to make a joke – and now all at once I didn't have a single word on my tongue. He took my silence to mean I didn't want him. He later married *pre čeranki*, which means he married the sister of the boy his own sister married. That was very, very common among Roma.

He lives not far from me in Prešov. He has a lot of children and grandchildren. When we run into each other, we look at the ground, then we lift our heads and greet each other, and each one goes their way.

A boy is born with a bow in his hand, a girl grows up with song

The most sought-after husband was a musician and the most sought-after bride was a girl from a musician's family. If she was white on top of that, the parents could have their pick of husbands, since it was worth more than riches. The girls who knew how to sing especially nicely were also in demand – though we all knew how to sing, because *čhaja* sang every day from morning till night.

Our father was a musician, but at the time we were looking to get married his band was threatened by strong competition – Rudaľis and his musicians. In our settlement there were two bands: Papa's and Rudaľis'. Rudaľis was actually a relative of ours, since his brother married my sister Ema. And Rudaľis himself had learned to play the violin from our Papa. He was a outstanding musician!

These two bands competed with one another. Two or three times a week the musicians brought their instruments out *pre vatra*, the whole settlement went quiet around them and Papa said: "So then, boy, play, show what you can do."

"You first, uncle, you are the elder," said Rudaľis and Papa's band started to play. Rudaľis just lay in wait until Papa started to play. Then he peeped at his people – which meant: we're better! And Rudaľis' band started in. My father shook his head and smiled indulgently. What did they think? Whose leg were they trying to pull? It's got the wrong feeling to it, it's a wild animal! "Yes, my boy, you're a good musician, I'm not saying you're not, but it lacks fantasticality!" Then with his eyes squinting and with elegant gestures, my father conjured up some truly fantastic notes, his band took it up, and began to accompany him fantastically. When they finished, Rudaľis said: "But uncle, it's a different world today! People want a little more wild animal, modern songs!" And so they argued in a friendly way, each one thinking he was better than the other, each outdoing the other the whole afternoon and late into the night, us singing and dancing all the while and having a good time.

The *gadže* brought their chairs, took their seats on the bridge like in a theater balcony, and listened.

The *gadže* said of us: those Gypsies live like shneps. A shnep is supposed to be some kind of small bird that doesn't eat anything at all and only sings. I don't think there is any such bird. But the truth is that if there were nothing to eat, we would play and sing and forget about our wretchedness.

During the *bašaviben*, that is, during our Romani entertainments, at some moment a woman who had something on her heart would step up to the hammer dulcimer and say: "Now play my song." She started and the band took it up. For example, there was one person from our settlement who beat his wife cruelly. He had a face disfigured by pits from smallpox, and we called him Bela Rapavo. I remember how it was just his wife who called for quiet once during a *bašaviben* and then began to sing: "Man, what are you doing, you walk around drunk night and day, you drink through all the money that you make, and then you come home and beat up your wife!" Bela was publicly shamed and couldn't do anything because, as I said, a song was untouchable.

We were sorry for Bela's wife. As children we used to run around their shanty, throw rocks and mud on their roof and call out: "Bela Rapavo, you crawl outside when you beat your wife, we'll break your windows!" He chased us through the settlement, cursed, swore, but in the end he repented, started to be ashamed, and no longer beat his wife so much.

And there's one more story I often think of. There was one other lead violinist who played with Papa in the band. He was young, still learning, but he had a great talent. His wife was beautiful, but not exactly tidy. One time they had our boys play at a wedding, and she didn't wash his shirt. Going out in a dirty shirt was an enormous embarrassment for a musician. Borrowing a shirt would also have been shameful and what's more, there wasn't anyone to borrow from. No one but the musicians had a white shirt; in fact, the poor musicians didn't even have a shirt and underneath their jackets they wore only a *jepašgad* – a collar with a shirt-front and no back. When that young lead violinist found out he had nothing to play in, he beat his wife. At the very next *bašaviben* she sang

72

about it in public. But then one of his sisters asked for the floor and sang that a woman who didn't know how to wash her husband's shirt deserves to be beaten. After that she washed his shirt so he wouldn't be embarrassed. A Romani song had enormous power! Without arguing and without cursing, people told each other what they wanted, and meanwhile everyone else got to laugh or cry on top of that. It was mostly the girls and women who sang. And if a man felt like unbosoming himself about something sensitive in public, some woman from among his relatives sang it for him.

In our settlement there was one young woman who sang the best; you would feel chills up and down your spine when she sang. Her husband was an outstanding musician, they had four children together, and her husband died when the oldest one was nine years old. She wept like the rain, and we thought she wouldn't survive his death. Then, when her sorrow was spent and she was able to sing again, she would always come up to the hammer dulcimer and sing about how her husband left her. The whole settlement wept with her. Their oldest boy had his father's gift. As a seven-year-old he was already playing the dulcimer and the musicians took him with them to weddings. They split their earnings with him as with a adult. But this boy also died young. At the age of twenty-five he had come to the end of his road.

Playing at a wedding was an adventure sometimes. Few village weddings went by without a fight. The bigger the fight, the more people talked about the wedding and the more famous the bride was. Often our musicians were carried away by the fights. A big, robust fellow would come up to the lead violinist and say: "Now play my song!" and give him the melody. The musicians then had to pick it up right away, even if they'd never heard the song before in their lives. If ever they didn't pick it up and the big fellow was quick-tempered, he'd break the violinist's instrument over his head. They did it to show off, so they'd be talked about. Or a couple dancing would come up as ask for this or that song, and another would come up and say: "No, not that one, play this one!" – And then they started to argue and scuffle among themselves – but they'd break a violin over our musicians' heads. Even my father came home with his violin broken.

Even worse was breaking a double bass or a hammer dulcimer. A dulcimer cost big money. My husband told me how at one time at these nuptials they just carried the dulcimer out of the room, because the slivovitz bottles had started to fly. The dulcimer-player was crying and trembling, because losing his dulcimer meant losing his daily bread.

But wonder of wonders, in Kapušany, where my husband came from, there was one Rom who broke his violin over some peasants' sons' heads. That was unheard of and something you never saw. His name was Movač. He could afford it, he was an outstanding musician, a big rowdy, and a real Midas. He dealt in pigs. He'd killed his own brother, my husband's father, over pigs. Jozef was three years old at the time. His shameful Uncle Movač didn't do a minute's worth of time, because he gave the judge a hundred thousand.

Movač always had a valuable violin and played it divinely. When some big fellow came up to him at a wedding and wanted him to play his song, Movač would summon quiet in the hall with a single word and tell the young man: "Sing!" If the big fellow sang well, Movač would praise him and play the song. If ever he sang off-key, Movač would shout: "Enough, Janek, enough! I can't even listen to that!" The hall had some fun at the expense of the humbled singer. Some fellows kept singing, because they wanted to show that he wasn't going to let some Gypsy order him around, and broke Movač's

No-nose, Lina's grand-daughter, 1984.

violin over his head to boot. Then he left the hall and the fun was over. No one dared do anything for Movač, and people said he was in league with the devil. The next day he bought a new violin, even better and more expensive than the other one. Some people say that he'd broken a hundred violins over fellows' heads, some claim it was two – God knows what the truth is. But one thing's for sure: that Movač played divinely and that at the same time he was a real rowdy in league with the devil. How can it be?

I still have to finish the story about what it was like with my father's band. Papa was getting old, he was really sick, suffered from bronchitis and bouts of pneumonia, and his art went down with him. Maybe it didn't, even, but Rudaľis' band worked their way up and got better and better. The young men stopped inviting Papa for the weddings and started inviting Rudaľis.

In our family we believed that no-nose Lina had cast a spell on Papa's band. Lina was the only woman in the settlement who didn't have a husband. No one married her, because she didn't have a nose. (But she has a beautiful grandson by her daughter who was born to her no one knows how.) People said of Lina that she knew how to cast spells. She enchanted a boy to come to a girl or, the other way around, she was able to get a boy out of a young girl's way.

A girl who wanted to win a boy's love had to bring Lina a *kotor*, a piece of the boy's shirt, and Lina burnt it in the fire saying three times, one after the other: "May your heart burn for me like this piece of cloth." Then the boy would want the girl even if he didn't.

Lina was one of Rudaľis' relatives and they said that, when Rudaľis couldn't defeat Papa's art honestly, he had a spell cast on him. They say Lina brought some clay from the graveyard at midnight, having gathered it from nine graves, and then threw it over her shoulder at our musicians so people wouldn't take so much notice of them, the way they didn't take notice of the dead in their graves.

Papa never left off playing the violin. When he no longer had to play for his living, he played for his and our enjoyment.

Suitors

We were *čhaja*, and so the boys tried to win us. Our Maruša more than anyone else. She was beautiful, white, and had as many suitors as hairs on her head. But I couldn't complain either.

Once a cart drawn by two horses stopped before our house, and on top of the cart were lots of spirits and food – and women; behind the cart were a bunch of men on bicycles. The horses whinnied, the women slid off the cart and tumbled into our apartment with the spirits and the food. Papa and Mama could only stare; they didn't know what to make of it all. They kept in the back room and so did I. But those Roma had come politely to invite them to a feast. Then Papa, as a well-mannered person, also went outside with his violin, summoned his band and while they played, people danced, ate, and drank. They were Roma from Lipjany, and we knew each other from the fair. They were an exalted family, because the woman's sister had married a veterinarian.

At twelve midnight Papa asked: "Look, people, is this all about?"

The veterinarian's sister-in-law, who had organized the whole trip from the beginning, said: "That tomorrow we would be happy to take your Ilona away with us."

"What for and where?" Papa persisted, though it was clear to him what it was all about.

"We would like her to come to our house as a *bori*, as a bride, in short. Our Lajko would consent to live with her."

Jožka had just started to court me. There was a woman from our settlement who'd gotten married in Lipjany, and she wanted to win Jožka for her daughter. That's why those people set out come to me and *te mangavel*, to win me over, for their son: hey, hey, in our Šariš there's such and such a family, Mikluš, a refined man, an outstanding musician, their daughters go around dressed like countesses and Ilona's been to school! She's going to council school! That'd be something for your boy. So they'd nudged them and nudged them until the family had horses in harness – saying they had horses and a cart, because they took coal to the train station – and so they came to see us to win me over.

Mama said: "Look, our Ilona is barely seventeen years old. She'll get married when she's eighteen, and in a church!"

"Aii!" lamented their mother. "Sixteen years old! A normal girl should already be married by then! Do you want her to turn into stinking curd cheese on you?"

"You needn't be afraid of that, because Lackaňa's son from Kapušany is courting her!"

"Aii, Mikluš!" their mama shouted. "We'll give you the cart, we'll give you both horses, if only you give us your daughter as a bride!"

"Listen, people," said Papa, "I didn't raise a cow so I could barter her for horses with you. Our Ilona is not going with you as a bride!"

"Aii, Mikluš," shrieked their mother like a madwoman, "tomorrow morning we have to take your daughter to Lipjany, no matter what! She must be in our house tomorrow as a *bori!*"

"Listen, people," Papa shouted, though he was a very mild-mannered person, "I didn't invite you here, I never called you into my home. If you have any idea what honor is, leave in peace and quiet before something happens."

This whole time I was shut up in the back room and only listening to what was going on. I was awfully curious, but I was afraid to go outside because Mama had ordered me not to move from that room. But when all the screaming and yelling broke out, I couldn't resist and I crept out. At that moment I came upon a young man next to me whom I was seeing for the first time in my life. "Ilon, don't you want me?" he asked. It was their boy Lajko.

"I've already got a fiancé and I don't want you!"

"We've got to go back to Lipjany tomorrow with a bride! We've got to go back to Lipjany tomorrow with a bride! Aaaai!" shrieked their mother. "I'll give you twenty thousand for her! Oh, the shame, if we come back without a bride!"

"Listen, people, if you gave us all of Prešov and threw in your fucking Lipjany on top of that, we wouldn't give you our daughter as a bride for your household!" said Papa, uttering the last word, and they had to leave. They crawled into their cart that very night, the men got on their bicycles, and they left. And as they were leaving, that female kept shouting: "We're not going back to Lipjany without a bride! Aaaai!"

Then the son of the Polish woman, Špacajka, who lived near us in the settlement with her drunk of a husband, wanted me for his wife. His parents had four children, two boys and two girls. One boy went to study to become a priest and the other one said over and over again: "Ilon, will you marry me?" I thought he was kidding. We had grown up together since we were little, we went for mushrooms and raspberries together, he was like a brother to me, and it never occurred to me to marry him! Then he went off to do his military service, and when he came back, he asked: "Did you wait for me?"

I goggled my eyes at him. "How was I to know you meant it seriously? I'm going to marry Lackaňa's son from Kapušany. And besides, you're a *gadžo* and I'm a Gypsy girl and those don't go together!

From the time we were little Mama drummed into us: *Rom Romeha, gadžo gadžeha* – Rom with Rom and *gadžo* with *gadžo*. She used to say: "You're not marrying a *gadžo*, you're marrying a Gypsy boy!" She herself was Polish, but she felt like a Romani woman. "What do you think you are?" she said to me. "A stinking Gypsy girl! If ever you do something a *gadžo* boy doesn't like, he'll start cursing you up and down as a Gypsy. What do you need that for? You'll marry a Rom and that's that!"

When I was sixteen years old I rode a train for the first time in my life. A ticket from our town to Prešov cost twenty crowns. That was big money, and that's why we went on foot. There was a fair in Košice and that time everyone went by train, so that's how I went too. I really liked it! I liked the way the trees and telegraph poles flew past the window, I listened to the way the wheels clattered against the rails, and I was awfully proud that I was traveling by train.

And can you believe what happened next? There was a seminarian traveling on the same train, a young boy who was studying to become an Orthodox priest. He was wearing a vestment and had a shaved head and enormous, black eyes – and those eyes burned like two fires. The seminarian's head was hurting so badly he fainted. I set off through the train asking people: "Do you have any headache medicine?" I got him some medicine, gave it to him, and said: "Try to relax!" He looked at me the whole trip through, until it started to make me feel uncomfortable.

I was in the hospital for a few days afterwards, because I got a cut on my leg. The day they let me out I was walking along the corridor and who did I see? The seminary student from the train! He was wearing hospital pajamas. His eyes flared up and he said: "I cannot forget how you got me that medicine in the train, miss!" I just stared at the way his eyes were burning and kept quiet. "I would very much like to marry you!" he said. "My fiancé is waiting for me at the gate," I replied. He shut his eyes and walked away.

A few days later I went to Prešov and a whole band of seminarians came walking toward me. He was one of them. He walked around me with his head cast down. I never saw him again after that.

And there was also a clarinetist of high renown who courted me strenuously. I had heard of him even before we met by chance during a Sunday stroll in Prešov. The Roma from the whole area knew all about each other, even if they didn't know each other personally. And this boy was especially famous, because he went to the high school. But he was awfully black!

He came all the way to our house to see me once, his clarinet under his arm, a briefcase with books in his hand. Mama was hospitable, invited him in, and sent me to the store for some bread and something to munch on.

I came back from the store and who'd come to see us? My fiancé Jožka. "Why are you so startled?" he said, "aren't you even going to say hello? Aren't you happy I've come?"

I couldn't get even one word out. They were already playing music at our house. The boys had brought a violin, a bass, and my black suitor had joined in with his clarinet. Papiňori was singing. I went inside with Jozef. "Ahaaa!" he said. "Ahaaa!" And in reply my mother said: "Listen, boy, I'm not going to throw someone God has brought to my door out of my house. My daughters are decent girls and they know what honor is. So they can have fun with anyone they want. It's no skin off your nose."

All the same she pulled me aside after a while and said: "Walk the clarinet player to the train!"

"Your train's leaving soon," I said. He grasped the situation and said good-bye. I went to walk him to the station. We were clambering up the slope to the bridge and he said: "Ilonka, I've already spoken about you at home. I said: Mama, Papa, you'll be surprised at what kind of bride I'll come home with! One who's been to school! She goes to the council school – and how proper she is!"

And I said: "But after all, you know I've been betrothed to Jozef. He started courting me before you did."

At that moment Jozef crawled out from under the bridge, following us in secret because he wanted to know what we were talking about with each other. "Well, you're just lucky, Blackie, that you said what you said! If you'd promised him that you'd marry him, you'd no longer be among the living! Not you, not him, not me!" Then he sent me home and went to walk the clarinet player to the train station by himself.

Later the clarinet player married a girl from Kežmarok. She was, begging your pardon, a tramp. She lived with her husband and at the same time with his father – with her own father-in-law! They fought over her like dogs, cut each other with razor blades. She was as beautiful as a saint on the altar, and yet what a slut! Then the two of them realized that the depth of their shamefulness and sent the girl home to her parents. Her father dealt in pigs and was awfully rich, offering fifty thousand to anyone who'd marry her. A lot of good that did, because everyone shunned her for living with a son and his father at the same time. Then they snagged that black clarinetist for her. He came from another area and didn't know what kind of girl she was. Or maybe he didn't want to know? Was he glad he'd have a white girl when he himself was so black? I don't know. They weren't happy together.

After the war he worked somewhere in an office and one time he got together with Jozef at some kind of conference in Bratislava. After the conference the clarinet player wanted to go home, but Jozef told him: "Don't go, brother, the driver's drunk."

He said: "It's just a little ways to Trenčín and I want to be home tonight." So he left. Hardly had they gotten out of Bratislava when the driver ran into a tree and both of them died on the spot.

How my sister Ema was married off

Mama chose potential husbands by her instincts, as it was done among decent Roma. And when a boy had found a girl, he was able to marry her only when the family had given its consent. Sometimes it happened that two young people fell in love with each other and the parents wouldn't allow the wedding. If the two were especially daring, they ran away. They hid with some relatives as far away from home as possible. When they came back with a child, the parents usually took them in. Of course running away was an act of real daring. The authority of the parents was sacred. And also, the members of a family loved each other and your heart wouldn't allow you to cause your relatives pain or shame.

Our grandmother chose Ema's husband. He was a boy from our settlement, an outstanding blacksmith who forged horseshoes, bits for horses, plowshares, and door jambs. His name was Laci. Laci's mother made friends with our grandmother, and so they made an agreement that Laci would marry Ema. Ema knew nothing about it. The engagement feast had already been planned and Ema still didn't know anything about it.

One day Laci's family came to our house with bottles of spirits and Ema asked: "Who'd they come for?"

"For you, girl!"

Ema howled and screamed that she didn't want to, that she wouldn't marry him! A lot of good that did, because the wedding took place a few weeks later. Relatives set them up in a shanty on the other end of our settlement and bought them a pig. Once Ema had an argument with Laci and, as was the custom in such cases, she ran home to Mother. She took the pig with her. She left him in the sitting-room and the pig squealed as if he were on the cutting block. After a while the door opened, Laci appeared on the other side, and said he'd come for the pig. Obviously, he hadn't come for the pig, but for Ema. And can you believe what happened next? At the moment he showed up in the doorway, the pig stopped squealing, and the whole rest of the time it sat in our house, with not a peep out of it. Mama could easily say that neither Ema nor the pig was there. Except she couldn't keep from laughing at how smart the pig was, knowing when to squeal and when not to. Three days later Ema went back to Laci's house and the pig with her.

Today they've got kids named Lacek, Zoli, Rudi – Paľi died – then Magda and Haňuša. They grew old together in love and peace.

How Marga got married

There was a boy from the settlement who fell in love with Marga, and she liked him too, but Mama said: no! She could have been happy the girl was leaving home and there'd be one less hungry mouth to feed. Marga was ripe for marriage, but there was no potential husband that Mama liked.

Until one day when two boys on bicycles came riding by Šariš. They were from Solivar. And the way they were looking at the girls, one of them fell off his bike and tore his pants. "Hey, you nice girl, you, will you sew up my pants for me?" he asked the girls from our settlement, who were standing around gaping. "I can't go home like this!"

Naturally, the girls sent him to our mother. Mama said: "Go into the room next door, take off your pants, give them to me through the door, and wait there in the room while I sew them for you."

My mother took a great liking to this boy, and when he'd put his newly-sewn trousers back on, he said: "Auntie, you're such a nice lady that I'd like to have you for my mother-in-law. Do you have a daughter who's ready to get married by any chance?"

Mama also liked this polite young man, so she said: "In fact, Marga's ready to get married." Ema was already married, Jozef was courting me, and my other sisters still weren't old enough to get married.

And so the boy married our Marga.

My wedding and what kind of family I married into

Jozef was from Kapušany. The Roma from Kapušany had a reputation for being rowdies and brawlers. Šariš Roma, by contrast, were decent, refined people, acknowledged everyone they met, had great manners, and didn't even know how to scuffle, because they were musicians.

Mama and Papa were afraid that if I refused Jozef, some Kapušany Roma would come and beat us up. If I ever had an argument with Jozef, Mama said: "Forget about it, girl, please, forget about it, or those people will come from Kapušany to beat us up!"

I had a wedding like eastern Slovakia had never seen before. I used to go to choir and the priest cultivated me as his only Gypsy child of God. He allowed me to decorate the church with flowers. Even the peasant women loved me, because I had worked hard on the fields. And so the whole village took up my wedding as if it were its own affair.

Jožka's relatives were awfully rich. They dealt in pigs. They became poor during the war, when the Hlinka Guards took away their livelihood because they were gypsies. They came to the wedding in automobiles. Gypsies in automobiles – at a time when not even the peasants had cars! Well, they were trucks to transport pigs in, but they had been scrubbed out until they were clean and decorated with garlands. Jožka's girl-cousin looked like a Russian czarina. She was also just as fat and her middle was laced up in a bodice. Her clothes went down to the floor, and a great big green four-leaf clover was stuck on her breast, as was the fashion then.

And because I was getting married as a virgin, the priest had the carpet rolled out in the church. Crowds lined the whole way from the bridge to the church, both Roma and *gadže*, and the choir sang to me out by the church. It was such an aristocratic wedding. But for all the good that did …

Ilona Lacková under her wedding photo, 1984.

Jožka's relatives were rich all right, but his mother was poor. She became a widow at the age of twenty, since her husband was killed by his own brother over some curly-tailed pig! My mother-in-law had lived by herself for twenty-two years and brought up two sons. She worked herself ragged on the peasants' land.

Jožka's relatives didn't end well. God avenged the sin of Jožka's father's murderer on his children. When the Fascists took away their livelihood, they grew poor. They sold their fields, then their horses, cows, pigs, and finally even their house. That was it for their riches and their glory.

The other man's girl-cousin ended badly even before the war started. Her husband got colon cancer. They started selling their property to get money for the doctors. They sold absolutely everything, even their house – they lived in a multi-story house and at that time only the richest people in the village had multi-story houses! Still, it didn't do any good and the doctors themselves said: "You're throwing your money away, there's no help for him." But the man who was sick had decided he wasn't going to die until he'd found a son-in-law who would elevate the family name again a little.

He had a daughter as beautiful as a saint on an altar, and her name was Jolana. A boy from Čemerny fell in love with her. He wasn't rich, but he was capable and from a family of musicians. Jožka's cousin's husband said: "All right! Now I can die in peace, I've got a son-in-law here!" And he died. Prematurely, unfortunately!

The future son-in-law came one day to look around Kapušany at how the wedding preparations were going. He came in a buggy with his sister. He stopped the buggy in front of the house. Right next door there was another family that dealt in livestock – awfully rich! This livestock dealer was as black as if they'd brought him straight from Africa, and he had a girl who was even blacker. They couldn't get a bride for her because she was so black. Not even their riches tempted anyone.

That black girl's mother had thought up a terrible plan. As soon as she heard the buggy stop in front of her neighbor's house, she ran outside and in a sweet voice she said: "Come inside for a bit of conversation, good people! You won't be sorry!" The young man suspected nothing and stopped in at their house. And there the livestock handler's wife started to sing her daughter's praises to him. "You can't marry a girl as desperately poor as the one next door! What good is it her being white when she hasn't got a thing to wear? Her father died of cancer, and she'll kick the bucket soon herself! What good will that cunt of a beggar-girl do you? Marry my girl and you'll get twenty thousand cash!"

The young man turned his buggy around, went home, and told his mother: "There's a house there where they're offering me twenty thousand if I marry their girl. She's little, ugly, fat, and black. What should I do?"

Both his mother and father went on and on about it for so long that he canceled his engagement with my husband's cousin's daughter and married the black one. But how many times he cried afterwards! He used to go cry where no one could see him. That's how people who break their solemn promises end up.

There's one story about growing poor that's such a nice one that Roma even composed a song about it, and the song went round the whole region for two or three years. It happened in Lučka. That was also one of those rich settlements where they dealt in pigs. Naturally, it happened to a widow who had suddenly become poor and supposedly didn't deserve to. But what does anyone know? The paths of fate are difficult to understand.

In Haniska near Prešov there used to be these enormous livestock markets. They sold horses there, cows, and a lot of Vlach Roma who traded in horses gathered there. All kinds of hucksters did a good business there: the Bosnians sold knives and nails, they used to carry dossers on their bellies and had their wares all spread out on them. There were also organ-grinders with chimpanzees and parrots, who followed their lucky planets. And they also played *bľaški* there, a gambling game.

The poor widow was still rich enough then that she had a cow. But the cow didn't give milk anymore, so the widow said to her son: "Sonny, go to Haniska, sell this cow, and with the money buy another one that'll give milk."

The boy went, sold the cow – and the *bľaškaris*, the man with the gambling setup, saw that the boy had money. That's where the mistake was: "Young man, sir, come play, you'll get rich!"

The widow's son let himself be tempted and the *bľaškaris* let him win. Once, twice. The young man from Lučka thought he'd win a third time and bet again. But this time he lost. And he kept on betting until he didn't have even a kreutzer left.

What now? He couldn't go home without a cow. There were also Jews who sold at the marketplace. They hired some poor young fellows who drove the livestock home at night, slept in the tavern, and the next day there was the sale. The cows were tied up around the tavern overnight. The young man from Lučka went and untied one cow. He drove it home. His mother was beside herself with happiness: "Aii, my golden little cow!" She gave the cow fodder to eat, milked it, and fell completely in love with it. "Aii, my boy, I had no idea I had such a clever son!" And that very night the gendarmes came for her clever son with the Jew the cow belonged to. They beat him so badly he was more dead than alive.

People across the whole region knew of stories like this. They were told at fairs, at weddings, relatives discussed them endlessly when they came visiting, and songs were composed about them. One day something happened and the next day the whole of eastern Slovakia knew about it. After a year or two the sensation died down and after three years no one even knew about it any longer – partly because it had been supplanted and overshadowed by some new spine-tingling thrill of a story that fate had dealt people.

When I married into Kapušany

Whenever someone brought a wife from another village, people were beside themselves with curiosity over what she was like. I came to Kapušany and everyone took a good look at me. I walked through the hamlet and saw how the curtains in the windows were pulled aside and how behind the curtains were inquisitive eyes. Šariš was a town, but Kapušany was only a village. The people were curious what the Gypsy "city" girl would look like. In our parts the women went around in full outfits, but the Kapušany women had only skirts. The peasant women would stop me on the village green: "Oooh, the lady has gone and married into the Gypsies!" They couldn't get through their skulls that a Gypsy woman could be dressed like a proper lady.

"Where else should I have gotten married, since I'm a Gypsy woman myself?" Obviously it made me feel good that they saw me as a lady – and so I was ashamed to ask the Kapušany peasants' wives for work. A proper lady and she'll go begging them to let her dig potatoes. In secret I went as far away as Fuľanka to ask for work. It was about seven kilometers through the forest. The peasant women in Fuľanka praised me because I was used to working and on top of that, I told them all kinds of adventures, cowboy stories, and folk tales. The lady of the grounds where I worked always asked me in the evening: "Do you have something to eat at home?"

I'd say: "In our house in Šariš we have food to eat, but my mother-in-law in Kapušany isn't exactly in the best shape that way." She wanted to give me potatoes, but I said: "Ma'am, how am I going to bring those potatoes all that way?" And so she gave me butter and curd cheese – and we were happy.

When I married into Kapušany, I had to submit to a test like every young bride. The husband brought his wife home and his relatives immediately subjected their new *bori* to entrance examinations. First of all they sent her for water. The whole family stood out in front of the shanty and watched how the girl carried herself in doing it. She was supposed to step nimbly, lightly, like a dancer, yet also not too coquettishly. If she dawdled, the comments started: "What kind of a girl did your son bring you? That one might as well be carrying shit in the graveyard!" If the girl had too much of a wiggle in her walk, her new sisters-in-law would taunt her: "Little brother, that girl's going to need you to tighten her screws a little! So you're not made a laughing-stock for bringing home a slut!"

Then the female relatives watched to see if the new daughter-in-law was clean, if she wiped the bucket before she dipped it in the well, if she let debris get into the water. If the *bori* passed muster, the mother-in-law would be satisfied but wouldn't say anything out loud so she didn't spoil her daughter-in-law. She only boasted about her in front of other people, while at home she was tough and strict toward her.

As her next task the bride had to make *haluški*. If the male relatives didn't like them for any reason, the girl would have a hard time of it. Her mother-in-law and sisters-in-law would poke her and push her around until they'd made a decent, hard-working, devoted, and above all, subservient wife out of her. Every daughter-in-law had to spend five or six difficult years as an apprentice in her mother-in-law's house.

Not long after I came to Kapušany, Jožka said: "Ilon, make some *kikimen haluški*." *Kikimen haluški* is a dish that's enormously easy yet also enormously difficult. Only a master chef can pull it off. *Kikimen haluški* are made out of pure potatoes. You grate raw potatoes, carefully press all the water out of them, and you knead what's left into dough. All the art is in kneading the dough. You have to knead the dough expertly and just long enough so you can rub it with your hands into thin noodles. It's a wonderful dish, but a lot of work! Then you boil the noodles in water and flavor them with curd cheese, butter, or cabbage – just like ordinary *haluški*.

I had never made *kikimen haluški* in my life. Jožka went off to work, but his brother Jani and his male cousin Štefi stayed home and watched to see how I'd begin. It didn't work for me as quickly as for my mother-in-law, of course, since I was making them for the first time in my life. "It's taking long enough!" the boys mocked. "Hey, look at how she's dawdling with them! Such a young female and she moves like she's walking behind a coffin!"

Tears came welling into my eyes, and I kept from crying only with difficulty. But then I got angry: "You runny little snot-face!" I shouted at Jani, though he was two years older than Jožka. "Just you wait until Jožka comes home, he'll give it to you! You won't get a single *haluška*, even if you're dying of hunger!"

Ilona Lacková with her mother-in-law, Mária Cinová, 1984.

Jani and Štefi snickered at me until they were slapping their thighs. Then Jožka came home and he liked the *haluški*. Finally I served those two snot-faces as well.

A few days later I made them yeast dumplings, Šariš style. They weren't familiar with that dish either. Štefan and Jani just rolled their eyes at what I was doing. I gave them a full bowl. "You know, Ilon," said Štefan, "if I get a wife who makes me this kind of dumplings, I'll be happy." But the Hlinka Guards killed him before he'd managed to find a wife.

Like every normal Romani wife I also ran away from Jožka. If a young *bori* couldn't take the way she was being treated in her mother-in-law's house in their efforts to make an ideal being out of her, she ran away to her mother. The mother-in-law, sisters-in-law, and young husband realized that they had overdone it with their retraining, the husband went to get his wife after a few days, and then she was left in peace for a while.

I ran away from Jožka eleven months after I came to Kapušany. Our first child had just been born, little Milánek. He was about three weeks old, I held him in my arms and ran away across the fields; it was pouring rain, the wind was blowing, my good mother-in-law had just dug potatoes, and she called after me: "Where are you running to, you silly girl, stay inside here at home! You know, you'll kill that child, the innocent wretch!" But I was crying so hard I couldn't even answer and I ran on, running almost the whole ten kilometers from Kapušany to Šariš.

Jožka had given me a beating. And why? After the birth my sister Maruša had come to see me in Kapušany to help out a bit with the little one. After a few days she wanted to go home and just then it was raining terribly hard. I walked her part of the way to the other side of the village and said: "If I had the money I'd buy you a train ticket, but I don't have even a crown." A Romani woman heard us and said: "Ilonka, here's five

85

crowns, you can give it back to me tomorrow." I thanked her and bought Maruša a ticket for the train so she wouldn't have to go on foot in the rain.

But then I completely forgot about the five crowns and that woman spread the story among the people. My brother-in-law Jani said to Jožka: "What've you brought into our house? You see how she shames us among the Roma!" And Jozef gave me a terrible beating so everyone could see that he was a big guy and that he knew how to deal with a wife who was out of line.

I had a very kind mother-in-law. I can't say a single unkind word about her. She did backbreaking work for the peasants because her rich relatives made like they didn't know her. She had raised two sons by herself, lived twenty-two years as a widow, and didn't so much as look at a man, even when they courted her. She'd say: "I knew what kind of a father he'd make. My children don't need to experience what I went through."

We used to be home alone together all the time, because her sons were either at work or sitting in the beer house playing cards. We went to the forest together for wood, for mushrooms, for berries, and spent the time happily. She used to say: "Look, girl, at how young I've grown around you!"

At first the Kapušany Roma would make fun of me – this also belonged to that consecrating ritual before which a person would not be accepted as a member of the group. They used to shout at me: "Fiddle-dee, fiddle-dee, Šariš!" As if all we Šariš Roma ever did was fiddle on our violins and never worked. "Fiddle-dee, fiddle-dee, Šariš, not a heller in their pocket, when they've got some guests at home, all they've got to eat are bones!" I'd break out crying, but my mother-in-law would hound them: "I'll show you bones! I'll break your bones in two if you don't leave her alone!" She always stood up for me. And my husband, whatever else he may have been, defended me in front of other people as well.

The Second World War

Marel o Del marel, kas korkoro kamel,
soske ša jov marel mire kale čhaven ...

God punishes whomever He wishes,
but why is He after my black children ...

March 14, 1939

On that day the church bells began to ring in the village. They rang for about two hours. The peasants came running outdoors, listened, and shouted that they were free now. That they had an independent state!

We Roma were in the settlement waiting to see what would come next. Every change made us afraid. We did not believe that any such change could mean a turn for the better for us. Then when someone so much as ran outside the settlement, the peasants mocked: "Now they'll gather you all up and boil you into soap, you dirty Gypsies, so you'll have something to wash with!"

I went to the choir to sing, the only Romani girl among all the peasants' children. Two or three days after they proclaimed the Slovak state we had a rehearsal. I went as usual. One boy stepped on my shoe from behind and made the heel come off my foot. He said: "Now they'll make soap out of all you gyps." I ran home in tears and stayed away from the *gadžo* young people from then on.

One day in the settlement there appeared a drummer, drumming like a wild man, and when we had all come out of our shanties, he announced that the gypsies were now outside the law. That meant they weren't allowed into the ale houses and public places, they weren't allowed in the town except for two hours daily – between twelve and two in the afternoon – and they weren't allowed to use public transporation. Gypsies were completely forbidden to enter Prešov. This order was given because the Gypsies were an asocial element which spread infections and lice. Anyone who disobeyed the order would be sent to a forced labor camp.

The Eržička

Everyone really did stay away from Prešov for a few days. But then people forgot about the order and set off for the flea market. There used to be a flea market every Monday and Friday in an old square in Prešov. They sold mostly used clothes there. The Romani women went there to sell the rags they got from the peasant's wife in exchange for chopping firewood or sweeping the courtyard. Or they'd buy some cheap skirt here for themselves. Our people also picked up the news at the flea market, because every Monday and Friday there were loads of Roma here from all the nearby villages and towns.

But the Eržička was out on the streets. That was a blue paddy wagon without windows, named after a famous Prešov prostitute. Some time before, the Hlinka Guards had made a raid on the prostitutes and named the prison vehicle after the most notorious of them. They gathered all the Roma they caught in Prešov into the Eržička. They surrounded the old square and the Eržička wasn't big enough to take all the Roma to the police station. There they shaved the women's heads half-bare and onto the men's heads they shaved a cross, as punishment. Or they just chucked them in the work camp in Petič.

One time my sister Ema headed off to Prešov. She wanted to buy her children some clothes at the flea market. Papiňori and I went with her. It never used to happen that a Rom would go somewhere by themselves, there was always a bunch of us together.

Ema was picking over the old rags and some *gadžo* next to her said: "Run, quick, it's the secret police!" There were also good-hearted *gadže* who felt sorry for us Roma. Papiňori and I squirmed out of the crowd and flew as fast as our feet could carry us. But poor Ema wasn't at the ready, and before she knew it she'd found herself in the Eržička, in the dark, squeezed in with a mishmash of other Roma.

Papiňori and I ran the whole way back to Šariš. Ema arrived a few hours later, completely disfigured. They took her to the police and shaved half her head bare. On one side she had long hair hanging down and the other side was completely bare. We didn't know whether to laugh or cry. A peasant from Šariš took a photograph of Ema. He said she should keep the photo as a keepsake and as a historical document. But who among the Roma worried about historical documents?

One time my grandmother went to the flea market in Prešov. Not even the fact that Ema had come with half her hair shaved off was enough to dissuade her. My grandmother said: "They'll go after a young girl, but to show disrespect to an old woman is going against God." We tried to persuade her, pleaded with her, but Grandma was stubborn and wouldn't let anyone tell her what to do. She was pushing eighty, but she didn't have a single grey hair. She wore her hair tied in a knot, and when she let it down it reached to her knees.

Grandma walked all over town as if no decree had anything to do with her. Then the Eržička braked right in front of her and the gendarmes threw Grandma inside with the other Roma. They took them to the police station, drove them into the yard, and from there they called them into the office one after the other. There they decided whom they would shave, whom they would give a beating, and whom they would send to the work camp. Pačaj himself, the captain of the secret police, oversaw the whole operation.

The day they caught Grandma there was a one-eared gendarme who was shaving the

Roma. He lost his ear in some kind of fight. Grandma's turn came and the one-eared man stepped up to her with the shaver in his hand. Grandma began cursing him in her spirit: may your other ear fall off, may the arm you reach for me with rot, may your eyes pour out of your head before you get close to me! As if the curses started to take effect, Pačaj stopped the one-eared gendarme, turned his ugly, oniony eyes on Grandma and said: "Let down your hair, Gypsy woman!" The best thing of all was that Pajča was a half-Rom himself.

Grandma let down her hair and it fell all the way to her knees. She saw that the gendarmes' breath had been taken away. That gave her courage: "You just look and see if you can find a single louse on my head! You try touching me! I'll put such a spell on you that your arms will shrivel up!" Grandma spoke with such certainty that the simple gendarme stepped backwards. Then Pačaj took a long ruler and began to rake through Grandma's hair. He couldn't find a single nit. My mother was very careful that none of us ever got lice, and she kept especially careful watch over Grandma's hair. Pačaj turned to the simple gendarme and said: "The old witch is right. Hair like that – and not a single louse!" Then he asked Grandma: "Do you know how to cast spells?"

"You want to see?" Grandma asked, yielding a little. She sensed that she had won. Naturally she didn't know how to cast spells.

"Tie up your hair and get out of here!" ordered Pačaj.

Grandma ran home and collapsed in a chair. Only now when she was safe did she shudder with her fear. "What's the matter, Grandma, what's the matter?" We washed her with water, but for the longest time she was unable to utter a word. Then she told us the whole story, down to the smallest details. "Children, I'm not going to the city anymore at all!" And she didn't go. She didn't want to tempt fate.

It also happened to me once that I escaped Pačaj by the skin of my teeth. Sometimes a person risks everything so that for at least a while he can have the feeling he is living in freedom, like a human being. I set off for Prešov for I forget what reason. I walked along the wall so I wouldn't stand out so much. I needed to cross the street, so I was standing on the sidewalk waiting for the light to turn green when a car stopped right next to me, and who was sitting next to the driver but Pačaj! Fortunately he was staring straight ahead of him and he didn't see me. At that moment my legs felt like they were made of lead, and I couldn't move. I was twenty years old and I still felt like a newlywed, I wanted Jozef to like me, and now he was going to see me with half my hair shaved off! But then their light turned green and the driver took off. Pačaj hadn't noticed me! And I fell down. My knees just plain gave way under me and I collapsed on the sidewalk. By sheer force of will I got a hold of myself so that pedestrians wouldn't come running up and then have one of them turn out to be a gendarme or a Hlinka Guard. They didn't catch me. I walked all the way to my mother-in-law's in Kapušany more dead than alive. I don't know how it is, but in my life I've always had good luck.

The one who paid most dearly for his daring was Feriček, whose father was Feri from our settlement in Šariš. Feri was a very wise man, although he could neither read nor write. If someone had no idea what to do in some serious life situation, he went to see Feri. Feri also took the role of justice of the peace at Romani weddings – few Roma got married in a church or in the town hall. We organized our own Romani wedding, *bijav*, and for us it was just as binding as an official wedding in a church. The *gadže* used to tell us not just to live together, but that was because they didn't understand our customs. The function of master of ceremonies at our *bijav* was taken by a respected person, one who knew how to speak beautifully and wisely. He tied the bride's and groom's hands with a red scarf, poured a little spirits into each one's palm, and then the groom had to drink out of the bride's hand and the bride from the groom's. Then the justice of the peace at the wedding delivered a beautiful speech to them and wished them happiness to the end of their days. In Šariš everyone wanted Feri for their wedding.

Feri had a lot of children, just like other Roma. His oldest son, Feriček, was a real devil. He had no respect for anything, not even for the war! One time some German soldiers were riding through the village on horseback, Feriček conspired with some fellows, each as big as he was himself, and they clambered up the slope onto the bridge, stuck out their bare behinds at the soldiers and called out: "*Schießen! Schießen!*" – shoot! shoot! – "If you can hit me!" Fortunately the soldiers just laughed.

Feriček once said he was going to Prešov and that the Hlinka Guards and the gendarmes could kiss his ass. Everyone tried to talk him out of it, he wouldn't let anyone tell him what to do, and he went. In Prešov they caught him and beat him so badly that he was left lying on the sidewalk. A kind-hearted *gadžo* brought him home on his truck; he lay bleeding and unconscious. For two months he couldn't move. The old women washed his wounds with chamomile and burnet and applied wraps made of healing leaves. He was more or less all right after about two months. All the same, the young man died not long after the war.

The steamer

At first the gendarmes shaved only those Roma they caught in town, as a punishment and as a warning. Later the "hygiene patrol" began traveling around the settlements and they shaved everyone. They said it was so they wouldn't spread typhus. They traveled in a big vehicle they called the "steamer," because inside it they steamed "Gypsy rags." The soldiers and the gendarmes strong-armed their way into every shanty with their guns aimed while the "hygiene patrol" gathered up all the clothes, coats, and feather blankets – not even a single foot-wrap escaped their attention. Then they steamed them in the steamer, threw them in a pile, and we were left to sort out what was whose.

I experienced the "hygiene patrol" when I was living at my mother-in-law's in Kapušany. Even if the racist laws forbade us from leaving the settlement where we had our "right of domicile," people took risks and late at night secretly went through the forest to visit their relatives in other settlements. I can't tell you how many times I traveled that way from Kapušany to Šariš and from Šariš to Kapušany! We found out what they were doing with Roma elsewhere – and that was how we found out the steamer was going around. Jožka went to the gendarmes' station right away and said: "My wife goes around wearing clean clothes and so does my mother, neither has a single louse, and I won't let them be shaved!" As it happened, the leader of the gendarmes was a decent man and my mother-in-law had worked in their home as a cleaning woman before the war, so he knew her and what she was like. He told Jozef: "Don't worry, I know that you're respectable Gypsies, and I won't let them shave you."

The next day I was going through the field to the peasant's place and I saw the "hygiene patrol" coming down the road at me from the opposite direction! I turned around and hurried all the way home: "Mother dear, Mother dear, they're on their way to shave us! Come quick and hide in the peasants' courtyard."

But my mother-in-law said: "I'm not going!" She always did whatever she felt like doing. I don't know if she was brave that way or if she was resigned to her fate. She said simply that she wasn't going and kept puttering around in the kitchen as if absolutely nothing was wrong. I didn't want to go to the peasant's house without her, I was a stranger there, and Jozef had brought me there from Šariš only recently. I had long, thick hair, waves and waves of it – I think my hair was as beautiful then as it's ever been. I wanted to look beautiful in that village full of strangers so that my husband could be proud of me. What now? This fellow was coming into the yard, turning the shaver in his hand and mocking me in this western Slovak dialect: "We'll find something nice to shave!" He was approaching me. In the yard we had a chopping block, and there was an ax stuck in it. I grabbed it and positioned myself facing him: "What are you going to shave? What are you going to shave? You'd better get lost, or ...!" and I took a swipe with the ax. "Nononononono!" he howled, and he took off running. When he was gone I realized what I'd done. I dashed into the kitchen: "Mother dear, we've got to get out of here! Quick! For God's sake please, I just tried to kill a gendarme with an ax!"

My mother-in-law looked at me: "Where do you want to run?" The steamer stood in the road and the gendarmes and a Hlinka Guard commander were coming toward the house. The man with the western accent who wanted to shave me was keeping well behind them.

There was nowhere to run, so I went toward them. I stepped up to them and said: "You can't shave either me or my mother-in-law, because neither one of us has any lice! That's an order from the commander of the gendarmes!" This brashness somehow came pouring out of me. Out of nothing! The Hlinka Guard commander sized me up and then he turned to the gendarmes and said they really didn't have to shave the two of us, that he would vouch for us.

Not long after the war that westerner who shaved us during the war showed up in a pub near our place. And in Kapušany there was a Rom named Bugi. He was the most decent and sensitive person in the whole village. The peasants loved him and said: "If only every Gypsy were like Bugi! There aren't even any Slovaks like him!" Bugi never fought, and he'd never beaten anyone in his life, not even his wife! He never hurt anyone. And Bugi came into the pub just when the westerner who had shaved his wife and daughter was sitting there. As soon as he saw him, he jumped into the kitchen, grabbed a long-handled brush, and beat him so badly there wasn't a single part of him that came out unscathed. "I had to do it! I had to do it!" the westerner defended himself. "I was paid to. It was an order!" No one stood up for him.

Pačaj

Most of the anti-Gypsy laws and edicts were valid throughout the whole Slovak state, but I am convinced that some of them were made up by Pačaj himself. Or at least Pačaj was responsible for the drastic way they were enforced in our area. They say make a dog out of a hare and it'll chase hares worse than a dog. One who has been Turkicized is worse than a Turk. This was all true of Pačaj.

Pačaj, who was half-Romani, came from Gelnice like my sister Vilma's husband, and some nephew of Pačaj's even learned to play the violin from my brother-in-law – so we knew everything about their family. Although Pačaj had a house in Gelnice, he started building himself a political career, married a Slovak woman, and moved to Košice. He wanted to become a member of parliament, but I don't remember what party slate he ran on. All of a sudden before the elections he remembered the Gypsies, so he started campaigning among us so we would vote for him. He even sank so low as to stand on the edge of the Gypsy settlement and explain how he wanted to elevate us. At the same time you got the impression he felt superior to those Gypsy beggars. The Roma didn't vote for him, he lost the elections, and didn't become a member of parliament. That was why he took such revenge on us during the war. He became a captain in the secret police and persecuted his own flesh and blood worse than any Hlinka Guard or German Nazi.

After the war Pačaj escaped conviction because he'd hidden two Jews. They'd given him good money for doing it.

One time, I think it was in the year 1949, our Romani theater was performing in Spišské Vlachy. After the performance we were waiting for the train to Prešov and who was standing there but Pačaj. The boys recognized him. There was one man among the actors whom Pačaj had ordered beaten, another he had locked up in a work camp, and a third whose mother he'd had shaved. Our actors threw themselves onto him and wanted to beat him up. He was as pale as a corpse, just shifting those oniony eyes of his and howling. There were a lot of people at the train station, and I didn't want them to go around saying that gypsies were always brawling. I talked our people into leaving Pačaj in peace.

His shoes never left Gelnice after that happened, and they say he didn't even go outside. He was an awfully ugly man, fat, obese, his eyes sticking out of their sockets. He died not long after that.

Why didn't the Roma take revenge against him? Why didn't some old woman put a spell on him so he'd be covered in worms? Well, the suffering he'd caused our people was enough! Roma believe – or at least they used to believe – that everyone would get recompensed for what they'd done, whether in this world or some other one, whether in this life or the next one. Fate is just, even if it doesn't seem like it sometimes. *Thovav tut Devleske*, a Rom will say, I'll leave it up to the Lord God – and that's enough for the person who's done something wrong to be eaten up with fear in anticipation of a just punishment. The fear in and of itself is sufficient punishment, and that's why merciful Roma forgive those who've done them wrong before they die. It's not up to human beings to take revenge, because they would defile themselves that way. Recompense is God's affair.

The transports

In 'forty-one the transports came through Kapušany. Jožka was working at the train station loading and unloading the cars, and I used to go bring him his lunch. One time there was a long train that had stopped at the station, all cattle cars, and they were using them to move Jews. It was awful! All they were wearing was pajamas, squeezed in so they could hardly stand. Right at that time I was expecting with Milánek. Jožka said: "Don't look at this, go home so you don't lose the baby. We can't help those people anyway!" I didn't listen and stayed there, and it was as if someone whispered to me: go look in the rear boxcars! I asked Jožka to go with me and so he went. The rear cars were filled with Roma! As soon as they saw us they started groaning and begging: "Water, water, take pity, people, give us a little water!" Their accent was different from ours and I didn't know where they were from. I said: "Jožka, for heaven's sake, come on, we'll ask for a bucket somewhere, we can't leave these people to suffer like this!" and I was already running inside the station building to get a pail or a can. But just then the German who was accompanying the transport came running up and drove us away with the butt-end of his gun: "*Weg! Weg! Weg!*" The train moved on. For several nights I couldn't sleep, and I was ashamed that I hadn't given those people a little water.

Fortunately I was luckier the next time, although they weren't Roma but Russian prisoners of war. My mother had sent a bed to Kapušany for me. My mother-in-law had only two beds, and the two of us, my mother-in-law and I, slept on one and Jožka and his brother Jani slept on the other. My mother-in-law didn't want a third bed in the house, saying: "Girl, there won't be room to turn around in here!" But my mother sent it all the same and one evening my husband and I went to the train station to get it. Another transport was just coming through, this time with Russian prisoners of war. They were leaning out of the boxcars and calling: "Little mother, water! Water!" This time I did a better job of it than the last time, being careful that the transport's German guard didn't see me. I asked the woman who was the station attendant for a bucket, pumped the water, and carried it to the first boxcar. The prisoners took the water into their mess tins and drank until they were choking. I wanted to bring water to another car, but the German had already come and was driving me away with the butt-end of his gun.

One time late at night, Papa was going home from Prešov, where he had traveled in secret in order to learn the news. Just when he meant to change trains, a transport with Jews came up. Papa hid in the bushes so they wouldn't see him. The train stopped in the middle of the fields. Three German soldiers were watching every boxcar. When the train stopped, the soldiers from the first car went to relieve the guards from the second one. Right in the middle of that the Jews started jumping out of the train, running away in all different directions, and two or three ran right by Papa – but the Germans were right there, bullets were flying, and they beat anyone they got a hold of with the butt-end of their gun. Papa was petrified with fear. And that was good, because if the soldiers had seen something moving in the bushes they would have taken a shot at it and Papa wouldn't have gotten home alive.

Toward morning when he came home, his whole body was shaking. He said: "It'd be better if we killed ourselves than wait for that kind of horror!" But Roma consider suicide to be the greatest sin.

Home defense training

I had the misfortune or the good luck that I always turned up where something was going on. Once I'd stopped in Šariš in secret to see my family when I was expecting a little one, I was scared, and Mama always knew how to get me to snap out of it. I had barely come in when my parents started in with the news: "Just imagine, the village *gadže* have compulsory home defense drill, the Hlinka Guards are organizing it, and they've left us out because we're outside the law. How's that for you, eh?" Mama also

93

made fun of certain Roma – it was as if they'd fallen on their heads, they were actually offended: "Yet again, the *gadže* are leaving us out! Yet again they've got something more than we have!" Of course, most Roma were normal human beings and were glad that being outside the law had finally brought them some kind of advantage: they didn't have to do home defense drills. They went to sleep with the feeling that fate was kinder to us than to the *gadže*.

We hadn't even gotten a good night's sleep when outside someone shouted: "Get up! Get up! Everyone outside! Home defense drill!" and someone was already banging on our door. Our mother only whispered: "Quiet! Don't move!" We kept as still as the dead. Meanwhile Hlinka Guards were running from shanty to shanty, banging on the doors and the windows, there were sounds of people running outside, the women were yelling and shrieking: "What are they going to do with us?" The children were crying. There, I thought, now the people who felt offended that they weren't allowed to do home defense drill have something to be happy about. The Guards banged on our window two more times but then they stopped, thinking we were already outside with the others.

Then they drove our people under the bridge and used tear gas on them. No one had any idea what it was! In our whole lives we had never heard that such a thing existed! Desperate cries of "mama, I'm dying!" rang out. The Guards still weren't satisfied, so they forced their way into the shanties and soon the whole settlement was bathed in tear gas. It was a miracle they left our house alone. People were choking, jumping into the river, children were drowning, gasping for breath – and the Hlinka Guards scrambled up the slope onto the bridge and laughed until they shook. They stamped and clapped like madmen at the show the gypsies were putting on for them.

I went to complain

Milánek still hadn't been born yet and I was having strange feelings. On one hand I was more fearful – for his health, for his life – and on the other hand it was as if I were bolder. Maybe I'll manage to protect us and to save us if I don't give in! In the novels I had read there were heroes fighting against injustice, and I had adopted them as my ideal. My heroes always won, and I was convinced that I would win out as well. I resolved to go to the provincial chief in Prešov and ask him why we Roma were persecuted in this way. The provincial chief was the biggest man in the area – or in the Iupa, as they said then.

I said nothing to anyone, since I knew that my mother wouldn't want to let me go and would cry. I went all by myself. Several times I wanted to turn back, telling myself: if Pačaj catches me this time, there's no way I'll manage to avoid getting shaved! What would Jozef say? Or Lieskovský, the provincial chief himself, would order me shaved. In my spirit I prayed that the Lord God would give me the strength to reach the end of my journey, and at that moment it became clear to me: "nothing will happen to you!" resounded within me, and I went to the provincial office. I was dressed like a city woman and I asked the gatekeeper where I would find the *úri*. At that time we called high officials *úri*, in Hungarian. The gatekeeper looked at me with amazement and then he explained to me which way to go. I walked up the stairs, went from door to door until I found the right one, knocked, and stepped inside. I greeted the official there and said

I would like to speak to the *úri* – with the provincial chief, Mr. Lieskovský. I must have said it with great decision, because the official didn't even ask me what I wanted of him, opened another door, and I caught sight of a man behind an enormous desk and two Roma standing in front of him – then the official closed the door behind him, and when he came back into the room where I was waiting, he said: "Right away, right away." In a moment the two Roma left, terribly sad, because Lieskovský had sent them to a forced-labor camp. I wanted to back out, but it didn't work. The *úri* had beckoned me inside.

I greeted him politely. I knew how to speak because I had read a good deal. I asked him why they were doing all these things with the Roma. Why were they shaving our heads? Why weren't they allowing us to go into town? Why couldn't we leave the settlement?

He sat looking at me with his mouth open. He left me standing and didn't tell me to sit down. And at that time it didn't even occur to me that I could sit down in the presence of such a great man as the provincial chief. He asked me who I was. I said I was the daughter of the Romani mayor in Šariš and that I had completed council school. Besides that I had married into a decent and well-off family of Roma from Kapušany.

He asked if I wasn't afraid to come to Prešov, afraid they would bundle me into the Erľiǎka and shave my head. I said that they tried to shave my head a couple of days ago but found no reason to, because I didn't have any lice. That wasn't the truth, they wanted to shave my grandmother's head, but it didn't matter whether it was my grandmother or me.

He used the familiar pronoun with me. In those days it was unheard of for a *gadžo* to be on formal terms with a Gypsy and address him, say, as "Mr. Horváth" or "Mr. Lacko." They typically called us by saying "Gypsy, c'mere, you, Gypsy girl, c'mere." At best "our" *gadže* said "Mikluš," "Máňa," or "Ilonka," but only with the familiar pronoun. Never formally! Naturally we were formal with them. Even long after the war the "white folks" in our parts couldn't get used to the fact that people had begun to use the formal pronoun with us Roma, just like with everyone else.

The provincial chief asked me again what my reason for coming was, and I repeated that it was a matter of justice. And that I believed that he was a just man, otherwise he couldn't fulfill such a responsible function. I complained once again how they had boiled my English outfit in Kapušany, and now if I wanted to go out dressed like a lady I couldn't, because what good is an outfit that's been boiled in water? I told him how they had made a radio program about me because I wrote poems, but they didn't print the article in the magazine because in the meantime Gypsies had been placed outside the law. And so no matter how good a Gypsy was or how much he tried, he could necessarily, always be only a Gypsy, because the "white folks" wouldn't accept him as one of them.

He offered me a seat and started to use the formal pronoun with me. He said that these were all edicts from Bratislava, that he hadn't thought up any measures to persecute Gypsies, that he was too small an official for that, and that there was nothing that could be done about it.

"And so what am I supposed to do?" I asked him, and I wanted to cry.

"Go home and be careful that they don't catch you. Last time you were lucky they didn't shave your head, and that didn't mean you were going to be lucky again today and go home with your head unshaven. That'd be a shame, with such hair!" Then he added: "But don't you give up, because I'm listening to you," and with that he let me go. I went home feeling as if I were in a swoon and there were two feelings pounding in me: absolute helplessness and hopelessness, and pride over the fact that the provincial chief himself, Mr. Lieskovský, had used the formal pronoun with me, that he had said "please be seated." That he had acknowledged the humanity in me.

The next day the gendarmes picked up my husband, took him to the station, and beat him so badly that I went to Lieskovský's office to complain. I went with Milánek at my breast, so they didn't dare touch me. But as punishment for that they beat up Jozef. And as a warning to the rest: so we'd lose our taste for complaining. Jozef crawled home looking like one big bruise. I soothed him, kissed him, and begged him to forgive me. He said: "You stupid woman, if they'd beat you like that you wouldn't have survived! I can take more."

Petič: the forced-labor camp

In 'forty-two they started laying a track from Prešov to Strážský. The German army wanted to get to the east. The track led through Kapušany. They had to build tunnels and tall viaducts, like they had in Hanušovce, and to do that they needed a lot of workers. They'd taken the Slovaks into the army, not trusting the Gypsies with weapons, made the Gypsy recruits into work squads, and put them on projects important to the war. But there was still a labor shortage. And so it occurred to the higher-ups to establish forced-labor camps where asocial, subversive elements and work-shy individuals would construct the track of victory over bolshevism...

I was twenty-one years old then, my husband twenty-two, and Milánek was a year old. Jozef and his brother Jani were working at the train station loading coal. They worked from early in the morning until ten at night, often coming home after eleven o'clock. I waited for them so I could heat up some water for them to wash up and cook something warm to put in their stomachs.

One evening – I had just poured the warm water into the sink for them – pounding on the door! I asked who it was. "Open up in the name of the law!" I was shaking all over and didn't go to open the door. They kept pummeling so furiously that my mother-in-law said: "They're going to break our door!" She pulled herself together and went to open it. In came four gendarmes, with two more standing by the entrance. Two of them went up to Jozef and two up to Jani, slapped some chains on their wrists, the kind they used to tie up pigs' legs at the slaughtering-feast, and without a word of explanation led them outside. That night they picked up all the Roma in Kapušany, plus one poor *gadžo* who'd married a Romani girl. They picked up Jožka, Jani, Franc, Ferenc, Baro Šero, Feri, Deža – in short, everyone, down to the last man, from eighteen to sixty years old. They led them off to the gendarmes' station.

I didn't sleep all night, I only cried. Milánek cried with me, because he sensed my fear and my desperation. My mother-in-law said: "Don't cry, my girl. They picked up the Jews and it came the Gypsies' turn. It could have been expected, so what are you crying for? You won't do either yourself or them any good. And you're making the child cry along with you."

In the morning I got up, got dressed, and went to the train station. At that time there was a train that went from Bardejov to Prešov, and we suspected they would take them away on that train. And that's what they did. The gendarmes led our men in a procession through the village, and all of them had chains on their arms like criminals. We women just cried and tore our hair. Some *gadže* were sorry for us and some mocked us: "They're bringing the Gypsies! They'll boil you into soap!"

They drove the men into the train and the train departed. That didn't stop me, and I set off for Prešov on foot with two other Romani women from Kapušany. When we arrived, the people told us they'd put all the gypsies together in the stockade next to the fire station.

They'd rounded up the Roma from the whole area there, because the night they took away Joïka, Jani, and the other men from Kapušany, they'd raided the other settlements around Prešov, in Šariš, in Vagaš, in Chmiňany, in Solivar, in Chmeľov – in short, absolutely everywhere.

All the women, mothers, sisters, and daughters, were pressing around the stockade. They were looking through the cracks between the boards and I was looking through a hole where a knot had been. The stockade was full of Roma. Gendarmes on horseback were riding around among them. In the middle there was a table, and behind the table a doctor who was carrying out some examinations. Then they lined the Roma up four deep and took them to the main train station in Prešov. We followed them at a distance. We wanted to know where they were taking them on the train. But they wouldn't let us in the station. A gendarme on a horse came up, made us scalter with the butt of his gun, and threatened to pick us up too. There was nothing left for us to do but go home.

In the evening a train came in from Prešov. All through the village you could hear people shouting: "They're bringing the gypsies! They're bringing the Gypsies!" They made them get off the train in Kapušany and drove the whole, endless procession to Hanušovce and into Petič. It isn't far, only about eight kilometers. Petič is a hill and on the hill they'd put up wooden barracks for prisoners.

The men hadn't had a bite to eat since the evening before and hadn't slept at all. Some of them couldn't even eat, having been weakened so. The stronger ones held them up. Once again I ran outside and several women came after me. We walked next to the procession along a trench, and one woman was wailing awfully that she had seven children, and how was she going to feed them? A gendarme on horseback came up to her and struck her with the butt of his gun. She fell down. They told us that we had to turn back right away. Two women picked up the one the gendarme had struck and led her home. One other woman waited with me for the gendarme to go away, and again we set off after the marching column. We got as far as Petič. There they drove the Roma into a stockade. It was hard for us, but at least we knew where our husbands were. It was about two in the morning when we got back to Kapušany.

The next day I set off for Petič again. I wanted to know what they were going to do with my husband, and if they weren't going to kill him. I stood by the gate and didn't know what to do. I just stood there and waited. Today, when I look back at that time, it seems to me that we Roma had that waiting in our blood since time immemorial. We stood and waited, stood and waited, the universe revolving around us as we stood and waited or walked and waited and perhaps didn't even notice that we were alive, and that in that endless waiting there was a spark of certainty that a miracle would happen that would change our lives. I don't know how long I stood and waited at the gate, but a miracle happened: some Slovak woman from western Slovakia addressed me, kindly. She asked if I had my husband here. I said I did, and that yesterday they had brought him here. She told me how her husband also worked here, but not as a prisoner. As a tunnel blaster, she said. Their firm had sent them here for a job. They lived in caravans – though the job was inside the camp, after work they had free time and could go where they wanted to, and they were allowed to bring their wives. Then that kind woman invited me into their caravan and said I could see through the window what they were doing with our people. I was well-dressed, wearing clothes my mother had sewn me, and no one could tell from my clothing that I was a Gypsy woman. But I'd pulled my kerchief up to my forehead so no one could see how black I was. The western Slovak woman led me through the gate to her home in the caravan. I stayed at their place overnight. Morning had barely broken when people started lining up for breakfast. The men gathered around an enormous cauldron. Everyone got something poured into their mess tin. They said it was ersatz coffee without sugar and without milk. They also got a piece of dry bread. Gendarmes with clubs in their hands were walking around the crowd, and you could constantly hear: "Quick now! Quick! Hurry up! Hurry up!" Anyone who dawdled got it with the club. After breakfast the men went in a group to work. They were made to march. Anyone who didn't keep step got it with the club again. And on top of everything they were made to sing.

Then the kind Slovak woman led me outside through the gate, I thanked her, and went home. I told my mother-in-law through my tears what I had seen. "At least they're not shooting them!" she comforted me.

Still, I had good luck in my life! They let my husband out about a month afterwards, because he couldn't move his right arm properly. When he was little, his cousin was carrying him on horseback, and Jozef fell and broke his arm. My mother-in-law didn't take him to the doctor's because she was a widow with no money, and just bound up his arm tightly. The arm healed, but my husband never could move it properly. And that was a great piece of luck, because they let him out of the camp while his brother Jani had to stay there.

There was another Rom from Kapušany whose name was Ferenc. He was a real tough guy, brave, and the whole village was afraid of him. He was gutsy because he'd traded in pigs before the war, and those rich pig traders had an altogether different place in the scheme of things than other gypsies. Even the peasants often borrowed money from them, and that's why they were polite to them. But according to the laws of the Hlinka Guards, a Gypsy was a Gypsy, and so they took Ferenc to the camp as well. Ferenc was desperate, since his wife was due to give birth any minute and he was looking forward to having a little girl. He was rock-solid certain it would be a little girl, because they'd already had about five boys and so far not a single girl. His wife gave birth – and it really was a little girl. Somehow Ferenc found out in the camp and decided he was going to have a look at his little daughter. He escaped from the camp. But if he had only escaped and gone home nice and quiet to have a look at the little girl! No! Ferenc was a flashy guy, so he went to the pub to have a beer. "Don't go there, don't show yourself in public!" his wife begged him, but Ferenc cut her short and said he ought to be able to celebrate the birth of his daughter! He just up and went to the pub! Luckily there were no gendarmes there at the time, just peasants who'd enlisted in the Hlinka Guards.

"How come you aren't in the camp?" one of them bawled out. "You escaped, didn't you?"

That wasn't something Ferenc was going to take lying down. He lived only a short way from the pub. He ran out, grabbed an ax at his house, and came tearing back into the pub. "Who used to lend you money before the war, you *gadžo* nobody! You're making a big noise, aren't you, now that you've got Mr. Hlinka and the gendarmes standing behind you!" He just wanted to brawl with some of the Hlinka Guards. They didn't have any weapons and took off running. Ferenc ran after the commander with his ax in his hand, chased him as far as the yard of his house, and the guy just barely managed to jump in the door and slam it behind him. In the meantime the other members of the Guards had gone to get the gendarmes. But Ferenc didn't wait for them and ran into the forest. He crept along through the creek so the dogs wouldn't be able to follow his tracks.

He hid that way for a couple of days. Maybe the gendarmes wouldn't have even found him, except Ferenc had fallen in love with his newborn little girl. He couldn't stay away, and one night he went to have a look at her. Their house had been occupied by the gendarmes, of course. They caught him. They didn't shoot him, because he was a big, strong guy and they wanted to use him to work. But they took him away to the camp and beat him so badly that he couldn't move for three weeks. When he lost consciousness, they poured water over him and started beating him all over again. After that he was afraid to run away. "If they kill me, I'll never see her again," he said. He meant that little girl of his.

Among the Roma in the camp, the gendarmes also found an informer. His name was Holub and he came from Košice. They gave him more to eat than the others, didn't beat him, and in exchange he told them who was planning to escape. Then the gendarmes tied those Roma to the bench, one after the other, and four men beat each one. Until they were unconscious. So they would lose all thought of escaping. It didn't do much good, because the Roma were always escaping.

After the war that informer disappeared. He ran off to somewhere in Bohemia. Ferenc survived the camp, went home, looked around for that man, but couldn't find him. Maybe he would have found him, but finally he gave up. "What am I going to mess with him for? It'll all come back to him and justice will find him."

One of the Roma who was always escaping from camp was my mother-in-law's other son, Jožka's brother Jani. He ran away twenty-two times and they caught him twenty-one times. If anyone else had done what Jani did, he would have been long dead, beaten to death, but maybe it was because my mother-in-law was an upright woman who never hurt anyone either in deed, word, or thought, because she worked so hard and wasn't afraid of anyone, that she was fortunate and her son stayed alive.

But even so we suffered plenty. Day after day the gendarmes came to our house, turned everything upside down, ripped open the straw mattresses – looking for Jani. Our nerves were completely shot. Sometimes they tyrannized us by coming at night, driving all the Roma into the icy creek and asking where Jani was or where this or that Rom who'd escaped was. Of course, they learned nothing.

Jani hid in the forest, his mother brought food to an agreed upon place for him, but sometimes he came sneaking home to eat. One time he came, his mother had made him scrambled eggs, and he started to eat them. He had hardly put two or three spoonfuls into his mouth when the gendarmes burst in through the door. They had come quietly, not even using a flashlight. They wanted to surprise us – and so they did. But they didn't really surprise us, because we were prepared for everything. Jani ran the other way, smashed a window that was closed, jumped outside, and escaped into the fields. A fat gendarme behind him. But how could he have done it? On the road there was a peasant, probably coming back from the pub, and he laughed at the gendarme: "With a belly like that you want to catch him?" The gendarme was so angry he was foaming at the mouth.

They didn't catch Jani. He kept hiding in the forest, but he didn't dare go home. Until one time he got a craving for cigarettes and couldn't stand it. God knows if he didn't get mixed up in that head from being alone so much – he just up and went to the pub! Just like that crazy Ferenc, the flashy guy, that other time. The pub owner was from western Slovakia, a really good man, I can't tell you how many times he let me have sugar on account. Jani was sitting in the pub and there were gendarmes in the yard. They were asking the peasants where this and that Gypsy was. Well, and the peasants told them that one who'd run away, Lackaňa's son, was sitting inside in the pub there. The gendarmes – there were four of them – burst into the room. Jani ran all around, pushed one out of the way on one side, the other on the other side, and he managed to escape again. The gendarmes went after him. And there was a peasant standing there, a really good man, name of Séman, and he said to them: "Aren't you ashamed to be chasing an honest boy? Did he kill anybody? Rob a bank? Why don't you leave him alone? And his mother, you could kneel at her feet, an honest woman like that!"

The gendarmes were also human beings who lived in the village with everyone else, and they were ashamed. Only the fat one told himself that he'd catch Jani one way or another. And so he did. One time when Jani just couldn't resist temptation and went to see his mother, they caught him from behind and took him off to the camp at Revúce. There they beat him so badly that he barely survived it. He couldn't move for a month. And a month later he ran away again.

Things went worse for Jani's cousin, Štefi. Štefi Bílý was the oldest of five children. A terribly poor family. His father walked eighteen kilometers a day to his job in the quarry. Eighteen kilometers there, eighteen back, all on foot. He went lame and died. The oldest son, that was Štefi, took care of the family, because his mother had tuberculosis. When they took him off to the camp, his mother was desperate – what would she do by herself, a sick woman, with four children? And so Štefi ran away. He hid himself and always managed to bring some potatoes from somewhere and wood to keep the house warm. But one time they caught him. They bound him hand and foot and threw him in the back of a freight truck. But the truck didn't have any sides. It was clear from the beginning that it would be certain death. When the truck took a curve near Chmeľov, Štefi fell off, hit his head on a rock and was dead on the spot.

Tobacco broth

There was a forced-labor camp at Petič for something over a year. Then they liquidated it, because they'd finished work on the Prešov-Strážská line. They took most of the prisoners elsewhere, but they let some of them go. Among them they let go two fellows from Šariš, the son-in-law of the storyteller Feri, and Ema.

In Šariš we had one young man whose name was Ema. His mother had given birth to all boys, she'd had twelve of them, and her husband was just sick of it. He wanted a little girl at any cost. When the mother went into labor the thirteenth time, she said that she wasn't going to let another boy loose on the world and that whatever she gave birth to would have to be a little girl. But then, of course, another male child was born! "For

God's sake, old woman," the mother moaned, "tell my husband that we've got an Ema!" And the midwife really did lie to her husband and said that this time it was an Ema. Out of sheer joy he got drunk and ran through the settlement shouting: "We've got an Ema! We've got an Ema!" The mother managed to keep the fact that Ema was a boy secret for a few days, and later when the husband found out, the name Ema stayed with the boy.

Poor Ema paid dearly for the fact that he wasn't a girl! They took him to Petič like all the other men, and let him go home when they liquidated the facility, but they immediately started to pick the men they'd released up again and throw them into other camps. Before that, of course, they all underwent medical examinations, because many had been so decimated by the hunger, beatings, insects, and backbreaking work that they were useless for other projects. Naturally, people realized in an instant that they could make themselves even more infirm than they were in reality and so avoid going to another camp. Roma hate pain terribly and can't even look when someone is bleeding, but in those days you found people who even chopped off their finger. But most often of all they drank a broth made from tobacco. They thought it would make spots on their lungs as if they had tuberculosis, and they didn't take tuberculars to the camps. I don't know whether you get spots on your lungs after drinking that kind of broth, but the fact is that anyone who drank it was so sick afterwards that after the examination they usually sent him home. When Ema and Feri's son-in-law were called up for another camp, Feri advised them to drink tobacco broth as well. Unfortunately, they listened to him. They drank the broth and the next day both were dead.

Jantotis

The only personn that neither the gendarmes nor the Guards dared lay a finger on was Jantotis from Kapušany. He was a man in league with the devil. He was getting on toward eighty years old, but he walked erect, tall, and straight as a poplar tree, his back like a gate. He used to carry a gnarled stick with him and stand on the crossroads where the road leads to Šarišské Lúky, and as soon as any man came walking round, whether Rom or *gadžo*, Jantotis asked him: "Do you know me, boy?" When the person in question greeted him and said his name, Jantotis let him pass. But woe if someone said: "I don't know who you are, uncle!" He immediately got it in his back with the gnarled stick. It went even worse for the bigheaded peasants who said something in the manner of: "How the hell am I supposed to know what every Gypsy's name is?" Jantotis beat them with his stick so badly they could hardly crawl home. God knows what he said to them in the meantime, because as far as I know, no one dared complain about him. And at the same time there were a lot of people who passed through that crossroads, because they went that way to the marketplace in Prešov to sell chickens.

During the war Jantotis informed on his own relatives. There was no wood and nothing to heat the house with – and in the nobleman's forest there was a dry old beech tree. Completely dry, not a single little leaf on it. An enormous tree, not even three men could reach all the way around it. And so our men agreed – even Jantotis' own sons and sons-in-law – that they would cut the tree down late one night, chop it up, and everyone would cart their share of the wood home. They really did set off for the wood late one night, and when they had felled the beech tree, it broke into little pieces, since it was so dry and moldy. Fortunately they had a pushcart, so all night long they carted the pieces of wood that hadn't disintegrated completely. There was at least something for every Romani household. But then in the morning the gendarmes were right there in the yard when we'd barely just put the last little branch in place. "Where have you got the wood from that beech tree?!" Could I have said we didn't have any wood, when they were looking right at it? "Then kindly get yourselves together and take all of it to the train station, right away!"

I pulled myself together and started denying it: "How do you know it's wood from the beech tree? And from which beech tree?"

"It's no good denying it, old Jantotis came to us this morning to say that you'd cut down the beech tree in the nobleman's forest. That's quite a devil you've got there!" It bothered even the gendarmes that Jantotis had informed on his own flesh and blood. But it didn't do any good. We had to take the wood to the train station.

Jantotis not only acted like a devil, he even looked like a devil. One time a Rom didn't like his bad manners and he cut him with a razor. As a result, Jantotis was disfigured for the rest of his life. People used to say he was in league with the devil because of one other thing: the way he was able to build brick ovens. And in general for how he was so handy.

Jantotis couldn't bear to see any of his own children eating. If he ever came home and the children had so much as a smidgen of bread in their mouth, he grabbed the ax, shattered the windows, the doors, demolished the oven, in short, he destroyed the shanty. His wife lamented, tore her hair, and the children ran away and hid in the forest. But the next morning Jantotis woke up, and by evening everything was like new: new windows, new doors, a new brick wall, and a new oven. If people came running up during Jantotis' raging and saw that work of destruction, the shattered windows, splinters on every side, the shanty in pieces – they couldn't believe that anyone could manage all that in five minutes. But then the next day when they saw the brand-new shanty, they ceased to believe that Jantotis was human.

Even the gendarmes and the Guards were afraid of Jantotis. As I've been telling you, during the war Gypsies weren't allowed to go to the pub, but Jantotis went, as if nothing at all had happened, and the gendarmes and the Guards greeted him respectfully. That's the way he lived until he died. He died a terrible death – and I don't feel like talking about that.

Korpáš

When the Germans started losing at Stalingrad, the Hlinka Guards and the gendarmes left us alone for a while. They apparently had other things to worry about. We took advantage of the situation and went to live at my mother's in Šariš, although we really didn't have permission to, because Jozef's residence permit was for Kapušany. We moved because little Milánek had an acute inflammation of the joints with a high fever, and when I went with him to the doctor, the doctor said: "Don't be angry, but I have strict orders not to examine any Gypsies." And so, desperate, I went to see old Cibrikaňa in Šariš, and she treated the boy with compresses of nettle and peat. Jozef came after us and we ended up staying.

We had to stay, if only because fate wanted me to experience what happened to me there. One night we were woken up by car horns. The Hlinka Guards had descended upon the village. They were like a flock of crows. With them were gendarmes with guns and bayonets. They drove us out of our houses. "Get up! March outside, you Gypsy scum!" It was November and there was snow flying in the icy wind. The gendarmes' commander reported to our father that under law number such-and-such the Gypsy element would no longer be tolerated among the regular citizenry and must be moved away from proximity to the towns and public roads to remote places so as not to spread infection and provoke offense. The responsible offices had assigned us to live in Korpáš. Korpáš was a wooded hill about two kilometers from a small town. According to the responsible offices' directive, the move was to take place immediately and without delay. Any Roma who couldn't understand officialese grasped quickly what was going on when the gendarmes and the Guards started throwing people, their children, pots, and bedcovers out of the shanties. "Move it, you black brood, get off to where you belong! Get going!" The children were crying, the women were wailing and tearing their hair. Then the wiser ones who saw there was nothing left to do started to wrap what they could into blankets, their bedcovers, and dishes, and set off in a sad procession for Korpáš, driven there by half the gendarmerie. The other half stayed in the settlement and started to demolish our shanties. Today I can no longer recall how we got to Korpáš at all, because we were simply out of our senses with horror, cold, and suffering. I remember only the wailing of the women, which blended with the howling of the wind, and I also remember the cries of grief, answered by the croaking of the rooks.

We dragged ourselves to Korpáš. It was late at night. Rain mixed with snow was falling. Every family partook of a common fire and somehow we endured that terrible night. In the morning we began to build shanties. From whatever came to hand. One kindhearted peasant lent us a horse and cart, and so we gradually transported what was still useable from our houses laid waste.

Godfather Bango, who had twelve children, lost his head, afraid they would die in the cold, and so as quickly as he could he build a shanty with no foundations. Three days later the water had taken it to pieces from below and he had to build it all over again.

Our father found a small cave with an overgrown raspberry thicket inside. He put boards over the opening, covered them with clay, and on them we built our shanty. He made this hiding place on account of us girls, in case it became necessary to hide us from the Germans. There were four of us, me, Maruša, Haňa, and Vilma. And my sisters were young and beautiful. The Germans were wild about Gypsy girls.

We hadn't even finished building our shanty when Papa got pneumonia. We lay him on the ground on the bedcovers. Bedcovers underneath him, bedcovers on top of him. They were heavy, stuffed duvets that Mama had intended for our trousseaus. Papa lay in the warmth and Mama went into the village to beg something for food. Meanwhile we built the shanty and kept looking down the hill toward the village to see if Mama had come with food. We were afraid Papa would die if he didn't get something to eat.

And can you believe what happened next? A peasant woman we'd worked for in summer on the field gave Mama some beans and potatoes and let her cook up some soup in her house. It was still impossible to do any real cooking in the forest on the hill, there were people milling about among the half-built shanties, children getting tangled underfoot, the fires wouldn't start because the wood was damp, and every so often it began to rain. Mama cooked at the peasant woman's and the woman was so kind that she lent her a pail: "At least you'll all have a little soup so as to get something in your stomach!" And we looked and saw Mama hurrying up the hill to Korpáš with a pail. All so that Papa could have something to eat as soon as possible. But since it was drizzling constantly and raining intermittently, it was slippery everywhere, Mama slipped and fell, the pail flew out of her hand and all the soup spilled out. Mama stayed sitting on the ground and tore at her hair. She cried so awfully that we were afraid she had broken something. We all ran up to her. Fortunately nothing had happened to her, but she was bitter over the spilled soup. And I will never forget this about my husband Jozef: he bent down to my mother, picked her up, and kissed her hands. Then he sent me to the village to cadge a few potatoes somewhere.

In a few days we were all getting by somehow or other – at least we had a roof over our heads. In our other settlement there was only one house that had been saved – and that house is still standing. A Rom as black as an African used to live there, his face pitted from smallpox on top of everything else. His wife died and he was left alone, with four small children. He worked in the mill and there a poor little girl, the cleaning woman, a *gadžo* girl and also widowed with two children, got on his good side. She came to live in the settlement. She was unkind to her stepchildren, so they went off to live with relatives. The pockmarked African died shortly before the Hlinka Guards demolished our settlement. In his little house only the Slovak woman and her two Slovak children were left, so the gendarmes let her keep on living in the town.

Kharasho

In Nižní Šebastová there lived a man named Varga. He was the director of a school and spoke Romani very nicely. He was interested in our history and knew more about us than we did ourselves. He had learned somewhere that we came from India, and when he told us about it we just goggled our eyes. Who had any idea at that time that there was an India? Plenty of Roma didn't know there was a Bratislava or a Prague, let alone in India. Even for the peasants, India was something doubtful, because there was nothing about it in the Bible. According to the peasants' way of thinking, Egypt, which had the Bible's sanction, was where the Moors lived, and that's why people generally believed that we were a "Pharaonic tribe out of Egypt." Really, it was an honor that they considered us descendants of the Pharaohs, but that was only because they didn't know who the Pharaohs were.

This man Varga came to see us once in Korpáš. Papa welcomed him and they shook hands. Varga was amazed that I already had a son, praised him to me, and was sorry for us for what the Hlinka Guards had done to us. They gossiped for a little while longer about everything under the sun while we just waited to find out the real reason Varga had come. It certainly wasn't for me reason at all. Finally he said to my father: "Everything bad leads to some good. Really, you can be glad that they moved you out of the way. You're not around for people to see, and when the Russians start chasing the Germans – and it won't be long – you'll be safe. And the ones who drove you here will get what's coming to them."

Papa kept nodding his head. The same thought had occurred to many of us. Though we were living in unbelievable poverty, we felt safer. We had almost no contact with *gadže*, nor did we see their dogged faces, so we were spared their constant mocking.

104

"I have a Russian I need to hide!" Varga finally came out with the truth. During World War I he was in Russia, got as far as Georgia, lived there with some family and had corresponded with them ever since.

Fate had wished that these people's son came all the way to Slovakia as a partisan. They threw him out of an airplane in our area. Though the Germans caught him, took away his weapons, transmitter, and everything, he managed to escape and find Varga.

"I can't keep him at my place," Varga was saying. There was a German unit in Nižní Šebastová, a military hospital, and it was full of Hlinka Guards. "And you're all the way out here in the forest." And that was how he said that he was really asking us to take his Russian into our household. At that time they called all the people in the Soviet Union Russians, whether they were Georgians, Ukrainians, Kazakhs, or cross-eyed and from Chukots.

Papa said fine, and late at night my husband set out with my sister Maruša for Nižní Šebastová for the Russian Georgian. They brought him through the forest to our place. We fell in love with him at first sight, because he was just as black as we were. And he hugged and kissed my husband most of all, because both of them were named Jozef.

It was decided that he would stay with us. For one thing, our shanty was right on the hill and we could see if anyone was coming from a distance, and for another we had the little cave underneath the floor, an excellent hiding place.

We called the Georgian Kharasho, because he didn't understand anything, just nodded his head at everything and said: "*Kharasho, kharasho.*"

One day late in the afternoon the children came bursting into the shanty:

"Uncle, the Germans are coming!" Papa ran outside. There really were two German soldiers clambering up the hill. Kharasho had to hurry inside the cave. "Sure, but what if they've come for the girls?" said Mama, afraid. "Where will we hide Haňa?" Haňuša, my brother Toňu, Jozef, little Milánek, and I were all living there. By that time Maruša, already married, had her own shanty and eleven-year-old Vilma was living with her. "What about Haňa?" Mama insisted. In the corner there was a divan. "Get on top of the divan!" she ordered Haňa. Then she threw one of her enormous, heavy bedcovers, which we kept stacked on top of the bed, over her. Barely had Haňa been buried underneath the bedcover when the soldiers came in. We recognized by their uniforms that one was an Austrian and the other a German.

"*Partisanen! Partisanen! Wo sind die Partisanen?*" the German blurted out.

"*Partisanen nix!*" Papa shook his head. "Wife, bring the chair, the gentlemen want to have a little fun!" and he started taking his violin down from the wall. We only had one chair, Mama wiped it with her scarf and offered it to the soldiers. The German sat down, since he had a higher rank, and the Austrian sat on the bench next to my husband. It was obvious they'd come looking for girls. We all hoped they had no idea about Kharasho.

Dad knew a few German songs, from as far back as the First World War, and he knew that Germans loved marches. He started playing. He played sweetly, obligingly into their ear and we knew he couldn't do otherwise. The Austrian pulled out a field flask and handed it to Jozef. My husband gladly took a good swig, and I got scared. He restrained himself that time, though, aware of what the situation was, and only drank a little. Meanwhile the soldiers were drinking and getting into a good mood. The German even jumped up and started stamping his foot to the rhythm. Kharasho huddled in the cave underneath him.

The Austrian kept looking around the room and our teeth were set on edge. Had he heard something about Kharasho? Or was he looking for girls? Finally he asked – his tongue was getting a little tangled: *"Tochter wo?"* Meaning where were the daughters keeping themselves?

"That black girl there, that's our daughter," Papa pointed at me. I was sitting on the edge of the divan, breastfeeding Milánek, and Haňa was under the bedcover behind me. *"Noch Tochter! Noch Tochter!"* the Austrian insisted. *"Nix Tochter!"* said Mama, and Papa was just playing those marches of theirs like a wild man. The German got tired, rolled onto the chair, put his head on the table, and fell asleep. The Austrian leaned in toward Jozef and started telling him the story of how he hated the German. He knew a couple of Czech words and said that before the war he was studying in Prague. He was drunk and had the hiccups. Then he started showing Jozef how they could slit the German's throat.

"Listen!" Jozef was saying – and I got scared, because my husband was very sharp-tempered, wild, and also straightforward. "Listen, this friend of yours is sitting here nicely and snoring and I've got no reason to slit his throat. And you, if you studied in Prague, you should know that you don't go visiting this late!"

The Austrian probably didn't understand him, but he recognized by Jozef's tone of voice that something was wrong, and tried to intimidate us by threatening us. "Where have you got her? Where have you hidden her?" – Later Mama found out from our peasant woman that the Austrian had seen Haňa in the village and asked the fellows where he'd find her. I was dying of fear that Haňa would stir under the bedcover. Fortunately the German woke up at this point, looked at his watch, and said: *"Drei Uhr! Drei Uhr!"* meaning it was three o'clock. They got up and left.

Only after we saw their dark figures down the slope at the bottom of the hill did we let Haňuša out from under the bedcover, and Papa moved the board to one side so Kharasho could crawl out of the small cave. He was all blue, chilled to the bone, and frozen, and Haňuša couldn't catch her breath, she'd been suffocating, and she was dripping in sweat. We slowly got a hold of ourselves. "That's enough for today," Papa said.

Kharasho stayed with us for three more months. The school director, Vargas, sent him food and clean shirts. The Russians were advancing. Kharasho wanted to get to them. We tried to stop him, telling him: "Wait until they're closer." He wouldn't let himself be persuaded. One dark night my husband led him across the Torysa and told him which secret paths to take through the forest. When he got home, he had tears in his eyes. He told how they embraced, kissed, and couldn't say goodbye. "Farewell, Jozef!" "Farewell, Jozef!" It really was the last farewell, because after the war we never heard from Kharasho again. If he'd stayed alive, he surely would have let us know about himself.

At least let the children survive

Sometimes when we get together with relatives or with people we know and those of us who survived the war happen to start remembering those times, the young people say: "That must have been horrible! How could you even live in that kind of fear and uncertainty? How did you ever survive?" I don't know, it would be hard for me to describe precisely our feelings and states of mind and body then – but I think we Roma have always taken everything as the judgments of fate, against which people can do nothing. *So kampel te avel, oda ela* – whatever will be, will be. Or: *so o Del dela, oda ela* – whatever God wills, will be. *So tut hin dino, ňiko tutar na lela* – no one can change what has been ordained for you. And in one of the oldest songs, one which all the Roma in the whole world know, they sing: *Marel o Del marel, kas korkoro kamel ...* – the Lord God will punish whomever he wishes ... And that is why, even if we cried and suffered, we knew that things were the way they were supposed to be, this way and no different, and that's why we really are able to be content. On the other hand, even the longest period of time divides into an infinite number of "nows" – and every "now" when nobody was beating us, when our guts weren't twisting up with hunger, when we could touch each other and feel the life-giving warmth of our relatives right there, was a time of happiness for us. As best we could, we tried hard to live in accordance with *pativ* – with honor, a good reputation, and decency, which we were constantly reminded of in *vitejziko paramisa* – in stories of heroes, in songs, in sayings, in the wise words of old Roma. But when we got into a situation where our very lives were at stake, many people, rather than be led by the demands of *pativ* were led by a more manageable precept: *dživ sar pes del* – live as best you can. An example with the well in Korpáš occurs to me. When we were still living near the town, we had two wells in the settlement. Two wells for five hundred, maybe six hundred people wasn't enough, of course, and that's why we were as careful with our water as with the sacrament. A girl who went for water was watched by dozens of eyes to make sure she didn't put a dirty bucket in the well. Every girl had to make a ceremony, literally, of rinsing the bucket in the special tub of water that had been prepared at a sufficient distance from the well, and only then could she draw the water. As I've told you, the pride of a new bride was the elegant way she was able to draw water from a well. And any girl who didn't know how – shame on her!

But they packed us off to Korpáš and there was no well in Korpáš. We got our water from the stream. It was good, clean water, but when it rained there was nothing for us to do but draw it with mud in there too. It came about that typhus broke out in the settlement. Maybe it wasn't even typhus, because only seven people died, and with typhus you would have expected more deaths – and in any case it was some kind of intestinal epidemic, probably from unclean water. Vilma and Haňuša from our family got sick and lost weight down to the bone, but Mama and Cibrikaňa managed to cure them with herbs. When the typhus had passed, the town had a well dug for us, afraid that next time we would infect the peasants as well. Although we had taken anxious care to keep the water clean when we were living in a town, here all of a sudden nothing mattered to us. The path to the well led down the hill and it was usually slippery, and when some female slipped and fell, it didn't even occur to her to look and see if she hadn't gotten the bucket dirty! She just knelt and drew water with the muddy bucket. After a while the water in the well was worse than in the stream when it overflowed its banks.

Why did the people let themselves go? Was it that they stopped believing in life? Or else did they tell themselves: if we're meant to survive, we'll survive, and if we're not, not even clean water will save us? I don't know, myself. And yet again we were guided by the truth that everything bad leads to something good. That experience was confirmed even in the case of typhus. When the German soldiers came after our Haňa, the Roma had something else to be afraid of: that they would start coming around all the time. Typhus broke out at just the right time. That was because the Germans were even more afraid of typhus than they were of the Russians. As soon as they heard the word typhus, they'd rather escape to the front than loll around in Šariš. There was a Ukrainian doctor who lived in our Šariš, having emigrated from Russia after the revolution, and at the end of the war he got more and more nervous, afraid the Russians would shoot him when they came. He wanted to get on the Gypsies' good side, because he hoped he would be able to hide among us, and so he readily stuck on red signs all our shanties with the warning: danger, typhus! He willingly put up new ones, even when the intestinal epidemic had seen its last. From that time on the Germans didn't show their faces in our settlement.

Most of all it was the children who preserved our feeling of life, hope, and happiness. *Nane čhave, nane bacht* – where there are no children there is no joy, as people say. And on the contrary, where there are children, there is joy. Both joy and worries – but the worrying is really a strong wish for the children to survive and to live better than those who brought them into the world. Our small joys and small worries with the children helped us forget the strange world we were living in. If during the war I used to walk back and forth, in spite of all the risks, to stay for a while in Šariš, then for a while in Kapušany, and back to Šariš, and then back to Kapušany, it was really because of the children: because of little Milánek and later because of the twins.

I returned from Šariš to Kapušany with little Milánek just in time. Right before the typhus broke out in our village. As if I'd seen it coming! He definitely wouldn't have survived it. I thanked God for that saving inspiration and told myself: girl, you have one lucky life.

In Kapušany I started to work with my mother-in-law on the field. I was no longer making myself out to be a city lady and everyone knew I was a Gypsy girl like the rest of them. We were glad the peasant women gave us work to do. There was no Gypsy settlement in Kapušany. There were only a couple of Romani families living there among the *gadže*, and since most of them were from a rich clan that dealt in livestock, the Hlinka Guards let them stay in the village for the time being. The peasants gave us work here and there, so we didn't go hungry.

My mother-in-law was very kind and tried to spare me, saying: "Girl, you stay home, you take care of the child, cook, do laundry, chop wood, you already do plenty!" But I was always sorry for her and ultimately we went to the fields together, and I brought Milánek with me, he'd just been born. I was breast-feeding him. I breast-fed him for two years.

Milan was used to seeing horses, on the fields, from the time he was little, and he was crazy about them. He couldn't speak or walk, but when a horse came into the distance he started laughing, pointing with his little hand, and wriggling out of my arms, telling me he wanted to go up to the horse. As soon as he could stand up on his little legs, he went pitter-pattering after every horse that crossed his path. Everyone laughed, but I was horrified that some horse would kick him and kill him. Everyone assured me that a horse wouldn't hurt a child. I think that Milánek's love for horses made us favorites among the peasant farmers.

One time when he was about two years old, a peasant gave him some horse's reins to hold. He was ploughing over a bramble patch. The boy held the reins, stumbling behind the horse through the bramble patch, laughing at the whole world until he was jumping for happiness. When I picked him up in my arms afterwards, I saw that the child's little feet were all pricked and bloody. I cried for how much it must hurt him, and Milánek just laughed happily.

The peasant who lived next door to us was a good man. Sometimes when we was going somewhere, he would seat Milan on top of the cart and take him with him. The boy would always watch for the moment when the peasant hitched up his horses, jump up beside him, and wouldn't let himself be taken away. The peasants went for wood very early in the morning, hitching up the horses as early as two hours after midnight. When the sun had barely come out, Milan woke up while we were still sleeping, put his little chair next to the door, because he still couldn't reach the handle, opened the door, and just as he was, in his little shirt, with a bare bottom, he ran outside and straight to the neighbors' into their yard. But the cart was gone, the horses were gone, and our neighbor had already left. We were woken by Milánek's tearful crying: "Mama, the peasant's gone! Mama, the peasant's gone!" He couldn't be calmed down. I had to promise him that the peasant would take him with himself next time, and I hoped that this three-year-old child would forget about it. But Milánek started watching out for the peasant to come back from the forest, and as soon as he saw him he ran up to meet him and started telling him how he wasn't allowed to go the forest without him any more. Finally I had to explain it to the peasant myself, because we spoke Romani at home and the children didn't know much Slovak. They understood, but they couldn't speak it.

"I leave very early in the morning," said the peasant. "little tots like you are still curled up asleep at that hour!" Milan said nothing, and I thought he had abandoned the idea of his trip to the forest for wood. I went about my work, put the child to bed that evening as usual, and started cooking so dinner would be ready when Jozef returned from work. He sometimes came home from the train station at eleven o'clock, sometimes even later. I waited for him, falling asleep on the chair, but I didn't lie down on the bed, because that was unseemly for a good daughter-in-law. That night my husband came home at twelve o'clock, because I remember that the church clock was striking midnight. I poured him some water so he could wash up, gave him his dinner, he ate, and then he went to lie down. Jozef, Milánek, and I slept in the same bed. Jozef went up to the bed and asked: "Where's the boy?"

"Somewhere under the covers," I said.

Jozef took the covers off, but there was no Milánek. "Good grief!" I shouted, "where is the child?" I woke up my mother-in-law. "My dear, sweet mother-in-law, where is Milánek?" All three of us started looking. We gave the room a thorough search, looked under the beds, in the wardrobe, under the table – there was no other place to look in there, so we searched the hallway, the small yard in front of the shanty, and Milan was nowhere to be found. Jozef was beside himself and shouted at us: "Two women in the house and they can't keep an eye on one child!" For God's sake, if only he hadn't fallen in the stream! Under the house there was a little stream, and we'd beaten out a footpath to it. The stream was shallow, but in spite of that we'd closed off the entrance to it with a few boards.

What if he'd crawled through the cocklebur leaves? We ran to the creek with candles in our hands. He wasn't in the creek, he hadn't drowned. I heaved a sigh of relief, but only for a moment. Where was he?

Then my mother-in-law, who was a wise woman, said: "Listen, my children, the boy is always going off the neighbor's, over and over again, to borrow his horses. What if he's with the horses?" We all went running over to the neighbor's house. I banged on the window. After a while the peasant came out, and he didn't even get angry that we'd woken him up at that hour of the night after he saw us all worn out from weeping. "Mr. Farmer, we beg you, is our little Milan with you?"

"And where would he be?" the peasant asked, surprised.

"Well, in the stable!" said my mother-in-law.

He went with us to the stable and sleeping there between one of the horses' front legs was our Milan. Just in his little shirt, his bottom bare – and the horse was breathing on him.

I caught him up in my arms and kissed him all over. We tried to take him home, but the boy cried that he wouldn't go, because then the peasant would leave in the morning without him. Only when the peasant had promised him with him solemn oath that he would come to get him in the morning did he let himself be carried away. He really did come and get him, otherwise the child might have gotten sick.

When he grew up, Milan transferred his affection for horses to cars. His whole life long he was a driver by calling, until the time when he crippled his leg and had to retire as an invalid.

Máňa and Irenka

In 'forty-four our twins were born. First came Máňa, then Irenka. Máňa was a white little thing, and Irenka completely black. Everyone marveled at this a great deal.

When my mother sent us a bed from Šariš to Kapušany, we took pride in the fact that in my mother-in-law's house, our family had its own bed in the room. But at that time our family consisted only of Jozef and me, with Milánek in my belly. Then came Milánek and now there were the twins as well, filling the bed so full there wasn't an inch of room left. We had to reorganize our system: before, my husband and I slept next to each other, and Milánek at the other end, his feet facing us; now my husband slept next to Milánek, his feet facing me and the twins. Only when the twins were half a year old did we get an inexpensive, used cradle.

At the age of three months, Máňa got pneumonia. I said I wasn't going to let her die and went with her to the poor folks' hospital in Prešov. The edict saying that Gypsies weren't allowed to come to Prešov hadn't been rescinded, but the gendarmes and the Hlinka Guards were more lenient now. Things were going badly for them, the front was drawing closer and it was clear how the war would turn out.

I set off for Prešov. They wouldn't let my husband off of work, so I had to go by myself. I took both the girls, even Irenka who was healthy, because I was breast-feeding them. I dressed them up well – my mother was always sewing and knitting for us, mending and reweaving our old things – I packed them up and went to the train station. Except that during the war Gypsies were forbidden to travel by train. So they wouldn't spread typhus, they said. I knew the ticket seller, since Jozef and Jani loaded coal at the station, and the ticket seller wasn't a bad person, always had time for a few words with us. I stepped up to the window with both children in my arms. He looked at me and he said: "Aren't those pretty little children! And how you've got them all decked out, like princesses! So clean! Hey there, one's white and the other's black, how did you come by that?"

I said the white one was Máňa and the black one Irenka, and that Máňa wasn't white but completely red from fever, because she had pneumonia. And I gave him some money, saying I wanted a ticket to Prešov.

"Well," said the ticket seller. "It's true your children are clean, all dressed up, but what good is that? I can't sell you the ticket, after all, you know Gypsies are forbidden to travel by train. If an inspector come along, they'll lock me up for selling you tickets! And I've got two children too, you understand! If only you weren't so black! But like that everyone can see what you are."

I wasn't angry at him, he couldn't help it. "Well, forget it," I said, "I only came by to show you the twins." And I went to Prešov on foot.

The physician in charge at the poor folks' hospital in Prešov was a man named Hečko. He didn't ask what I was, who I was, didn't look at the fact I was black, let all three of us into the hospital, and treated my little girl Máňa for free. During the war you found out who had what kind of heart: who was chicken-hearted, who had a human heart – and who had none at all.

Máňa was always weak and thin, constantly sick. At the same time, Irenka was full of life and brimming with health. She was a great favorite of my mother's. Just imagine, little black Irenka! – and when I was born, she'd cried over how black I was. The front was drawing closer, the main road to Prešov led through Kapušany, and Mama said: "We're out here in the forest, the war isn't coming through here, who would go looking for anything in our parts? Put the children up with me, they'll be safe here." I kept saying I didn't want to, that I wanted to have them close by me. "At least put Irena up with me," my mother pleaded. I said all right, Irenka was strong and healthy and Mama wouldn't have any trouble with her. But I would keep Máňa with me, because she always needed something, she cried, she was fussy, wanted to be held – and you could treat her with the warmth from your body, if with nothing else. I took Irenka to Korpáš. But there was nothing to eat, and Irenka was always hungry. I don't know what she put in her mouth – she got an upset stomach and died. She died just before the end of the war.

The fiery rams

It was obvious that the war would be over soon and that the Germans would lose – but whether we would survive the war's end, alive and healthy, that wasn't so obvious. In January 1945 the Americans carpet-bombed Prešov. They wanted to bomb the Fascist headquarters there. Behind the headquarters there was a prison, and in the prison were a lot of political prisoners and Roma. Instead of the headquarters they bombed the prison to pieces. About five hundred people lost their lives. Among them were Romani partisans, like a father and three sons we knew from Hanušovec. Outstanding musicians.

At that time we were at Korpáš. I was crying and saying: "What's going to become of us? We won't live to see the end of the war. If only the children survived!" Old Cibrikaňa comforted me, saying: "There is no darkness that isn't followed by the dawn, little girl."

Today when I remember the carpet bombing, it makes me both laugh and cry, thinking how our children survived it from a distance. They ran outside, and the bomb explosions made them happy and excited. Little Milánek came running up and saying: "Mama, Mama, shiny rams are falling from the sky!" I don't know how he got that idea. "Mama, Mama, make them fall on us too! I want a red ram! I want a sun-ram!" I couldn't bring myself to utter a word. The Lord God ordained that no shiny rams fell on us, but when we went back to Kapušany, Milánek told everyone he met that seven sun-rams had fallen on his grandmother's yard in Šariš. He solemnly believed in his own imagination, and he cried when I tried to explain to him that things were different.

After the carpet bombing, I went back to Kapušany, uninvited, because I was losing my mind and kept telling myself, I want to save the children, I want to save the children, I have to be with them somewhere where it's safer.

Cina

But Cina from Stuľany had won over my mother-in-law and moved in with us. There were eight of us in one room, sleeping on three beds. My mother-in-law had been alone with her children for twenty-two years, and at the age of forty-two, like a crazy, young girl, she fell in love with Cina. I've raised my sons, they can take care of themselves, they don't need me, she told herself, and started to live with Cina. He used to walk from Stuľany through Kapušany to Prešov on foot, selling chickens. He bought up fifteen or twenty chickens from the peasant farmers and went to sell them at the marketplace. It worked well for the peasants by saving them a trip to Prešov. In Kapušany he caught sight of my mother-in-law a couple of times, asked around about her, and the Roma told him that she was an extremely honest and hardworking woman, and so he went to woo her. His wife had committed suicide. First he tried to cut off his own head with a scythe and then he jumped down a well.

Cina was a strange person. Light-skinned, he didn't look like a Rom, which is also why the gendarmes in Prešov didn't pay any attention to him. He was fearless and a rowdy, with a voice like a bull. He was the only one who wasn't afraid of that devil, Jantotis. When Jantotis died, his ghost started showing up on the crossroads where he used to beat travelers with his gnarled stick. People said he looked horribly frightening, even worse than when he was alive. Even the gendarmes and the Hlinka Guards were afraid to go there. Jantotis smoked a fiery pipe, the smoke from which was like a locomotive, and his eyes burned like glowing coals, although you couldn't see the rest of his face, because a *mulo* never shows his face to a living person. In that form he forced the gendarmes and the Hlinka Guards to play cards with him. When he was losing, he grabbed an ax and chased them around the area. Then people would say that the gendarmes and Hlika's Guards restrained themselves and no longer dared bother innocent people so much. Of course, wiser people believed that the gendarmes and the Hlinka Guards were restraining themselves because the Russians were getting closer.

In any event, Cina wasn't afraid of the dead Jantotis. Above all because he had never seen him before. And in fact, he didn't really believe that his ghost was back on earth. Cina was an unusually intelligent person. During World War I they stationed him in Italy, and he learned to speak perfect Italian. In Kapušany there were Italian prisoners who had somehow offended Mussolini. As punishment they were peeling potatoes and washing dishes at the German headquarters. They were completely in love with Cina and always found some opportunity when they could speak Italian with him. He even spoke German perfectly, and one time he used it to save our Haňňuša.

As I said, the Germans were wild about our Romani girls. Especially my sisters, Haňuša and Maruša, who had the unfortunate good luck that the Germans went crazy over them – but, thank God, they always managed to avoid that danger. One time

Haňuša came to stay with us in Kapušany for a couple of days. I was sick, my mother-in-law was in love with Cina, and the work wasn't getting done. Haňuša was chopping wood in the yard when the Germans came round! Obviously to knock on someone's door late at night. What did it matter that the war was coming to an end when it wasn't won yet? *"Aufstehn! Aufstehn!"* Meaning we were supposed to get up. Cina jumped out of bed and started roaring something in German in his bull's voice. At the same time he was wheezing and rattling like the most German of Germans. Suddenly, the pounding on the door stopped. We waited for another long while to see what would happen next, but nothing did. The Germans got frightened and left. They thought one of their commanders had beat them to the Romani girls.

The curly-headed German

Of course, there were good people to be found among the Germans as well. "Well why did they go to war, if they were good?" my little grandson Románek, the one who drowned, once asked me. I said then: "Because they would have shot them if they hadn't obeyed." "They could have shot them in the war, too! It's all the same whether you're shot by a German or by a Russian!" He was nine years old then, when he was talking with me that way. I've thought about that conversation many times since then. That child just asked me the questions people don't want to ask themselves, because the answer would expel them from the cozy dung-ball of their dung-beetle-like existence and into the insecurities and fearfully difficult road to understanding.

Unfortunately, little Románek died before I was able to answer his questions.

The German from the Šimeks' house saw our Maruša and was completely beside himself and how beautiful her hair was. He had just a few strands of hair on his own head himself. *"Schööön, schööön!"* he cried out, and pointed at his own bald pate, meaning he would have liked to have such beautiful, curly hair as Maruša's. Maruša wasn't afraid of him, because he had such kind eyes. She understood that this good-hearted old ugly puss wanted her to make him look better.

One such good German appeared in Šariš. He was an officer who was plenty tall, and they billeted him in his own private quarters in the Šimeks' house. Our Maruša used to go to the Šimeks' to chop wood and serve at table. Though we were forbidden to go into town except for two hours a day, from twelve til two, what did that matter when the peasant farmers needed us? Who was supposed to dig their potatoes? Who was supposed to shovel their manure? Who was supposed to chop their wood? Even Hlinka Guards would call us to come over and help out in the yard or on the field. Probably because they were having meetings and involved in politicking and didn't have time for honest work.

She was so sorry for him, for how ugly he was, that she borrowed Mrs.Šimek's curling-iron, heated it up, and went to curl his hair. The German kept still, smiling, and Maruša went about her curling. She curled and curled until she burned off all his hair and his head was as naked as a baby's behind. Maruša became frightened and ran home in tears. "They're going to shoot! They're going to shoot me!" She spoke too soon. But the German had a message brought to her that there was nothing to do for it, and that there was no denying he wasn't cut out to be a heartthrob. Some men have hair, some don't, what can you do?

There is no darkness not followed by the dawn

The front line came through our parts in January 1945 – and that really meant the end of the war for us. The Russians were already in Kapušany, but the Germans were still in Šariš. Obviously, I was in Šariš, because fate had ordained it that I would always be wherever the excitement was. I had left with the children because after Cina came, we couldn't all squeeze into my mother-in-law's place any more. Jozef stayed behind in Kapušany.

At Christmas time – you could already hear the rumbling of artillery fire in the distance – the peasants sent us word to come and carol them. That we come without fail and not pass over a single dwelling. Our menfolk went into the village and played from house to house, our womenfolk sang the old, time-honored Slovak carols: "Unto us is born the Son of God, and a new life hath come for us all." The children ran from one dwelling to another reciting the traditional Christmas greetings, and the peasant women threw them little five-heller pieces and gave them pies. In fact, we went Christmas caroling throughout the whole war. Not even the gendarmes, the Hlinka Guards, and the anti-Gypsy laws were strong enough to abolish this tradition. The peasants were convinced through and through that they would meet with bad luck if the Gypsies didn't come and carol them at Christmas. They must have sensed that the power they had gotten didn't promise them any eternal happiness, and that caroling from a Gypsy was a more reliable guarantee. Especially those last wartime Christmases when they saw their power drifting away with the current, they literally begged us not to forget to come caroling!

Our Ema was due to give birth in the middle of January. We kept a constant lookout down the hill and into the village for any sign of something going on. "The Germans are taking their heavy artillery to the cemetery!" I called out. They wanted to camouflage them there. There was nothing at all to eat, and we were afraid to go down the hill into town, God knew what could happen to someone at the last minute like this, they might shoot us just out of rage and helplessness! But we had to get some food, at least something more filling for Ema, after all she was due to go into labor any minute! "Eh, girl, you, go get a piece of bread!" our mother said to me. What was there to do? A couple of us came together, Papiňori, Maruša, and three or four other girls, and off we went. Hardly had we reached the edge of town when some Germans came walking in the other direction. Among them was a big, tall one, who shouted at us: "*Mutti, Russen morgen pum, pum!*" – meaning that the Russians would shoot us the next day. We got ourselves together and ran off to Korpáš. Without any food. "The Russians'll be here tomorrow!" I started calling out before we even got there.

"How do you know, you smartypants?" The people didn't want to believe me. All of a sudden a heavy artillery fire began. Balls of fire, yellow, crimson, green, came flying over Korpáš. The explosions blew our doors out. The shooting lasted the whole night long. It was dark – but there was such a glow from the shooting that we were able to gather pine needles.

On the slope there were a deep trenches hollowed out by water. The Roma ran outside and hid inside them. Mama said: "Eh, girl, you take your children and run and hide too. I'll stay with Ema." Ema was wailing, she'd started having birthing pains. I didn't go and hide. It was as if I'd become paralyzed, I was incapable of moving.

Someone had to run and get the midwife. Into the village. Mama made the sign of the cross over Ema's husband and he went running down the hill to bring the midwife. "For God's sake, mister, you want me to go out in this shooting?" said the old woman. A mine had exploded two houses from hers. "You'll have to give birth by yourselves!" The old woman didn't go. Ema's husband came dashing in, out of breath, exhausted. "There's nothing we can do," said Mama, "we'll have to help Ema by ourselves." Cibrikaňa and Pavlina came over – and by morning a beautiful, healthy little girl had been born.

Mama said: "Take the child to the church to be baptized." Roma believe that a witch can change an unbaptized child. A needle, knife, scissors, something made out of iron, or a small comb is put under its pillow. This is supposed to discourage the witch and protect the child until it is brought home from the baptism. Christenings usually take place after six weeks. But in those days we didn't know what would happen in the next second, and in six weeks we could all be dead and the child would die unbaptized. That was something my mother could not allow.

The firing grew weaker, with shots coming only once in a while. The Roma came back from the forest chilled to the bone – it was the nineteenth of January, 1945. I spent the night in the shanty. I got myself ready, along with my sister Haňa, and we went with the little girl off to the church. There wasn't a living soul in the village. We came up to the church – the windows were blown out. I looked around – and on the bridge under which our old settlement used to be, a bunch of Russians! On one side were men and on the other were Russian baryshni in pre-revolutionary dress. More *baryshni* than men. They were wearing old-fashioned high boots and military skirts. I told Haňuša: "Go and have the little girl baptized, I'm going to run to Korpáš and tell everyone the Russians are here!" Haňa didn't want to, but she was younger than I and had to listen to me.

I hurried off as fast as I could. The Roma, as if they suspected something was up, were standing and pacing around in front of the shanties. They were freezing, but their curiosity, uncertainty, and anticipation were stronger than their feeling of being cold. "Everyone!" I called as I was approaching. "The Russians are here!" And the people said: "You smartypants! Maybe they're just Germans in different uniforms!" "You're crazy! How the hell could so many Germans dress up like *baryshni*?"

My father caught me in his arms and kissed me all over. He'd been in Russia for four years, after all, and he got along with Russians very well.

They quickly got dressed and ran down the hill into town. Along the way they met Haňa, who was coming back with her little girl, baptized. The parish priest didn't even insist on the two customary godparents. He would have done anything in the world for us at that moment if only we wouldn't complain to the Russians how he'd been wild about Tiso and the Hlinka Guards during the war.

After a while Papa and Mama came back, completely crazy, saying they'd been embracing with the Russians and the *baryshni*, and Papa said: "The Russians are coming through Korpáš on their way to Svíňa, we have to prepare some kind of feast for them!" But what could we do when all we had at home were *kirňavki*, frozen potatoes gathered in the fields from under the snow? And so the men took out their dulcimer, double bass, and violin, and the girls pulled out pieces of red crepe paper and used them to color their lips and cheeks, and we tied the paper to one of the musicians' bows – and there were the Russians! They took our children into their arms, dirty, naked, runny-nosed, and lice-infested, kissed them, and cried. I don't know who cried more, the men or the *baryshni*. Then there was music, dancing, singing, Papa even played the Russian songs he remembered, and the Russians bawled even more. Then they asked us what our lives were like during the war. Feriček, who the gendarmes had beaten so badly he was left barely alive, took several soldiers to the gendarmes' station. But the gendarmes had disappeared like fog, like smoke, as if they had been swallowed up by the earth. The gendarmes' station was completely empty. Only the truncheons were left. "Those are the truncheons they used to beat us with," said Feriček, pointing. He said the Russians took the truncheons off their hooks and started smashing them against the table. "If the gendarmes had been there, they wouldn't have left alive!" Then they cursed, were sorry for Feriček, and kissed him.

We sang, danced, cried in each other's arms for a while, and then the soldiers and the *baryshni* had to go on, toward Svíňa. In a couple of days came another batch of Russians. There weren't any *baryshni* with them this time. By now the Guards had gotten a hold of themselves, and the worst ones, the most savage ones, began welcoming the Russians. They invited them to their homes, cooked up a storm, and fed them. The soldiers were famished and they were glad they could eat, and that they had a roof over their heads, at least for a while. We couldn't offer them anything but music and songs.

From all of Šariš there was only one member of the Hlinka Guards who was punished. The son of the richest landowner, whose name was Demeter. They sent him to some criminal camp in Russia for a year. When he came back, they wanted to elect him head of the local Communist Party. We had enough sense left to stand up and say how can you do this? But a *gadžo* won't put out a *gadžo*'s eye, as we say – and we were afraid to get involved with them. In the end they didn't elect Demeter Communist Party chief, but they made him secretary of the Czechoslovak Union of Friends of the Soviet Union, because he'd been in the Soviet Union for a year.

When the Russians came, old Cibrikaňa said: "It's the end of the war, we've survived. After every darkness comes the dawn. But after every dawn also comes the darkness. Who knows what's in store for us."

In reply my mother said: "And after that darkness comes the dawn, and then another darkness, and then another dawn, it's all in God's hands, and we have to have hope."

Performing with our Romani theatre

Bachtalo manuš, so angle leste o drom phundralo
Happy the man with an open road before him

The war was over

The war was over and everywhere you could hear: "Freedom! A new life! Equality! Our future is an open road" And we were still living at Korpáš, where the Hlinka Guards had driven us during the war. One room and a closet in the shanty. My father, mother, grandmother, brother Toňu, my sisters Haňuša and Vilma, and Jozef and I with our two children and a third on the way all squeezed inside. It wasn't any better at my mother-in-law's in Kapušany, because Jožka's brother Jani had gotten married and Cina had moved in. During the war we knew things had to be that way, but now after the liberation we thought to ourselves that things could be different, and right away. At least we young ones did. Old Cibrikaňa used to say: *so na del o ďives, del o berš, so na del o berš, dela o Del* – what the day doesn't give, the year will, what the year doesn't give, God will give. But we had forgotten the saying: *šun la da le dades, bo chale buter maro sar tu* – listen to your mother and father, because in their lives they have eaten more bread than you, and we cried out: we can't live the way we used to before! And our mother used to say: *na kereha tu korkoro, na šegetinela tuke aňi o Deloro* – if you don't make some effort on your own, not even God will help you. She didn't just say it into the wind in order to adorn the air with words of wisdom, she said it to us, and had in mind that Jozef should take care of his family and find us a place to live. But where? There were no flats in Prešov, and at that time no one even considered buying a house in the town, as some Roma managed to do later: we didn't have the money, there were no houses for sale, and even if there were, the peasants would have a hard time selling it to a Gypsy. And as for building a shanty at Korpáš and living on like savages, we didn't want to do that either.

Fortunately, at that time "the Czech lands opened up," as the Roma said. Before the war, many Roma from our parts in Slovakia didn't even know that the Czech lands even existed. Not even the peasants had any idea what kind of country it was. In those places where Czech gendarmes had been stationed, like in Šariš where we lived, at least people knew how Czech people spoke and sang, but that was all. After the war there was a labor shortage in the Czech industrial towns, and recruiters looking at least for seasonal workers started showing up in eastern Slovakia as early as 'forty-five. From the *gadže*, only the poor ones went, those who didn't have any land, while Roma were just flocking to the Czech lands, and when they came back to look in on their relatives, they sang the country's praises as if it were the promised land. A tenth of that was the real truth, but ninety percent was a truth that had been dreamed up, which for Roma always represented an inseparable part of reality. Possibly all the Roma around included songs like "The Roma in the Czech lands have nothing to do, they just sit in the pub and drink, drink, drink, and break the glasses" in their repertory. Or: "I've got no money, I'm going to get rich in the Czech lands, lend me the price of a ticket on the express or at least on the slow train." Obviously Roma were going to the Czech lands because they could make a living there and get a place to live, but as they say: *na ča maro the paťiv manušeske kampel* – man does not live by bread alone, he also needs honor, and so our people were also drawn to the Czech lands by enthusiastic reports of how the Czechs didn't call gypsies "gypsies" but "Mr. Horváth" and "Mrs. Kalej" – and they addressed us with the formal pronoun! A Gypsy, and "Mr." and "Mrs."! Something that didn't go together with "Gypsy" in Slovakia stuck to it completely naturally in the Czech lands. The Czech lands really did become the promised land.

Evička was born in the promised land – in Kladno

The largest number of people we knew from Prešov and the surrounding villages went to Kladno. Jozef said he would go too, and if he found a good job and place to live, he would send us ticket money for the express train so I could come after him with the children. In a few days a letter from him arrived saying that although he had work, since he'd gotten a job in the steel works, housing was more difficult. They put him in a hostel for unmarried men, but they didn't take family members there. My mother complained: "It isn't good to leave your husband alone! *Romňi sajekh pal o rom džal* – a wife should always go with her husband. Don't forget you've got two children and a third one on the way!" I was in my eighth month. We were getting reports that Czech girls were crazy about our men, and that the Romani men were having a great time with all the *rakľija* – white girls – going after them. And so one day I packed up Milan and Máňa and left for Kladno to follow my husband. The furthest I'd ever been in my life was Košice, forty kilometers from where we lived.

We reached Prague in the evening, and we had to change trains there. We were beat, dead tired, the children were sleepy, but the thought that I would see Prague got me up on my feet. People told me that the train to Kladno left from Masaryk Station, and that from where we were at Wilson Station it was just a short ways, across the park, and they showed me how to get there. I had to carry Máňa, she had just turned two years old, and she didn't want to toddle it by herself. I pulled Milan with one hand, had my suitcase in the other, and in front of me I had this enormous belly. "Children, we're going to see Prague!" I tried to rouse them, but what meaning did Prague have for them? They would have been happier seeing a bed. And, to be honest, I would have too. We went through the park near the train station and I was telling myself: so this is what Prague looks like!

Jozef came to meet us in Kladno, because I had sent him a telegram saying I was coming. He wasn't especially enthusiastic. "Where am I going to find you a place to sleep? Where are we going to live? They won't let you into the dormitory with me!" A Rom from Prešov took us in. We didn't even know him, but in those days Roma all treated each other like they were relatives. He had a room and a kitchen in an old house, and there were ten of them living there. He told us: "Stay until you get something. Where are you going to go, girl, with a belly like that?" But we thanked him and first thing in the morning we went to the housing office. The foreman gave my husband the day off, he was a very kind person.

At the housing office they told us to wait. We waited in the hallway for about an hour. Then an official came out and told us: "Listen, I might have something, but it's only an emergency shelter. So your child will have someplace to be born. There's a rich woman with a house, and she'll let you live there in the laundry room if you want." Obviously, we wanted to! The official wrote the name and address for us on a piece of paper and we set off to find the woman.

We arrived at a small villa with a garden. At that moment it looked like a palace to us. We rang the bell, the woman came outside and stood there just looking at us. Jozef explained to her who we were, but she just kept looking at the children and at my belly. "So you're expecting a third little one?" she said. "Aren't you lucky!" Then she led us into the laundry room. It was a basement room with a little window near the ceiling and a cement floor. A water tap and some washtubs stacked up by the wall. The lady called in her renters to take the washtubs away, because we were going to be living there now. When the room had been emptied out, I broke down in tears out of sheer happiness. For the first time in the six years I had been living with Jozef, we were going to have our own flat! And with running water on top of everything else. Right inside the flat!

On the other side of the hallway, opposite the laundry room, there was another basement flat and inside it lived an awfully nice Czech woman. As soon as she saw us, she came out and said she would help me. Before I could say boo, she had brought a bucket, a scrub brush, and a piece of soap, and we started scrubbing the floor. Because of my amazement, I didn't talk to her. The neighbor woman had a little boy the same age as Máňa, and while we were cleaning up, those two children went walking round and round the garden holding each other's hand.

It was a couple of days before we had a real talk with the lady from across the hall. I didn't speak Czech and she didn't understand our easterner talk. She asked me: "Do you need some washtubs?" "No, thank you, I brought some washtubs with me from Slovakia!" I said, so she wouldn't think we were just plain old beggars and that we couldn't even afford our own washtubs. But I didn't know what "washtubs" were. And a minute later I said: "But I could use a *bodvana*! So I'd have something to wash the diapers in when the baby's born." "You wash your diapers in a *bodvana* and a washtub isn't good enough for you?" she said, amazed. Finally we got through to one another and understood that the thing Czechs call a washtub, we called a *bodvana* – and we had a good laugh over that.

The laundry room had been scrubbed out, but it was four bare walls. My goodhearted neighbor walked through the streets with me and asked people if someone didn't have some old furniture for sale. Finally one young man sold us a sofa, a bed, a table, and four chairs. All that for only four hundred-notes in the old money.

Hardly had I gotten the furniture in place – it was the fourth of April – when I started having birthing pains. It was a very warm spring and we had the door open, because the little window near the ceiling scarcely drew the air out. The lady across the hall also had her door open. I started moaning and she came running: "What's the matter? What's the matter?" She called an ambulance right away. I was wailing that I couldn't go, where would I put the children, and my husband was at work. "Don't worry, I'll take care of the children," my neighbor reassured me. The ambulance came, I tried to get in, but Máňa started crying to break your heart. She was only used to me and couldn't speak anything but Romani, because we spoke only Romani at home. She cried and started pulling at her hair the way she'd seen our womenfolk do in the settlement. She ran the whole way down the street and people were looking at how the child was carrying on. They had never seen anything like it in their lives. Finally the ambulance took me away, because it was the only thing we could do. We had hardly gotten there when Evička was born. Evička with the miraculous head. She had thick, long, black hair, and the entire hospital staff came running up and they even called the head doctor in to look at this marvel. The head doctor said that such cases were rare. They said that in the morning some other experts would be in to have a look at her, but in the meantime I ran away from the maternity ward. Half a day after giving birth. After all, I couldn't leave the children home by themselves.

The whole street was talking about how in such and such a laundry room a little girl had been born with a head that was a miracle. People came to look at her. Every day ten or twenty people came. They stood in line so they could hold her. The factory sent us a crib, blanket, and sheets.

Across the street from us there was a pub, and the pubkeeper was a young man. He was still single. The pub opened at ten in the morning. Early one morning I heard a knocking on the door, and in walked the pubkeeper. He said: "Good morning, I heard that you have a pretty little girl with long hair. May I look at her?" I showed him Evička. "And could I hold her for a little bit?" he asked. I lent her to him. He walked around the room with her and sang to her softly. He didn't utter a single word to me, just thanked me, said goodbye, and left. The next morning all over again. A knocking, in comes the pubkeeper: "May I hold Evička?" Once again I lent her to him. And once again he walked around the laundry room, singing to her ever so softly, not saying a word to me, said goodbye, and left. He came like that every day. The interesting thing was that he always came when Evička was starting to whimper, as if he could hear her from a distance. He calmed her down and then he left. And in my heart I said to myself: "Good Lord, what is this supposed to mean? He'll spoil that child for me yet! Evička will get used to being held and then what am I going to do when the pubkeeper stops coming? I have to cook, do the laundry, clean, and I don't have time to hold her like he does. And why does he do it anyway? He doesn't say a word, just hello when he comes and goodbye when he leaves. And what about Jozef, when the people tell him about it all?"

One time Jozef came home, and after he'd eaten his fill, I said: "Listen, there's this pubkeeper from across the street who keeps coming over to hold our little girl Evička. He doesn't say a word to me. But if it bothers you, I'll tell him not to come anymore. Or you can tell him yourself."

Jozef just laughed and said: "Don't be afraid, I know all about it. I've watched those two. It's a pretty sight, the way the pubkeeper carries the child around the room and sings to her. Let him come whenever he wants." Besides, Jozef knew how I'd been raised, and that I wouldn't do anything untoward with another man. The young man kept coming for about another month and then he moved away somewhere.

We would have stayed in Kladno. My husband was bringing in big money, he was hardworking, sharp, and made more than the other seasonal workers, whether they were Slovaks or Roma. And, remember, he had an arm that'd been partly disabled after a childhood injury! But when he wanted to, he knew how to manage with it. And when he didn't want to, he knew how to use it as an excuse.

We had a good life in Kladno, except for the lady who lived upstairs from us and didn't have any children. I won't say what her name was, although I remember it to this day. She kept a lookout for those times when I went out to do the shopping or have a chat with other Roma, and then she was right there in our place. She came running in a thin little robe and always sat down in such a way that you could see everything. She wanted to have a child with my husband at any cost. She tried to get him to send me home to Slovakia, because the air was bad in Kladno and our children would get asthma. She kept at him for so long that one day she even said to me: "Anyone can see how tired you are. Go on home, your mother will take care of the children for you and you can have a little rest."

And I was so stupid that I packed up the three children and took off for home. With those three children I had to change trains three times: in Prague, in Kysak, and in Prešov. And I had to walk three kilometers on foot from the train station. Milan was six, Máňa three, and Evička was in her little blanket.

I was home for three months and didn't get a single letter from my husband. He didn't send a crown from his wages. My father went out playing again and made a little money, but Vilma, Haňuša, and Toňu were home as well. Mama drudged away for the peasants as she had her whole life long. For a long time after the war, everything stayed the same where we lived in Slovakia. It didn't bother my parents that I was in their house, people believed then that *famiľija paš famiľijate* – members of a family belong together, but one day my mother said: "Little girl, I won't drive you out, but if you don't want to lose your husband and if you don't want to deprive your children of a father, get yourself together as quick as you can and go after him."

And so once again I packed up the three children – Vilma and Haňuša helped me carry the suitcase to the train station – and I went back to Kladno. We came to the main train station in Prague like last time, it was still called Wilson Station in those days, and I had to get to Masaryk Station to catch the train to Kladno. Evička on one arm, the suitcase in my other, Máňa and Milan holding on to my skirt. But Máňa was three years old and didn't want to walk by herself, she was sleepy and tired from the train ride. She started crying. When Milan saw her, he let himself go off too. They sat down on the sidewalk and bawled. And I was standing over them and bawling as well, because my nerves were all unstrung. Two policemen came up and asked me what was the matter. I said that I had to get to Masaryk Station, the children didn't feel like walking, and I didn't know how I would get us all there. The policemen looked around, nabbed a gentleman and a lady who were together, and asked them to accompany me to Masaryk Station. The lady took Evička in her arms, the gentleman took the suitcase, I grabbed Máňa with one hand and Milan with the other, and we made it to the Masaryk – just as the train was leaving for Kladno. The next one wasn't until the following morning and the waiting room was closed because they were painting. We had to spend the night on the platform. It was cold, but there was nothing else we could do. I had an entire outfit on, so I took it off and wrapped the children in it. I lay them down on a bench and sat beside them in my blouse and slip. I didn't sleep a wink, because I was afraid someone would take Evička from me. I was shivering with cold, crying, and cursing my husband.

In the morning we arrived at the station in Kladno, from there we got on a bus, and from the bus stop it was another kilometer on foot. I was dragging myself, step by step. We got to the flat in the laundry room and he was sleeping. I broke down crying. I cried until I was shaking with sobs. He saw that things were not all right and was ashamed. Later people told me that little lady of his hung around the bars and that he paid for her. He was making himself out to be a real grandee. It flattered him that a lady like her was crazy over him. Over an ordinary Gypsy. But when he saw me like that with the children, he came to his senses and said to himself that this wasn't worth it, and that we would go home to Slovakia.

An idea for a play is born

We returned to Korpáš and it was as if everything we had lived through there was gone, like something from a play. The journey to the Czech lands was the end of the story. Now we were back, but the year in Kladno had broken the continuity, and a kind of border stood between the past and the present. My past became a closed compartment, a theatural play we could perform again and again onstage, always the same and always a little different, depending on the mood of the actor's life in the present.

On the other hand, of course, the past wasn't gone at all in those places where it should have been, and it was constantly seeping through into our "days of happiness," which they wrote about all the time in the newspapers. For example, one time it happened where we were living at Korpáš that the gendarmes came bursting in – that is, the guardians of our "national security" – and with truncheons in hand they began driving our people out of their shanties: "Move it! Move it! You lazy Gypsy scum! You think building the homeland doesn't apply to you?" The womenfolk were shrieking the same way as when the Hlinka Guards and the gendarmes used to "pay us a call" during the war, and the women tore at their hair and ran headlong into the shanties to hide. "They're taking us to the camp! They're taking us to the camp!" They'd really come to get us to join the work brigade. The Germans had ploughed up the airstrip in Šebešová so the Russians couldn't land there, and the people were putting it back together again in work brigades.

After the war they locked up the worst Fascists or absolved them of their functions, but there were still lots of sly folk hanging on in various positions of responsibility who'd just traded one uniform for another. They started calling each other "comrade," but inside they were still the same old Fascists and racists.

Fortunately my husband was home with us. We ran out of the shanty and stood in the cops' way. They came to a halt. They weren't used to a Gypsy standing up to them in defiance or speaking with them rationally. Our people were always just afraid and let themselves be beaten, and they wailed and begged, or cursed and swore foully. They didn't know any other way to defend themselves. My husband wasn't afraid, didn't wail, didn't beg, and didn't curse. He spoke rationally, used words he read in the newspaper, and above all – after what we'd seen in Kladno, that even a Gypsy could be treated with respect and called "Mr. Lacko," he really acted like a "Mr. Lacko." And who do you think started to be afraid all of a sudden? The gendarmes. They apologized, saying they were only joking. Then they explained to us politely what it was all about. And my husband and I said that we ourselves would organize a work brigade to rebuild the airport.

Then all of us in the settlement, young, old, men, women, and children went to the airport in work brigades. We went through the forest to Prešov, and from Prešov to Šebešová. There were lots of people there, loads of them, *gadže* and Roma. We always had less food than the others. We had three or four cubes of sugar and a dry pancake for the whole day. But there were goodhearted *gadže* working with us, and even if we didn't know them they shared their food with us. They didn't pay work brigades then, the people did it for nothing and were glad that they could do something for their country.

We had our biggest disappointment when we tried to join the party. His whole life long my father said: "The Communist Party is for poor people. Only Lenin can help us Gypsies!" In Russia he saw that there were many nationalities, black and white, and that all of them were comrades. He used to tell us all: "Remember, it's only in the Communist Party that you won't find people saying: I'm a gentleman and you're a Gypsy! In the Communist Party you're a comrade just like me!" And he kept after us so persistently that the whole bunch of us decided to join the party. I found out when the party meeting was in the village, and off we went. People dressed in the best clothes they had, with only godfather Bukoro saying: "If it's a party of poor people, we have to dress poor! Otherwise they'll say we're a bunch of moneybags and won't let us in!" So he went in his workmen's overalls and left his best outfit – a threadbare, hand-me-down loden coat from the gamekeeper – at home.

We arrived at the meeting, I knocked on the door, and we went inside. The man behind the speaker's podium – I don't want to say his name – started shouting: "What do you Gypsies want here? Who invited you?" My tears came rolling down, and I said: "Before the war we were 'Gypsies,' during the war we were 'gypsies' – and now, after the war, in our republic, in our Communist Party we're supposed to stay just 'gypsies' all over again?" Our people started to leave. *Rom Romeha, gadžo gadžeha* – Rom with Rom, *gadžo* with *gadžo*. There would never be room for a Rom among the *gadže*! But just then another comrade jumped up – I won't name him either – and ran up to us, saying: "Comrade! Gypsy comrades! That's not how our comrade meant it! Come right in among your comrades! Come in among us!" "Thank you, comrade Slovaks," said my father, and tears of real joy came welling out of his eyes. And that was how we joined the party. After that the peasants didn't want to give us work and they didn't want to give us milk and potatoes, saying: "Go on after the Communists!"

We built up our hopes that the party would help us find better housing and that we would be able to get out of Korpáš and into the village, or into Prešov, just somewhere in among other people. But all we ever heard was: "We don't have anything, there aren't any apartments, there's nothing, you have to wait, our republic has more important things to worry about these days than Gypsies." All the families that gradually moved away from Korpáš found their own path to better housing. The Korpáš settlement disappeared only in 1965. At the end there were only two families there, and they didn't want to leave the forest for the city. They kept goats, and there was a tall, juicy grass that grew at Korpáš. When they came in 'sixty-five to force them to move into the opulence of prefabricated housing, they all cried because they would have to part with their little goats.

At night I couldn't sleep, so I used to spend time sitting by the window and thinking about why everything was the was it was. Everywhere people were talking about "equality, equality!" – and the Gypsies were still in the same place they were before. It occurred to me that it was probably difficult for people to change all at once. Like Šudaňa – she didn't stop begging, even though she had enough money and pork trotters. Begging was in her blood, that's all. Just like the *gadže* had it in their blood that the Gypsy was last in line, and they couldn't imagine things any other way. Equality, yes – but the kind of equality that meant gypsies had the right to become white, to stop speaking their gibberish, to stop having unacceptable numbers of children – and if they didn't make use of this right, let them stay at Korpáš.

I started thinking over the idea that we were going to have to force our way into human society some way other than how the *gadže* saw it. At the same time thoughts of our wartime experiences kept coming back to me, and composing themselves into scenes on a stage. Before the war I used to visit the amateur theatrical group among the village youth, so I knew what theater was. And so one night when the moon was full I decided that I would write a play for the theater. For our Romani theater! And that we would show the *gadže* who we were, what we had been through and what we were going through, the feelings we had, and how we wanted to live.

I bought a notebook with lined paper for writing. In the evening I put the children to sleep, sat down with the kerosene lamp, and started writing. It didn't go well. Whatever I wrote I tore up. I wrote something and tore it up and wrote something and tore it up. Two days later I had to go buy another notebook for writing. And all over again I wrote something and tore it up. I was writing in Slovak. It didn't occur to me that I could write differently. But in my head, my characters' lines came out in Romani. Whoever heard of a Romani woman getting angry in Slovak because her little daughter had grown up and fallen in love not with a fellow with a steady job, but with some swell of a musician? Those beautiful verbal skirmishes of ours, full of peace and good feeling, that I wanted to start my play with couldn't even be translated into Slovak. My husband was starting to get irritated with my efforts, getting angry and saying: "Give it a rest, girl, you can see it's too hard for you, so what are you working yourself up for?"

"But you don't understand, come off it now!" I shot back, flaring with rage, and tried to explain to him all over again what I really wanted this play to show. For a while he said write, write! – then for a while he said don't write! And I decided that I just had to listen to my own instinct. The worst thing was that Jozef was egged on by my mother: "It's a wonder you don't give her a good smack! A waste of money, you know how much kerosene she's burning up! And all those torn-up notebooks! If I were in her shoes I'd be embarrassed to keep going to the store and buying more and more notebooks! Take her pen away from her and give her a crochet hook and a needle, let her crochet and sew and make some money! Going on this way is just a big waste of time – the mother of three children!"

I thought that I would quit, but then the devil got into me and I finished the play in one session. I called Jozef and said: "Please, come sit down for a little while and listen!" I called the play *The Burning Gypsy Camp*. It was the story of how they took our men

124

off to work camps, how they moved us out of the village, how the mayor of the Romani settlement stood up to the gendarmes and how they shot him, and how his beautiful daughter Angela cried out, "dear father, don't die!" – but then together with her kindhearted, *gadžo* engineer, who loved her to death, incited a rebellion by the Roma against the gendarmes and the Hlinka Guards.

Jozef was curious and he really did settle in, and I began to read. I read with fire, getting into every character, and I had quite a time of it to keep from crying. I finished reading and was afraid to look at Jozef. He was quiet. He stayed quiet for a long time, until finally I carefully, slowly lifted up my eyes – and I saw tears as big as beads of glass rolling down his face. He said nothing, and then he asked straight out: "Who are we going to rehearse it with, girl?"

"With our own people, who else?" And right away we started dividing the roles among Maruša, Vilma, my brother-in-law Janči, in short, our relatives. Family members have an obligation to stick together, and so I knew none of them would refuse to take part, even if none of them had any idea what theater was. But we needed a good musican for the main role. We knew about one fellow from Gelnice. We hadn't met him personally, but he was famous throughout the whole area as an excellent lead violinist, so I decided to take a trip and go visit him. When I saw him I was frightened at how black he was. And maybe he was frightened at how black I was. He was very kind to me, and I explained to him what it was all about, and I said that I had a sister, Vilma, white-skinned, who he'd play the main role with. He promised to come visit and have a look. He came, fell in love with Vilma, and immediately accepted the role. Later he and Vilma got married.

There were fourteen characters in the play, and I didn't have enough sisters and brothers-in-law to fill all the roles. We had to look outside our family. But the old Roma were overwhelmingly against the play. They had no idea what it was. They had never been to a theater in their life. They were afraid that we would shame ourselves in front of the *gadže*. The womenfolk went around to the whole settlement shouting: "What kind of a circus are you making us out to be? Do you want to make us a laughing-stock for the *gadže*? Aren't you ashamed, the mother of three children?" And because young people used to be very attentive to what older people said, a lot of the boys and girls kept their distance from us, even though they would have been glad to be part of the play. There was nothing to do, people were bored, and with the theater they would have had some fun, at least. Then the braver ones just up and came, and in the end the casting looked like this: Angela (the daughter of the mayor, Mika) – my youngest, surpassingly beautiful, white-skinned sister Vilma; Anton (the kind-hearted engineer in the work camp, a Slovak, who falls in love with Angela) – Jan from Gelnice, later Vilma's husband; Andrej (another engineer, a Slovak, dead set against Gypsies) – Lacko, my sister Ema's son; a Rom in the work camp – Zoli, my sister Ema's other son; Mika (Angela's father) – Ďula, who wasn't a member of our family; Šeja – Marta from Šariš, who also wasn't a member of our family; Gejza, Šeja's suitor – Beveľis from Šariš, who in the end really did marry Marta; a girl – Magda, my sister Ema's daughter; Evelina – a girl from Šariš; the director of the work camp – my husband Jozef; a gendarme – Gejza from Šariš; a second gendarme – Berti from Šariš; and Lola (an old Romani woman I based on no-nose Lina). No one would play the role of Lola for anything. The girls all wanted only young roles, so they could swish and swirl around in their frilly skirts. Finally a *raklo*, a son from the poor *gadžo* family that lived in the settlement with us, came to see me and said: "Ilon, let me be in your play too!" And so this white, good-looking young man played the role of old, ugly, no-nose Lola. And he played her excellently.

We met for rehearsals in our shanty. We couldn't meet outside because it was too cold, the end of February. None of my actors knew how to read. Except for Jozef and Jana from Gelnice. I had to prompt them line by line. But Roma have good memories, and I didn't plan on them learning their roles so fast. And also, we Roma experience everything with great emotion. Everyone became so identified with their role that they completely forgot "I'm Vilma," or "I'm Janči" – they transformed themselves into Angela, into Anton, into the characters in the play.

Mama sat on the stool by the stove and listened. She wiped her eyes, and she was enjoying it. "You see, girl," she would say, "you didn't burn all that kerosene for nothing."

The word went through the settlement that our play had *čačipen* – meaning truth, righteousness, justice, reality – and all of a sudden all the Roma wanted to see what we were really up to and what a theater was. They squeezed into the shanty until none of us could even move. My mother was usually polite, welcoming each guest gladly, but that time she said sharply: "Forgive me, people, but you've got no business here! You can see this is something serious, and if you come in here jostling and shoving, nothing serious will get done." She just threw them out. And so they began crouching below the windows outside so they could at least overhear something.

March came, the snow melted, and it was beautifully warm that year. We decided to rehearse outside in the forest. We had to sneak out one by one so no one would see us, otherwise loads of curious onlookers would have come after us. We crept along the furrows left behind by the melting snows until we got to the top of the hill, and we finished rehearsing the play in a small hollow covered by bushes. But our people sniffed us out here, too, and in a while there were at least five pairs of eyes looking at us from every bush. Before, no one even wanted to hear about the play, and now all of a sudden they were coming all the way to my house to give me a hard time: "Now just a minute, you wouldn't let my girl be in your play – and my grandmother was your grandfather's mother's own sister! Is this how your show respect for your family?!" Or: "Ilonka, I kiss your dear feet, I lick your sweet heart, let my boy be in your play! You know that he was born with two teeth! Things like that don't happen even in Bratislava, it's a great miracle – and you're ignoring him!" In all this I again had help from my mother, who said: "Look, people, there's no room in this play for any more people, but after Ilonka writes another one, everyone will have a part!"

The spring rains came, and I decided to ask the school director for help. I went to see him and explained what the situation was, and asked him to lend us a classroom. He winced and made excuses; he didn't want to. Finally he said: "If you guarantee me that you won't break anything, damage anything, or steal anything ..." Inside me, my Gypsy blood started to boil, but I got a hold of myself and said: "Sir, comrade, we're neither going to eat, nor sleep, nor make a fire in the classroom, only rehearse." And so finally he let us use the room.

Inside the classroom there was a tall, tiled stove. Once when we'd finished and were ready to go home, the school director crept out from behind the stove. "Thank you, comrade Lacko, you've given me a beautiful experience to remember." He had been moved by our performance, shook each of our hands, and from that day on used the formal pronoun with me. And not only that – he even began to help us. He gave us paper, lent us paint along with a teacher, who painted signs for us: "*The Burning Gypsy Camp* – a play by Elena Lacko, a Gypsy theatrical presentation." With those posters in hand, we walked through the village singing Romani songs. The peasants came walking out of their yards and shook their heads: "The Gypsies are going to put on a play! Will wonders never cease!"

Our first performance

We had our first performance in Šariš in the Hall of Culture. That afternoon Roma started coming in from Prešov, Stuľan, Sabinov, and all the surrounding villages. An hour before the presentation the hall was packed so full you couldn't breathe. Only now did the *gadže* start to arrive. Our people stood up and made room for them. First in the front rows, then in the ones behind it, and so on until all the chairs were occupied by the peasant farmers. The Roma stood underneath the windows, in the aisles, and behind the stage. Only my father and mother stayed seated in the front row. But at the last moment the parish priest arrived. He was fat and wheezy and a fan of Tiso's. Once when Tiso himself came to inspect the work camp at Petič, our parish priest was with him. He used to say you had to be strict with the gypsies. None of us liked him, but the parish priest is the parish priest. And because there wasn't a single empty chair in the whole room, Papa and Mama stood up and vacated their places for him. They both stood up through the whole performance.

In the second act, when they kill the old man, Mika, and his daughter Angela cries out, "Dear father, don't die!" there wasn't a dry eye in the house. Even the peasants who'd joined the Hlinka Guards during the war were wiping their tears away. Only the parish priest was dissatisfied. He had a message sent to me that after the times changed, there would be people who'd settle scores with me.

After the presentation there was great applause. The actors applauded as well, because they didn't know what they were supposed to do. They didn't know they were supposed to bow. Then the audience called me to the stage. I made a short speech. The first speech I'd made in my whole life. I said that we were human beings like anyone else, and that we wanted to live like human beings. Then we sang the "Gypsy wail." The audience applauded so much I can't even tell you. And for the first time in my life I felt that the *gadže* were looking at us like people.

A hundred and six performances

Word of our theater spread throughout the Prešov area. The newspapers wrote of us: "The first Gypsy theater!" Suddenly a letter arrived at the Cultural Center all the way from Prague, from the Ministry of Culture, asking me to come to Prague. At that time the deputy minister of social affairs was a man named Grünwald from Hanušovce – could it have been his hand behind this? True or not, Jozef and I set off for Prague. He wouldn't have let me go by myself. In Prague they offered to send us to political school for two years. But how could I leave my children? We refused, but we told them how we were living at Korpáš – four years after the war! – and that there was no hope of getting a flat. "That'll be taken care of, that'll be taken care of!" the Ministry of Culture crowed triumphantly, "we'll put you up in Karlovy Vary, we need to make an impression on your kinsmen!" We agreed to go to Karlovy Vary, because my sister Haňuša was in Cheb. And so our entire theater company packed up and we left for Karlovy Vary. The Ministry of Culture gave us fifty thousand crowns in the old money in exchange for our doing cultural work among citizens of Gypsy origin. At first glance it looks like a lot, but in reality most of the money went for costumes; we had to make our own money to live on. We lived on the money we took in selling tickets.

In the end we set up our center of operations in Cheb, because there was no one to look after my children in Karlovy Vary, while in Cheb I would leave them with my sister Haňuša. We slept in the House of Culture. Most nights we were off somewhere traveling. The cultural section of the national committee booked our shows for us, and paid for our train fares and nights' lodging in hotels. But many times it happened to us that we came to the hotel, they took one frightened look at us, and said they knew nothing about a reservation and that they were full up. They got scared when they saw Gypsies! And so then we slept in the waiting room at the train station. We spent the night that way a good many times.

Once we were performing on a state farm in Bor near Tachov. The workers there were all Roma. None of them had ever been to the theater in their lives. They thronged into the cultural center and all of them were very curious what was going to come next. The scene came in which the gendarmes kill the old man Mika. Someone in the audience let out a war cry and there were men jumping up on the stage and they pulled Mika out the policemen's arms, and some other men threw themselves tooth and nail at the wretched gendarmes. We dropped the curtain immediately, our boys shucked off their gendarmes' uniforms, and I started explaining that this wasn't reality but only playacting. Then the actors came out without their gendarmes' uniforms, with black eyes, bruised from head to toe. The audience was terribly apologetic, someone ran to buy bread, salami, candy, drinks, they made us eat up as a way of making amends, and only afterwards did we finish the play.

About a month later my husband and I went to Bor on a visit. The workers from the farm, Roma, came to see us and started to thank us. I asked: "For what?" One of the older people said: "For your play, girl! Ever since you showed us that *čačipen* – that justice and truth – the farm director hasn't dared be as rough on us as he used to be." They told us that before, he always went among the Romani workers with a stick, and if he didn't like something, he'd give someone a beating. We were performing in western Bohemia in 1949. Four years after the war. Roma still didn't know their rights. They thought a Gypsy was put on earth so he could be beaten, and a *gadžo* so he could beat him.

Once in Cheb we went into a museum, and what did we see but old guns! That would have been something for our gendarmes! "Ilonka, ask them to let us borrow them!" – and the gendarmes went after me about it for so long that I went to see the director, and I went after the museum director about it so long that he lent us the guns. In the morning we went through the town to the train station, the boys marching like swells with the guns on their shoulders. Little godfather Eštočak had chosen the biggest gun, dragging it along behind himself, but it made him feel good that he had such a large weapon. But some vigilant citizen called the district committee of the Communist Party to report that there was a band of armed, black bandits trolling across the square. And on top of everything else, little godfather Eštočak wanted to have a little fun with the comrade in the baggage check, so he aimed the gun at her. The poor woman didn't see the fun in all this, put her hands up, and shouted: "Dear Virgin Mary!" "I not shoot you, I only shoot at you!" Eštočak explained, in his peculiar Czech, and let her jiggle the trigger. The comrade expressed her happiness, saying: "Next time don't do that, or I'll have a heart attack!" and then she checked the guns willingly. We invited her to our show and parted in the best of moods.

We were walking out of the train station, and there was the party secretary running at us from the other direction: "Comrade, comrade, what have you all done? There's panic in the town that Cheb has been attacked by black bandits! The first thing I thought of was that you had your hands in it!" Fortunately the secretary was a reasonable person – his name was Hladík – and instead of taking disciplinary measures against us he let us stage a performance immediately; the people calmed down and saw that we weren't bandits.

Once they asked us to perform in the psychiatric hospital in Kynžvart. The patients sat there and watched us. It was so quiet throughout the performance that you could have heard a hair fall on the ground. The patients didn't applaud even once. That left our actors utterly confused. We were used to enormous ovations. It had never happened to us anywhere that we received no applause and that there was no sobbing to be heard from onstage. Every time Mika died, not only the women but also the men in the audience cried. And here, nothing! The actors lost confidence. I should have told them ahead of time who we were performing for – but I was afraid they'd be frightened of the loonies. Only after the performance I told them: "Do you have any idea who the audience was?" And our actors were utterly amazed that the loonies looked just like normal people, except for the fact that they were so quiet and didn't applaud at all.

They called me to the Ministry of Culture in Prague one more time. Mr. Toman, the writer, came and spoke with me personally, held out his hand to me, and said: "You deserve great credit for the work you're doing." To this day, scenes like that play out in my mind as if they happened yesterday. Again and again I have relished how great men have treated me with respect, offered me their hand, called me "comrade," and spoken well of my work. And when the word "Gypsy" was used, it had a completely different sound to it than when we heard it from the mouths of the peasants where we used to live. At the ministry they offered me work in Karlovy Vary in the cultural field. I couldn't accept it, because the people in the troupe wanted to go back to Slovakia. We all had relatives back there, and *fameľija pal e fameľija džal* – families stick together. They didn't write us, but in our hearts we could sense how they were calling after us: "Where have you been for so long? Come back!" We also missed them. And so we went back to Slovakia.

We kept on giving performances in Slovakia: there were about ten of them in Šariš, and also in Prešov, Vranov, Sabinov, Košice, and Humenný – we traveled round the whole area, and the house was always packed.

We also had some unpleasant things happen to us along the way – but today when I think back on our performances, I only remember our happiness that again and again, with every show, we experienced our human dignity, and how the audience's response made us feel, perhaps for the first time in our lives, a real sense of equality and of human solidarity, without regard for what color anyone's skin was and what nationality someone was.

We arrived in Humenný for a show just when they were having their annual meeting

VĎAČNÉ OBECENSTVO ODMEŇ. POTL. KOLE
KTIVA E. LACKOVÚ AUT HRY „CIG. TABOR."

At the première of "The Burning Gypsy Camp", Prešov, 1950. The author,
Ilona Lacková, is on the right, holding a plant. The play was revived in 1955.

of partisans. We didn't know about it. They came to watch, and after the show they organized a march through town and we had to go along with them. They sang a couple of marching songs, and then they wanted us to sing some Romani marching songs, but there simply weren't any such songs in our language because the Roma had never marched in their lives. In the evening they came to the hotel to surprise us, and they brought so many bouquets that I had never seen so many in one place in my entire life, except maybe in a flower shop or in a large garden park. They kissed us and said we brought back to their mind those beautiful times when people had a clear goal before them, and knew what they were living for.

One time we got a message that the theater commission from the town of Žatva wanted to see our show, and that they would come to Šariš to watch us. I resolved that we wouldn't put up any posters this time, and that we would tell only the Roma about it. We had given seven performances in Šariš, and every time the same thing happened as on opening night: our people came an hour or two before the start of the show and filled all the chairs, but as soon as the peasants started coming in, they would vacate their seats one after the other, and in the end everyone was left standing. I wanted the Roma to be able to sit down at least once. But – I don't know how word got out – the peasants came to the theater once again. And as usual, our people vacated their seats for them, stayed standing in the aisles, and pressed themselves up against the walls. "Well there you go, Ilonka," sighed old Brugaňa, "and I thought that I would finally know what it is to sit down in the theater like a lady!" "And who told you to give your seat to a peasant woman, auntie?" I asked, angry. "You've got quite a job ahead of you, girl, that's the way it's been since the beginning of time: a gentleman is a gentleman and a Gypsy is a Gypsy." The editor of the newspaper *Práce* praised us in an article for how hospitable we were for offering our seats to the white theatergoers who had come to see the Gypsy show.

Once we were performing in the boarding school of the National Security Corps in Poprad. We won huge applause as usual, after the show they summoned me to the stage, the school director came up to me and gave a speech: "Comrade Lacko, in the name of the future policemen of the National Security Corps, I pledge to you that our comrades will treat your comrades like all other people, will not allow any groundless racial discrimination against you, and will not lay a hand on you if they do not have to." Then he kissed my hand, although he was a comrade, and handed me a bouquet of twenty-five carnations.

When we played in Kežmarok, the lady director of a school came up onstage and said in front of the whole audience: "Comrade Lacko, as a pedagogue I assure you that I will teach your Gypsy youth to follow in your footsteps."

Sometimes the theater was a real headache. Just before our departure for a show, a girl came to me once and said: "Ilon, I'm not going. I don't have a skirt." I looked at her, and she was wearing an apron. I moved the apron aside and saw that her skirt was torn. Before I could have sewn it up, we would have missed the train. She had one of the main roles, so how could we have done it without her? I opened up my wardrobe and gave her my skirt. She never returned it to me and I didn't even want it back from her, because I knew she needed it for her mother.

Once we had a performance in Giraltovice. There was an enormous settlement in Giraltovice, at least a thousand Roma – and the tickets were sold out, down to the last one. And all of a sudden Laci disappears. To this day I don't know where he went off to and why he went off – he just disappeared. And Laci was supposed to play one of the Hlinka Guards. Now what? There was nothing else to do but for me to put the uniform on and step in for him. It was no big deal, I knew the whole play by heart, and I'd prompted the actors with all their lines countless times in order to teach them their parts, and also given them cues – but would I have the voice for one of the Hlinka Guards? After all, I was a woman!

Before the performance we set up the scenery – we did it all by ourselves, and I can't tell you how many times my husband hurried to finish painting a shanty or some barbed wire on a piece of wrapping paper. I ran around onstage in men's clothing and spoke in a deep voice so I could get into my role. All of a sudden the head of the cultural committee came up to me and said: "Get me Mrs. Lacko, boy, I want to introduce her to the audience!" I said: "And who do you think you're speaking to?" "Yeah yeah yeah, don't be fresh, young man, get going and bring me Mrs. Lacko!" I took off my cap and explained to him that I was Mrs. Lacko. He was amazed – and I was glad that he didn't even know I was a woman.

Things were worse when they called up the boy who played the mayor, Mika, for military service. We had a number of tours planned – now what? Mika's part was a large one, and who could learn it quickly? We were done for. Then my husband got an idea: "You know what, girl? Come on, let's head for the barracks and go see the commander. Maybe he'll excuse our Mika from his military service." It was another piece of luck that Mika was doing his service in Prešov.

My husband and I set off for the barracks and asked them to call the chief for us, telling him that we had come on a cultural matter. After a while a middle-aged man came up, looked us over, and exclaimed: *So kamen, Romale?* (What do you want, Roma?) He spoke Romani perfectly. We just stood there utterly floored. "Where did you learn our language like that?" I asked. "You speak Slovak, so why shouldn't I speak Gypsy?" he laughed. Then he explained to us that as a child he played with Gypsy children, because he was poor and the Slovak children didn't want to have anything to do with him. He wanted to know who we were. We introduced ourselves.

"Ahaaa, so you're the Mrs. Lacko that puts on plays!" He said he'd heard a lot about our theater and read about it in the newspapers. It was true that there were a lot of articles that had come out about us. I was in the habit of saving them, but then there was always some director who wanted to make a film about Gypsies or a university student who wanted to write a thesis about gypsies, so I lent them what I had and never saw it again in my life. I usually didn't see either the film or the thesis later, either.

"I've wanted to meet you for a long time!" said the commander. "There's a favor I need to ask!" But then he asked us to say first what we had on our hearts. I told him that it was about Mika. Without Mika we couldn't perform, and we had a lot of tours coming up. I begged him to excuse Mika from his military service.

"My dear little lady, that's a serious matter, excusing a soldier from his military service!" he said. And then he added: "There may be some way to make it work. We'll let him out every time you have a performance, and after the performance he'll come back to the barracks... But one good turn deserves another. You'll have to do something for us as well: drive the Gypsy mothers away from the gate to the barracks grounds!" I gave a start. He laughed and explained to me what it was all about. The Romani mothers were flocking to the barracks with their milk-cans, large pots, and serving bowls, crying at the gate that they had brought their son some *haluški*, that he was a poor, thin little boy, and that he was hungry, and that they wanted to see him and prove to themselves with their own eyes that he hadn't been shot. I explained to him that it was only five years after the end of the war, and that the womenfolk still hadn't gotten over it yet. Easily every one of them had had someone in their family locked up in a work camp, and that these mothers had to bring food to their husbands or sons there, otherwise they really would have starved to death. My husband told him what people ate in the work camps. Though he'd only been there a month, that month was enough for him to come back bone-thin, lice-infested, and broken down. "These women are all illiterate," I said, "and most of them don't believe that the war is absolutely over and done with. They keep on thinking it's in hiding somewhere and that it can come back at any time. They get frightened that the war has come back every time they see a uniform."

The commander listened to us as if we were telling him about some newly discovered tribe from the African primeval forest, saying only: "Yes, yes. Yes, yes. I didn't know that. I didn't know that." But then he started saying: "Yes, yes, yes, but these scenes in front of the entrance must stop! You know how to speak well, explain to those worried mothers that we really aren't living in a Slovak state anymore, and that we won't shoot their poor little sons, and that we feed them and sometimes teach them to read and write."

Then he actually called a meeting, and all the soldiers and officers came. I gave a speech. Then a discussion began. The first one to speak was a boy so black that next to him, the blackest night was as white as day, and he said: "Dear Mrs. Lacko, the Slovak boys keep calling me Blondie! Please tell them, Mrs. Lacko, not to make fun of me! Otherwise I'll run away from this military service!" Then another *čhavo* – Romani boy – spoke out, saying they always made the Gypsies clean out the latrines. One after another they got up, and every one had a lot on his heart. Finally we reached agreement with the commander who knew Romani that our theatrical troupe would perform in the barracks. After the show a cultural worker came to me and said: "We promise you that we will try to make our soldiers not treat your soldiers like inferiors and not mock them – because, after all, we've got equality here! And after all, we're not going to nurture bourgeois-capitalist-imperialist incidents in our army like they do with the blacks in America! That'd be no good! Don't be afraid, discrimination won't rear its ugly head here, because you're people too, and as soon as you assimilate, no one will notice the color of your skin ever again! We're comrades, after all!" He pressed our hand with sincerity, and it made an enormous impression on me. But when we'd left the barracks, my husband said: "Did you see that? 'Our soldiers,' 'your soldiers'! And that's the way it's always going to be. As soon as we assimilate, they'll be gracious to us." At the time I argued with my husband, saying that we had to assimilate, that after all, our people couldn't stay illiterate forever and live in settlements, and we kept on arguing without really even knowing what we were arguing about.

The biggest success we had from the show in the barracks was that they let Mika out for our performances, even for two- and three-day trips. The other soldiers respected the fact that he was an actor.

Mika got married while he was in the army. When he came back from the service, he went to work in a brick factory. He worked in the same place for years, winning a couple of prizes for being a model worker and a bunch of honorary awards. He has eight children – and countless grandchildren. He raised his children right. None of his sons or daughters ever did time in the clink.

We took our theater to Košice. In Košice there were *rajkane* Roma – high-class Roma. For the most part they made their living as coffeehouse musicians. Gold rings on every finger and their women draped in gold. They walked around ordinary, village Roma as if they were shit by the side of the road. They shunned us more than the *gadže* did. Probably so people wouldn't ever associate them with the ragged Gypsy rabble. But it didn't do them any good. For the *gadže* they were just "Gypsies," even if they were wearing sixty kilos of gold. I thought they wouldn't come to see the show. But they did! There was even a celebrated lead violinist who was all the way from Budapest. After the performance he kissed my hand and said: "Dee-oh I-lohhh-nohh!" because those Roma have a funny way of talking; they draw out their words and instead of *a* they say *o*.

One afternoon we were performing for some university students in Prešov. They asked me to tell them how I wrote the play before the show started. I was standing on the stage, telling the story, and all of a sudden in the aisle running down the middle of the theater I saw two dirty, dishevelled little girls. They were holding each other by the hand and toddling toward the stage. It was Máňa and Evička! My own children! Grimy, ragged, runny-nosed – and I was going to tell the students how in the framework of today's people's democracy, even we Gypsies were working our way up and living better and more happily. I froze and couldn't say another word. Then I got a hold of myself a little, finished my speech, ran down from the stage, grabbed the children, took them to the dressing room, washed them, combed them, and cried. I can't tell you how many times I've cried over how the children had to suffer because of my work.

One time we were supposed to play in Vyšné Hágy for the patients in a sanatorium. I traveled on ahead to take care of the arrangements and check on things. I was sitting in the little electric train and in the compartment with me there were some athletes from the Czech lands. Both girls and boys. They were all wearing the same sports shirts. I was thinking about where we were going to play, how much they would want from us for the hall rental, where we were going to sleep – and wasn't paying attention to anything. All of a sudden one of the girls cried out: "Heyyy, look who we have here!"

I roused myself from my thoughts and looked around to see who they had there. The girl hugged me and I didn't know what was going on. Then they put a newspaper in my lap, and inside were my photograph, an article about our theater company, and some story about me. I don't even know who put it in the newspaper. I had no idea that an article like that had come out, no one had told me a thing. I looked over the photo – it was really me! Then the young athletes wanted me to tell them about myself. And so for the rest of the journey that was left to us before we got to Vyšné Hágy, I told them about our theater, about my life, and about Roma. They got off at the same station I did, wanting me to go with them to the hotel and keep telling them stories. But I didn't go. On one hand I was an assertive woman, but on the other hand I was always bashful. I know many Roma who are educated, who "made it" – as people say and write – and yet they never lose the anxiety they have in front of *gadže*. They're afraid that they're behaving somehow inappropriately, that they won't understand what the *gadže* are talking about, that they'll say something stupid, that they'll make a laughing stock of themselves, and that the *gadže* will laugh about them behind their backs. Even though the young athletes were friendly toward me and they hugged me, I said good-bye to them at the train station and went my own way. They cheered me on, the boys tossed their caps in the air, we kissed each other, and the people around us just stared, wondering what was going on.

134

Everything has its end and life goes on

We traveled with the theater for almost two years, first throughout eastern Slovakia, then in western Bohemia, and again back in eastern Slovakia. The actors loved performing. For at least the two hours of the performance they experienced the feeling of real equality and community with people of good will; obviously, the applause and the ovations also made us feel good. On the other hand, we were starting to get tired. Besides, the actors were gradually getting married and they wanted to start families.

There were two married couples who got together in our theater company. Both of them are still living together today. The first one was my sister Vilma and Jan the violinist from Gelnice. Vilma played Angela. I wrote the part of Angela partly with Vilma and partly with myself in mind. Like Vilma, she was beautiful, and like me she gathered no moss. The Slovak engineer Anton falls in love with Angela. He is idealistic, just, and humane. I was inspired to write his part by the character of Kalina from *The Lady of Čachtice*, the storybook hero of my childhood and youth. Anton has meetings with Angela in the woods and secretly brings her bread for the prisoners. Jan from Gelnice, who played Anton, really did start having meetings with Vilma, that is, with Angela, until finally there was a wedding. They've lived together for more than thirty years and have three children. Their daughter Marlena graduated from the conservatory and plays the organ in the Prešov cathedral, one son is also a musician, and the other graduated from seminary to become a priest. Vilma's husband has been performing for thirty years with the People's Art Ensemble in Prešov.

The other couple our theater group brought together was Marta and Bevelis from Šariš. Marta played Šeja and Bevelis, Gejza. Šeja comes from a family of musicians and her parents want her to marry a musician. It used to be that there was no work in Slovakia. If there was some construction going on, fifty or sixty Roma from the whole area would be outside waiting, starting at daybreak, until the foreman came, and one after another they would beg him insistently for a job. Only one or two got the work, because they didn't need more laborers. Marrying a day laborer meant marrying into a hungry family, as people said. In my play, Margita, Šeja's mother, sees her daughter enjoying herself with the day laborer Gejza. She runs outside and starts separating the two with a broom, cursing, and screaming that she didn't raise her daughter for the benefit of some stinking day laborer, and that her girl would only marry into an honorable family of musicians! Gejza stands up to her and announces: "The wedding will take place this very day!" And that's what happened. The young people got married. They got married in life just as they did onstage. Marta's mother cursed me at first for putting her daughter together with a day laborer, and that Bevelis couldn't play anything, and that he had to make his living as a worker, but then she calmed down because she saw how her daughter and Bevelis had a good life together. Bevelis and Marta bought themselves a little house in Šariš and set themselves up nicely. They have only one son, while that one has seven children. They all live in peace and good spirits.

We had given a hundred and six performances when the ensemble fell apart on us. We had traveled together more than two years. But none of us had an orderly life, and we wanted our families to be a little successful. As they say, *odoj manuš džal, kaj leske feder* – a person follows his bliss, and so everyone dispersed throughout the country in search of better wages and a better living.

In 1954, the Dilia publishing house put out my play. I rehearsed it again, this time with city Roma from Prešov. My husband Jozef didn't perform in it. He had a job as a hygienist, didn't feel like performing, and I didn't force it on him. Functionaries from cultural committees as far away as Bratislava came to the opening night. We got applause, and after the performance they organized a reception for us at the Dukla Hotel. Among the guests there were even actors from the Jonáš Záborský Theater. The functionaries were chummy with me, so much that I couldn't even look around to see where I was. My husband found himself on the other end of the table. I wanted to go to him, but the functionaries wouldn't let me. "You see him all the time at home! And now we need to you tell us how all about how you wrote the play ..." and talk like that. It was a big celebration, there were bouquets and pomp – we got home long after midnight.

We got home and Jozef said: "So you were ashamed to sit next to me!"

"Are you crazy? How did you ever get that idea? The gentlemen chummed up to me, I don't even know how, and they were asking me questions ..." I hadn't even finished speaking when the first slap hit me in the face. And a second, and a third. He beat me so that I more dead than alive. "So you're going to sit out the evening with the big comrades! Here's your gentlemen for you! Here's your comrades!" The bouquets I had gotten onstage went rolling on the ground.

That's the inner nature of Romani husbands.

Membership card for Ilona Lacková's theatre troupe, bearing her signature as troupe director.

In 1972 the director of the school in Drienov rehearsed my play with amateur Slovak actors. They got into the regional competition in Revúc and won an honorary award there. Suddenly, a car stopped in front of our house – I was cooking at the time – they rang the bell like there was a fire and the functionaries told me that I absolutely must go off to Revúc. That they had come in their car for me and that the public, the jury, the award, and who knows what else were waiting for me. Jozef was home, sitting sullenly at the table, and silent. I said I wasn't going anywhere, but the gentlemen said I just had to and that it wouldn't be comradely of me not to. I asked Jozef to go with me. He said no! Absolutely not! He said I should do what I wanted to do. I wanted to go, of course, but on the other hand I was afraid that it would turn out like the final show in Prešov. Finally I went, but I left on the clothes I was wearing while cooking so he wouldn't say I was going there to flirt. I got into the car wearing the same thing I had on by the stove.

At the conclusion of the theater competition they once again performed all the plays that had won some kind of prize. There was great applause after my play, and the audience called for the author. I said I wouldn't go if my life depended on it! How could I go out in front of the curtain in the clothes I cook in at home? They put me on the stage by force and even took pictures of me! It was an awful photo! I cried when I saw it. I tore it up and begged them not to show it anywhere, I was so ashamed.

Then there was a joint celebration, the jury was drinking, the actors were drinking, they poured wine into a huge vase and the vase made its way around the table, everyone drank, and I just sat there rooted to the spot, imagining what would happen once I got home. Toward morning they brought me home in the car. Jozef was sitting sullenly at the table, in the same place as when I left. He didn't say a word to me.

"It's a shame you didn't go," I said. "It was a big party ... But I just sat there in my kitchen clothes. A shameful sight. I was afraid to stand, afraid to move, so people wouldn't see how I looked. They took a picture of me, developed the photo right away, and I had to tear it up so no one could see how I looked. And all that so you wouldn't think I went to have a good time ..."

He looked at me completely startled and stayed that way. Then, with his eyes cast down, he said: "Well, don't be upset anymore. I don't know what I ought to do with this damned temper of mine." And he didn't beat me.

Even though my play has won prizes at various amateur competitions, I have never been so happy as when we were performing it with our original ensemble. The time we spent on tour was maybe the most beautiful time of my life. My mother was proud of me. It made her feel good when Roma from Sabinov, Vranov, or surrounding villages met her in town and said: "That's your girl, the one who wrote the play about us all? That's a fine daughter you have there."

Mama helped me a great deal. She watched my children. If it wasn't for her, I don't know how I would have done it all.

If I could start my life all over again, I'd like to live the life I've lived. When I think back to how proud and happy the Roma were when they left after a show of ours, I feel like my life has had meaning.

At the regional committee in Prešov, and working for the Roma in the settlements

Ko džanel avredženen bachtalen te kerel
prindžarel s'oda bachtalo te jel

True happiness belongs to one
who can make others happy

Y ou're an advanced Gypsy, comrade Lacko!

When I was small, I used to wish always that people would come to see me for advice and help the way they came to my mother. "Máňa, lend me a pair of scissors, Máňa, fix my skirt, Máňa, won't you sew our girl some bridesmaid's clothes for a wedding!" Though Mama cursed on the outside, that was only because it was the thing to do. Otherwise she helped where she could and never expected anything for it in return, not even thanks.

When we were performing in our theater and gathering applause, in my heart I told myself many times: maybe we're just a little bit useful to people! Although what I'm doing isn't as beautiful as the clothes Mama sewed for special occasions and spread out on the feather beds piled high, but maybe when someone's heart has been softened by my words it lasts for at least a week. But the ensemble had fallen apart and now what? Mama said: "You have no idea how happy I am! This is a sign from the heavens! It's high time for you to spend a little time with your family. I'm proud that you have such a clever head on your shoulders, but too much of anything is a bad thing. Take a look at how we're living! Use your mind to figure out how to get us a flat!"

As usual, my mother was right. In 'fifty we moved out of the settlement below Korpáš to Prešov. My sister Maruša – she already had five children by then – put her money together with Mama's and they bought something that had two little rooms and a small kitchen and called it a house. I don't know what people would call it today – maybe an emergency shelter – but at that time we were proud that we had a house. Maruša took us in with her, so in three rooms you had: Mama, Papa, that's two, Maruša's family – seven, all together that's nine – and the five of us, that makes fourteen.

One time I was walking along the street and thinking about what I was always thinking about in those days, in fact: where and how to get my own flat, one that I could start working on now, since our theater group had fallen apart, and whether I should start working on anything at all or whether I shouldn't take better care of the children instead! Just like that I was walking along, lost in thought, and not paying any attention to the world around me, and next to my ear I hear: "Comrade Lacko! Comrade Lacko! Where is your mind wondering?" Standing right there was Dr. Nagy from the health care department of the Prešov regional committee. In those days Prešov was still the regional capital. "I was just reading about you in the newspaper!" That was possible, because they really did write about us a lot: in the newspaper *Labor*, in the Slovak version of *Truth*, and in the magazines. Our theater was a sensation. First Gypsy play ever! First Gypsy woman writer ever! Gypsy woman rehearses theater troupe, and so on like that. Journalists came traveling to see us, take pictures, and they brought the news all the way to the government that in Prešov there were two advanced, socially-aware Gypsy citizens – by the name of Mr. and Mrs. Lacko – and that they should be used in political and cultural work. "Wouldn't you like to work for us in the health care department of the party's regional committee? Someone's got to come and work with your people – and who would be more suitable than you?" I was completely taken aback at the tempting offer fate had sent my way! Just at a time when I was thinking about what I should do next. But how could I work in health care when I didn't have the least notion what it was all about? And what about the children? When we were traveling out of town two or three times a week with the theater, Mama looked after the children for me, but to have them round her neck eight or nine hours a day while I was at the office – I couldn't ask that of her. "What if my husband – Mr. Lacko – were to take the job?" I asked. "He's had a bum right arm since he was five years old, he can't do heavy labor, he reads the newspaper every day, he's more socially aware than I am, and he doesn't have the children to worry about, because he's a guy – he meets all the requirements for a successful career in health care!"

"That's an excellent idea!" exulted comrade Nagy. They summoned my husband to the party regional committee right away, interviewed him, and sent him off to Bratislava for a six-month course on health care. He finished with straight A's. He had an excellent head on his shoulders. Then he graduated from a health care vocational school by taking correspondence courses. But that was when he was already working in the health care department of the party's regional committee in Prešov.

Thanks to the fact that Jozef had started working at the party regional committee, we got a flat. It was a relief for my sister Maruša – now there would only be nine people instead of fourteen in the two rooms and the kitchen – and we were proud that we had our own flat, on Železničiarská Street. It was originally a cellar. They put some families that didn't have anywhere to live in the house, which belonged to a reactionary woman in Prešov. They set us up in the basement. She had to clear out the coal, and we moved in. The room had a tiny window near the ceiling. We brought our big bed, all five of us slept on it, plus a table, four chairs, a wardrobe, and of course our stove. If I don't count the transitional housing in Kladno, we had our own apartment for the first time in our lives.

For us Gypsies, the greatest hope of that time was the Communist Party. It was something like an association of Robin Hoods, who took from the rich and gave to the poor. We were often satisfied with mere promises and words about equality. Because up to that time, we gypsies had never gotten anything but promises and words. We were grateful for every kind word. They have a saying: *te na des maro, de choča lačho lav* – if you can't give bread, at least give a kind word. And that time was extravagant with lavish words about equality. I can't even remember any awful news stories from those days like what you see now: "Citizen of Gypsy origin expropriates … Drunken citizen of Gypsy origin attacks …" and the like. In those days they were up against the kulaks, big landowners, black marketeers, petty bourgeois, we belonged to those who "had been exploited and bled dry by the advocates of imperialism through the centuries." But for us those phrases, which my youngest son Luboš makes fun of and wrinkles his nose at, were the bitter truth and reality of what we had lived through. What's more, the Slovak language had never been familiar enough to us to hear how false these words sounded. So, just like many Roma, I was a member of the Communist Party of Czechoslovakia and I firmly believed that only "our party" would ensure a better life for our children. And because I'm an action-oriented person and can't keep from speaking out, I often entered into public discussions at the party meetings. That's how it happened that they elected me to the district committee. The comrades in the district committee started working on me. "We have to convince Lacko to work in the cultural sphere," they'd say. And they really did set out to convince me! They said that working in the cultural sphere was my obligation to our entire people's democratic establishment, and that if I wanted to build a better life for my children, I should work in cultural affairs. I wasn't opposed to the idea, just the opposite. In my heart I told myself that this was how I could fulfill my childhood longing to do something for people. But I had no idea what it really meant to work in the cultural sphere, and on the other hand I had three children at home. But what was more important: building a better future for my children or doing their laundry every day, making sure they didn't have a single hole in their clothes, seeing to it that they had a warm meal at least twice a day, and keeping them entertained so they didn't go wandering in the streets …? Milan was nine years old and in the third grade. Máňa was just starting first grade, and Evička was two years old. Mama told me that above all else I was a mother – my comrades told me that above all else I had to build a new society. Jozef was off in Bratislava for the six-month course on health care and didn't know about any of this. Finally I said: "Fine. If you want me to, I'll work in the cultural sphere."

"We knew that you were a socially-conscious comrade!" my fellow party members praised me. "You'll go to Lipovec in a week, because you must be trained and ideologically armed." I stood there dumbstruck. Where was Lipovec? What was there? What were they going to do with me there? I got my explanation right away. In Lipovec in one week there was going to be a four-month training program for cultural workers, and the comrades had selected me for this training because they knew ahead of time that I would agree with their proposal. They also told me that this was a great honor for me, because they only accepted politically reliable people there, people who were sharp and intelligent, who within four months would be able to master material such as no college graduate would be able to cram into his head in four years. I was always happy to learn! If the war hadn't broken out, I would definitely have tried to enter the high school. The thought that I would find out more than I knew had an enormous draw for me. Just like the idea that I would become the first Gypsy woman functionary. Maybe I would be sitting in an office where some tall Hlinka Guard used to send our husbands to the work camps and had our women's heads shaved – if he only knew that now a Romani woman was going to be presiding at his table! The thought was enough to make me cry. In my heart I told myself that I must do what I could for our Romani people. But what would I do with my children? Who would take care of them for me?

I went into our basement flat, where Milan and Máňa were looking after Evička, who was sitting on the ground beating a spoon against a pot and laughing. I jumped over to her and kissed her, and with the thought that I wouldn't be seeing her for four months I began to sob. Milan and Máňa were looking at me all flabbergasted. Just then a car pulled up outside our place and there were two comrades all the way from the regional committee: "Hurry up, comrade Lacko, we're going to Lipovec and taking you with us, the training's starting, let's not miss the beginning!"

"What do you mean? The training's supposed to start a week from now!"

"Who told you a week from now? The opening ceremonies are tonight."

"But I can't go, where will I put my children?"

"So get someone, then! The important thing is that all the participants be on site this evening!" They took me in the car straight to my mother's so she would come for the children. Mama was glad that her daughter was being driven around in a car, but on the other hand she also told me in Romani: "You remember that I would have never left all of you to go off to some training!" In the end she agreed to come keep house at our place for a couple of days, but only until I worked something out with the children.

They took me away to Lipovec, but I wasn't at peace. The very next day I said: "Please, let me go and set my children up somewhere. I'll be back in two days." They let me go. I sat down in the train and went back to Prešov. I walked to the regional committee to ask them to tell me what I should do with my children. I ran into an older, reasonable comrade, and I could see that he understood the situation I was in. He said: "Not taking part in the training that the party is sending you to is a breach of party discipline. But your children are your children." He stopped and thought for a minute. "The little one, the two-year-old, put her temporarily in a children's home." Before I could say yes or no, he called a children's home in Humenný, and told them that he needed to place a child there for four months. Urgently. "The one who's going to first grade you can take with you. Normally we wouldn't allow something like this, but for you ... I know what you Gypsies suffered during the war. And I always love listening to Gypsy bands ...!" And right away he made another phone call to Lipovec to tell them that I was bringing a six-year-old child to the training with me, and that they should be ready for that. "And your mother will take care of the boy!" he decided. Of course, he couldn't call my mother on the telephone, because understandably, she didn't have a telephone. With her, I had to negotiate the business of looking after Milan myself.

The next morning I set off with Evička for Humenný, Evička was terribly attached to me. When the nurse wanted to take her in her arms, she caught me around the neck and screamed so the whole building could hear. She cried until she was choking on by her sobs. It took two nurses to tear her away from me. And when they had finally gotten hold of her, I fainted. I lost consciousness and fell on the floor. I pulled myself together only after they had poured some water over me. In the meantime they had taken Evička off somewhere so she wouldn't see me and I wouldn't see her. I left in tears. But what could I have done?

I took Máňa to the training with me. The women in the kitchen took charge of her. She helped them in the kitchen and they were very kind to her. They let her clean potatoes, put wood on the fire, and wipe with a dustcloth. When I had a free moment, I taught her how to read and write. And that way Máňa finished the first grade and didn't have to drop out.

My training went even worse. Up until that time I had read only novels like *Footsteps in the Mist, Eyes under a Veil,* and *The Lady of Čachtice* – and now I had to read political literature, economics, historical materialism, and Marxist philosophy. I didn't understand a thing. I didn't know what it was about. Most of the words felt like an incomprehensible magic spell to me. What good did it do reading the same paragraph five or six times if I didn't understand what the words meant? Many times I fell asleep over a book, exhausted. After a few days I went to the training director, in tears, and said: "It's no use trying, I'm going home! I don't understand anything! Do you have any idea what a Gypsy settlement is? Do you think that a girl from a Gypsy settlement can understand the three sources of Marxism and the roots of Leninism? And does a woman even have the kind of mind for something like this?" Because there were thirty-eight men there and only two women!

The director looked at me and she said: "You have to! You of all people must complete this training!" Then he started working with me, and over several days he explained all the unfamiliar terminology and incomprehensible concepts to me in his own words, until I slowly began to understand. It was as if some secret door, one that I hadn't known about before, had opened up in my brain, and there was new knowledge stored up in the open space behind that door. I was enormously grateful to the director for working with me and teaching me how to learn. And I was also enormously grateful to the Lord God for giving me a capable memory. I had always been able to remember a great deal. In the end I not only graduated from the training but I got A's in most of the subjects. I was like a devil, and there were no barriers for me.

I was glad that I finished the training, because they were able to hire me at the regional committee as an official. I don't know what I would have done otherwise. Getting a job in eastern Slovakia was very, very difficult, even many years after the war. Especially for women. There were almost no jobs for women doing manual labor. My husband could have supported me. But my husband had one weakness: he drank. And so two incomes weren't enough for us much of the time.

You want to be an official?

In 1951 they hired me at the regional committee in Prešov as a cultural inspector. I had barely come on board when my supervisor said to me: "You're coming with me to Humenný so you can learn how we carry out inspections of cultural activity in the district. You have to know what your work will consist of. We'll come back tomorrow night."

"For goodness' sake, what will my husband say?" I said, flabbergasted. "I have children at home! I have to be home in the evening!" Among Roma it was unheard of that a married woman would travel off somewhere with another man! If she so much as smiled at another man or said a word to him, people would start to say that she acted like a whore. I wanted to tell all this to my supervisor, but I was afraid that he would

143

think I was a backward Gypsy woman, or that he would say: why did the state invest money in your training? If you can't do what is necessary, stay home and darn your husband's socks! I tried making some kind of excuse – and the supervisor blew up just the way I thought he would: why did our society invest money in your education, comrade?

I broke down in tears and there was nothing I could do but come out with the truth. "My husband will kill me!" When the supervisor saw me bawling, he softened somewhat, but he didn't relent: "You're coming with me, don't be afraid of anything, after all, your husband isn't a backward Gypsy but is up to standard, we'll explain it to him! Or we'll explain some hard truths to him! – if something happens." In short order, they loaded me up in the car and took me off to Humenný. A good ways away it was, too. We got there and my head was spinning from all this cultural activity that I was supposed to oversee and inspect. On top of everything else, there were a number of localities in the Humenný district that were inhabited by the Hungarian minority, a different language, different requirements ... but after those two days I began to get the feel for things and I was glad that I had come to Humenný.

The next day I came home toward evening. My briefcase with official papers under my arm, I opened the door utterly aglow with the success of the trip. In the kitchen there were only my husband and Milan. Before I could even say: how are you – the first slap! "Looky here, madam official!" The second slap! The briefcase fell out of my hand. "So you want to be an official?" And another slap so hard I fell against the door. I don't know what hurt me more, the slap or the way I'd knocked my head in. "Don't you forget that I don't have any need for an official in my house! I don't need for you to go gadding about with strange fellows like some slut! Or for you to let them drive you around in their car! You're going to stay home! Cook! Do laundry! Take care of the children! This isn't why I got married, to cook over a hot stove and take care of an official!"

I felt my face swelling up, the world was spinning around me, I could barely stand on my feet, but somehow I pulled myself together and said: "Listen, Joža, now that they've given me training, now that they've made an official out of me, that's what I'm going to do whether you like it or not." He knew me well, and he understood that once I got something into my head there was no way I'd back away from it. "And what am I supposed to do by the stove, when you sink all your money into booze? All I can do is cook one empty pot inside another! ... And you know full well that I've never shamed myself with another fellow even in my thoughts." I felt him starting to cower at the force of my truth, and that confirmed it for me even more. "If you want, you go to see my supervisor tomorrow and tell him like a socially conscious Gypsy that you're not going to cook over a hot stove and take care of any official – and that they taught you that at the six-month hygiene course!" Then I slammed the door and went to my mother's to get Máňa and Evička.

The next day, Jozef really did go and see my supervisor. He went to make a scene in front of him and say he wasn't going to let me go to work. But all the supervisors in the place came running in and appealed to him for such a long time that he was an educated, intelligent, up-to-standard, progressive man, the first Gypsy who'd been saturated with the principles of Leninism – until they appealed him into complete silence. He came home ideologically suffocated, and he said: "All right then, you black jabberjaw, just so you don't go around saying I'm not as ideologically advanced as

Ilona Lacková at Prešov Cultural Centre, 1950.

you! Go work as an official. I give you my permission. But as soon as I hear anything about you, as soon as anyone betrays to me that you're flirting with some guy or that someone's got the hots for you – I'll grab an ax, and even if I had a hundred thousand health-care-and-hygiene training courses, I'd chop you up like cabbage. First you and then myself. And from the other world you can look down and see how I'm spending the rest of my life in the clink."

I took his words so much to heart that when my co-workers invited me for coffee or dessert after work, I said "thank you kindly," and raced on home. Then everyone knew how things were for me and said: we won't invite Ilona, because if Jožka found out she went to have coffee with us, he'd chop us all up like cabbage.

My heart drew me to the Gypsy settlements

I worked at the regional committee in Prešov in the capacity of a cultural inspector. There were fifteen districts in the Prešov region. I was supposed to oversee the districts and carry out control checks on the cultural work there: the people's ensembles, the amateur theater groups, the lecture circuit, the community discussion meetings, various training courses, cultural events marking important anniversaries and state holidays, the libraries, the public bulletin boards – in short, everything that came under the heading of culture. And because there was a shortage of people, at harvest time we helped out with the bulk purchase of potatoes and grain, dealt with the various problems of the collective farms they were starting to found in those days, and so on.

There was no center in the system for the so-called "Gypsy question," but any time some problem with Gypsies cropped up – that's how the authorities used to call it – everyone started running around: where's Lacko, where's Lacko? And they sent Lacko to "deal with the gypsies."

Even when no one sent me, of course, I was spending time with Roma. My heart drew me to the Gypsy settlements. As soon as my office hours were over, I went to see our people so I could speak in our language, learn a new song, hear the latest news, and see how the people were living. The hullaballoo of the children, the shouting of the women calling to each other from one end of the settlement to the other, the scent of dried mud, the smoke, the dark, unmoving figures of the old women sitting by the white walls of the shanties – *tel e fala*, it all reminded me of my childhood and youth in the settlement, which I had cursed countless times for its squalor and poverty, and which I loved above all else for the love and respect for one another that our people shared, for the art of taking life as it came, and for the art of joyousness. And then – in my heart I had a constant, secret longing – to write. To write about Roma. And so I – really from the time I was little, without even knowing it – loved to listen to the way people spoke, how they moved, what their life adventures were. When I was traveling by train on a business trip or when I couldn't fall asleep at night, the plays and stories I wanted to write would compose themselves in my head – but fate wished it otherwise, and so I haven't written most of them yet.

My life hasn't left me with a minute of free time. We had another child – a beautiful little boy, named Ďoďu. I put him in day care from the time he was little, because at the regional committee they didn't want to release me from my work for maternity leave. They reminded me constantly: don't forget that the party gave you an education, you're

146

obliged to build our society. To be honest, I have to say that I enjoyed my work enormously. And of course it made me feel good that I was the first Gypsy woman official. I couldn't even imagine staying home and puttering around the stove any more. I kept on the move, traveling around the districts, people asking me for advice, and sometimes I had the marvellous feeling that my childhood dream was being fulfilled: I was needed and useful to people. Naturally, sometimes I came home utterly exhausted, the heating hadn't been stoked up, the place was untidy, the children were hungry and dirty – and I had to pull myself together with all my strength to cook, clean, and do the laundry. I often went to sleep only toward morning, but I had to keep house – above all so people wouldn't say: hey, that Gypsy woman there, she's going to teach us things and her house is a mess! And so when I was falling asleep late at night with a hot iron in my hand over a heap of freshly-washed laundry, I told myself: do I need all this running around? What's it all for? By morning I had slept off such thoughts and I went out into the area all over again with the intention of doing something for our people, and with the faith that I would do just that. In the fifteen districts of the Prešov region there were about three hundred Gypsy settlements. Many of them had been slapped together from what was available after the Hlinka Guards drove them out of the towns. The conditions in the settlements were shocking, incomparably worse than before the war. The wretched shanties – cobbled together in some places from mud bricks, in others jointed together from the trunks and branches of young hornbeams or beeches – the walls bulging or sagging like the rickety little legs and bellies of the undernourished children who lived inside them, the roofs patched together from cardboard and rusty old sheet metal. Only by a miracle and against all natural laws did those crippled hunchbacks not collapse

In her capacity as a cultural inspector, Ilona Lacková awards a prize to Gypsy women for the high quality of their work.

before your very eyes. Most of the settlements were isolated, two or three kilometers from town, situated below a forest, in a gorge, or on a steep hill. The roads to the settlements were typically footpaths people had trampled out through meadows of sour grass, rusty red with sorrel blossom, or they led up a barren, infertile hillside. In rainy weather these footpaths turned into streams of mud. There were no wells in many settlements, and people drank water directly from the stream. I don't remember seeing electricity anywhere in those days. Of course, they often didn't have electricity even in the villages.

In the Romani language there is only one word for a house, an apartment, or a room – *kher*. This is because a shanty – grandly called a "house" – also represented an apartment, and an apartment in a shanty consisted of one room. In many, many shanties there was really no more than one room – and you entered it directly from the outside through a crooked opening that served as a doorway. And inside that room – sixteen square meters – there were fifteen or twenty people squeezed in together. In the most wretched shanties the only household appliances or furniture were the stove and the straw everyone slept on. Those who even then were called *feder Roma* or *barvale Roma*, the better class of Roma, rich Roma, had a bed, a sofa, perhaps a hutch for dishes, a table, and a chair. But even in the dwellings of those poor Roma, the semi-darkness of the shanty was brightened by large, colorful roses made out of crepe paper, and from the walls there looked down images of the Virgin Mary, who had a picture of Gottwald or Stalin cut out from some magazine stuck in the fringes of their greenish robes, and right next to it a photograph of a son in the army, the parents' wedding photograph, or that of a grandmother who had passed away.

I think that not even the most wretched peasant in the village in those days lived as wretchedly as the richest Rom in the settlement. But what was worse than the material poverty was the fact that after five years of constant fear, uncertainty, chicanery, and maltreatment, those hungry, dirty, sick, lice-infested, illiterate people had stopped taking care of themselves, and nothing mattered to them, because they had come to know that not a single one of their wishes would be listened to, and that their every effort was in vain. The girls didn't care if their hair looked like feathers and straw – and the greatest pride of Romani girls used to be their hair! The boys didn't care that they didn't know how to take a violin up in their hands – and the violin used to be the greatest aspiration of every young Rom. A bow would be put into the hand of a newborn baby boy with the wish that he would be a better musician than his father. People had begun to forget about even these beautiful customs. Bones, trash, and feces lay out in the open in the settlements, because the feeling of the home and responsibility toward the home was being destroyed in these people by the fact of their exile from civilization. The sacred tradition of *žužipen* – cleanliness, both real and ritual, was something people only talked about, but in reality no one took pains to keep it up. People had stopped believing, stopped trying, fallen into a kind of lethargy and living death.

*O*chmančaka

As is the case everywhere and always, inhuman creatures could be found who sponged off the wretchedness and poverty of the Roma and enriched themselves. I ran into a extreme case of this in Zborov. I arrived in Zborov in the winter. The Roma there lived on the other side of the stream. I hurried to finish my work at the regional committee while it was still daylight so I could head out to the settlement. I crossed the stream on a battered piece of board and drew close to the settlement. I could smell something strange even from a distance. It wasn't the stench of trash lying around, or even the slightly sweet smell of cooked ribs, the most frequent – and naturally the cheapest – Romani fare. It was something completely different. As in all the settlements, the children reached me first and milled around me. Then the women came closer, hesitantly. I was amazed. Some of the women's heads were completely bald. That was something you never saw among Roma. Their eyes were blurred by a dull, half-drunken glossiness. What what all this supposed to mean? Suddenly it occured to me: *ochmančaka*! – Hoffman's tincture. Distilled spirits were expensive, and Roma had no money to get drunk on spirits, so they doped themselves up on Hoffman's tincture. Not all of them, of course, but the habit had taken root in Zborov. I had heard about it, but that day I was seeing the horrible sight of a person doped up on Hoffman's tincture for the first time.

I said, in Romani: "Listen, you womenfolk, don't you want to live like human beings? Look at yourselves, can't you see what you look like? The *gadže* make fun of you and they're right! Do you want to wallow in this filth for all time to come?"

"What is this little lady telling us?" I heard behind me. Then an older person stepped out of the crowd, you could see that she still hadn't lost her humanity, and she said: "You're right, my girl, it's miserable! It's wretched. Finally someone has told us so to our faces. Every one of them wails and curses the fact that their old man drinks and beats them – but is there anything they deserve better? But tell us, what are we supposed to do?"

There was silence. The people sensed that the old woman was right. Many would be glad to kick the habit, but they didn't have the strength to do so. They needed someone who would help them, who would give them something to replace the *ochmančaka* – the chance to live like human beings.

"Where are you getting the Hoffman's tincture?" I asked. They told me that such and such a *gadžo* went to the Czech lands to buy it, brought it back by the jugful, and went round the settlements selling it. "Get yourselves together and come with me to the village!" I told them.

"I'm not going where the *gadže* live …! She's crazy …!" I heard all around me like a musical canon.

"What, are the *gadže* going to eat you up?!" I said, angry.

"What kind of a Gypsy woman are you that you don't know how the *gadže* treat us …? Ahem, yes, well-heeled shoes … pumps like you wear to a ball …silk blouse … she doesn't have any idea what Gypsy poverty is anymore …! Black as a crow, but the high and mighty folk have colored her heart white!"

Tears came to my eyes, I turned around, and felt like leaving. But the one wise woman saved the situation. "Forget about them! Their minds aren't worth rotten straw …! And don't be angry at them! The greater their powerlessness, the stronger the curse. The *gadže* hate us, and they won't go out of their way not to humiliate us. The cops beat that one old woman for coming to the village barefoot – said it was an embarrassment to our new regime … I'll go to the village with you." She took me by the arm and led the way herself. Among Roma the rule is "birds of a feather," so the rest of the women slowly started trickling along behind us. There were about twenty-five or thirty who reached the town. I had no plan, but I think that the Lord God was guiding my steps –

149

A typical Gypsy hamlet in the Prešov region where Ilona Lacková went to help people as a cultural inspector, 1984.

A lttle girl dancing to the music of a guitar and an accordion in the hamlet of Chmiňanské Jakubany, 1984.

Ilona Lacková and friends in a Gypsy hamlet, 1984.

A group of musicians in a Gypsy hamlet, 1984.

although I didn't believe in Him at the time, because at every training session and in every school they explained to us that God was a bourgeois anachronism. We got to the school, I quickly rounded up the director, and using my authority as a cultural inspector from the regional committee, I had them let the Roma into one of the classrooms. I sent the school employee off to bring the secretary of the local party committee, the teachers, and all the officials he could get, immediately. They came. They were afraid. They didn't know what was going on, but they knew that if they had a complaint from the regional headquarters, they could lose their jobs. The Roma just marveled at how a *gadžo* could obey a Gypsy! Then a debate began. The Zborov Roma felt more confidence with me standing behind them and they began to speak about what was troubling them. There was no drinking water and no work opportunities, and what were we supposed to live off of? The peasants didn't want to give us jobs because they were afraid! That was the truth – people in business for themselves were forbidden to hire labor, which was how the party wanted to force them to join a cooperative. There was no construction going on, and the industrialization of eastern Slovakia began only later. The Roma had really no way of making a living. It was worse than before the war. Before the war they could at least beg, and no one held it too much against them; on the contrary, when a peasant woman gave a Gypsy woman a few potatoes and a little curd cheese, she was happy to have one more good deed so as to be one step closer to heaven. Now people said: "Aren't you ashamed to beg now that we have a people's democratic regime? Today everyone has the right to work!" But where were they going to get the work? Anyone who had enough initiative to go off to the Czech lands was condemned to live just as meager an existence as the Zborov Roma. Any money they happened to make went for *ochmančaka*, because in their doped-up fogginess they forgot about their inescapable situation.

I paid attention to the way the Zborov functionaries were expressing themselves, and I even began to feel a little sorry for them. At first they responded to the demands of the Roma by putting on their usual air of amused superiority, marveling as if the foxes from the ancient forests were blaming them for not taking care of their food supply. But then their snootiness gave way to confusion and shame. "These people," I said, pointing at the Roma, who I'd seated on the schoolroom benches, "are citizens too. Although they live on the other side of the water, a stream is not an ocean and the barrenness on the other side of the stream is no barbaric, foreign land, but part of this state, and not only this state, but directly under the administration of this town. The elected functionaries are just as responsible for the Gypsy citizens as they are for the inhabitants of the village. Which of you," I asked, turning to one after another, "has ever, ever set foot in the Gypsy settlement?" I knew well that none of them had. The functionaries averted their eyes and didn't answer. Unfortunately, this apartheid, which has lasted centuries and centuries, persists to this day in some Slovak villages. Except for the gendarmes, no "white" person ever goes where the Gypsies live.

After about three hours, this altogether unusual meeting came to an end. The Zborov Roma had never in their lives sat on chairs in a public building in the village together with functionaries – and the Zborov functionaries had never in their lives had a discussion with gypsies, who for the moment were equal with them in the sense that they were sitting on chairs in their presence and speaking rationally about their situation – and they had their "black" representative all the way from regional headquarters with them to boot! The end result of the meeting was good will on both sides. The secretary of the local party committee promised that he would do everything necessary to get the men some kind of work, that he would include in the city plan the digging of two wells in the settlement, and that he would negotiate social support for the poorest families. At my urging, the Roma promised that they would join the Red Cross, send at least two of their members to basic training, and that they would bury in the garbage dump the bones and trash lying around in the settlement. I wanted to speak about the addiction to Hoffman's tincture, but at the last moment I swallowed my anger. What if someone right from the village had his hands in it? I resolved to catch the train, and I promised both the Roma and the officials that I would come back soon to check up on things. I ran for the train, several women came along to accompany me, and said: "Girl, you're a great partisan fighter!" They wouldn't listen to my protestations that I had never been a partisan fighter.

In Prešov I reported the case with the Hoffman's tincture to the party committee and insisted that the middleman be caught and punished. Within three weeks they really did find him out, and two accomplices as well.

After some time I came back to Zborov and literally wept with happiness that the settlement no longer looked so miserable. The party committee had a well dug, and though there was only one, they had at least that, there were no more bones lying around the settlement, they said some recruiter had taken a bunch of men to work somewhere in northern Bohemia, and one after another the women came up to me to boast of what they had gotten for themselves with the first paycheck – a shawl, a kerosene lamp, a holy picture, an old sofa, high-heeled shoes "like you've got, you partisan fighter!" and so on. I was most happy that the place no longer smelled like *ochmančaka*. The middlemen had been locked up and there was no one to buy from. The womenfolk betrayed to me that although there were some who cursed me, most of the people were glad they no longer had opportunity to continue in this awful addiction.

What are you cooking in that pot?

I went to one settlement and it was so poor I'm ashamed to give its name. In front of it there stood two overhangs it was barely possible to call a shanty. Beyond them were three underground shelters, and all the way in the back there was something indescribable: some collapsing boxes made of cardboard, boards, and sheet metal, and then a little off to the side the rusty chassis of a truck, a grey, broken-down delivery vehicle, painted with tulips. The underground shelter at least had a unified, time-tested traditional architectural style, but the two rear structures were something completely unparalleled. You didn't know whether to cry at the material poverty or to admire the resourcefulness with matter of the indomitable spirit which had managed to create something like that in defiance of all physical laws.

Every time I made out to visit a settlement, I bought candies for the children. They never disappeared as quickly as here. Hardly had I made my appearance when the children, who surrounded me as usual, literally dug the candies out of my purse as soon as I had opened it, and when they saw that I had nothing else to eat inside, they ran off to someplace at a distance and divided the candies up so everyone got some. A single candy was passed from mouth to mouth in the general, fraternal clamor.

It was temperate, early in the spring, and the sun was warm, but the snow still hadn't managed to melt entirely. The uneven area in front of the shanties shone with the irregular surfaces of puddles edged with dirty, slushy snow. Some of the children were completely naked. Not only the smallest ones – but also those who would be developing body hair any day now. Nakedness is considered highly shameful only from the time when the first hair appears on the private parts or under the arms. From then on, in the old-world settlements, a girl was not allowed to go out with even her arms bared, and a man in shorts with bare legs was considered either shameless or mad. The children here made use of the prerogatives of nakedness because they had nothing to wear.

While in other settlements the curious vanguard of children come to look over the new arrival was followed by the women and finally even the men, here the adults stood still as if cursed to remain unmoving specters. I began to walk around the dwellings with a little bit of an official air. Yet there was enough Romani propriety left in me not to cross the threshold of an entryway without being invited. I stood on the other side of the door and, as is proper, I waited for them to call me inside. *Te vičinel andro khe*r – an invitation to enter the home – is the basic, preliminary, and at the same time smallest expression of respect which a host wishes to or may show to a guest. Here no one invited me. Perhaps not even because they didn't want to, but because they couldn't. They were ashamed of their poverty. Naturally they asked me where I was from and who I was, and they even knew the name of my father, although we didn't even have any contact with these parts before the war. For us it was too far to walk on foot to the fairs, which was why not even one of our girls had gotten married here. But the names of the elder Roma, the representatives of the clan, were often borne beyond the borders of direct personal relationships.

Although I didn't enter a single dwelling, from the entryway I looked over the entire living area of the household. I didn't see a single piece of furniture. Everywhere there were two or three family members sleeping. Mostly the men. They slept on the floor of the dwelling in some sackcloth. For others the sackcloth – *parind* – served as a sweater, a coat, a shawl, or a wrap, just some kind of covering. Nowhere did I catch sight of a single, dry crust of bread or potato peel. *Ko čoreske na sal, čoreske na pat'a*s, one who is not poor does not believe the poor man, is a literal translation of the Romani saying. Only a white social worker could have been scandalized by the fact that gypsies slept even during the day – because she herself had never known hunger. I realized what all the households had in common: the cold, emanating from the stoves and hearths with the fire gone out.

I was all the more surprised when in front of the dwelling made out of the wrecked chassis of a truck I saw a small fire-pit with smoke rising from it. Even in our settlement, we used to cook in similar outdoor fire-pits in summer: two bricks one and a half hands' distance from each other, and on top of the bricks a pot, heated by kindling underneath. By the fire, a woman of about forty was squatting on her behind, in typical Romani posture, and adding to the kindling beneath an enormous black pot covered with a lid. Steam was escaping from underneath the lid.

"What are you cooking?" I asked. The question "what are you cooking?" is repeated among Romani women so often that it has become something like a greeting which doesn't even require an answer. Of course, I meant my question altogether seriously, because that woman was the only one from the whole settlement who not only had a fire that hadn't gone out but who was cooking, and what's more, in such an enormous pot to boot. To make sure she heard me I repeated my question one more time: "What are you cooking in that pot?"

"Can't you smell it?" laughed the woman, "take a whiff!" We didn't know each other, but Roma don't have to know each other in order to speak to one another like siblings. Only after her reply did I realize that the steam rising from the pot didn't smell like potatoes, or cabbage, much less like the broth you get from cooking bones. I sniffed and I sniffed, but I didn't smell anything. Not a thing. "Take a look, then," the woman said, "but be careful, don't scald yourself."

"Mama, are you done cooking yet?" asked a ten-year-old boy who came running up from out of a crowd of children when he saw something going on by the pot. He was one of the children who wasn't completely naked. He was wearing some bedraggled pants and a torn undershirt.

"Soon enough, little boy, but you'll have to wait just a moment longer! Go bring me some more kindling, run! But go all the way to the woods, you runny-nosed brat, you lazy boy, don't gather the twigs from the stream, those don't burn!" In her voice the mother had an enthusiasm which promised the children a feast if they took part in her culinary creation by bringing her kindling. Her enthusiasm was imparted to the boy, who ran over a shaky bench toward the woods with the whole gaggle of children behind him.

In the meantime I had carefully moved aside the lid, let the steam wash over me, and then tried to make out what was cooking inside that enormous pot. I didn't see anything. Nothing except water. Not even a single, naked *haluška*. "It's water!" I said, amazed, and involuntarily I looked around to see where the woman had dough or potatoes or at least a feed turnip to boil in the water. Nothing anywhere.

"That's right, it's water!" she confirmed.

"And what are you going to cook in it?" I asked.

"Nothing," she said.

"So why are you boiling it?" I asked, amazed.

"What kind of a Romani woman are you that you don't understand?" it was her turn to be amazed. "I'm boiling it so as not to disappoint the children. To make them happy. They're looking forward to getting something to eat, and so they're not constantly pleading 'give me something to eat, give me something to eat!' At least while the water is boiling in the pot I have some peace from them! They're not bawling 'I'm hungry, I'm hungry!' They're happy! Do you know how happy they are? It's belief! Belief! They believe I'll give them something to eat. The belief fills their bellies ... and I have peace in my soul." The woman abandoned herself to laughter, laughing like a lunatic, and against my will I laughed along with her. And then I asked, "what will you do when the children come back from the woods with the kindling and see that there's nothing in the pot except water?"

"Before then a miracle will happen!" she said, as an absolute truism. I had been trained in Marxist thought, and my knowledge, which our state had given me so graciously and free of charge, were weighing on my Romani Experience and Truth. "What miracle?" I asked, irritated. She didn't even have time to answer me, because the children were dashing back from the woods with the kindling, and even before they got there they called out: "Mama, is it done yet?" They ran up and threw the kindling on a pile next to the fireplace. Of course, they were not only the children she herself had brought into the world but all the rabble from the whole *bokhal'i vatra*, hungry settlement, because according to the traditional precept not to leave any child hungry, at that moment all the children were her own.

"C'mere!" I called the boy in the dirty undershirt, and poured everything I had in my purse into his palm. It wasn't much, because I remember that it was actually the day before payday. "Go to the village and buy some bread!" He didn't waste any time and wasn't bashful, grabbing the money and disappearing like smoke. A few children who were wearing at least some kind of torn rag ran after him.

Once again the boy's mother abandoned herself to laughter. "Don't you see, a miracle happened!" she said. "I kiss your golden little heart, I lick your little feet!"

"What kind of a miracle is that?" I staunchly defended my Marxist precepts, so impugned. "If it weren't for the fact that I'd given your boy all of my money, there would have been no miracle!" – Fortunately, I didn't say that! But a Rom doesn't even have to say what he's thinking for another Rom to read his thoughts precisely.

"Thank God" the woman said, "that this miracle was performed through you. This is a great kindness and mercy for you."

I said I had to hurry for the train. She wanted me to wait, saying they would share with me from what the children brought back from the village. I thanked her, wished her happiness, and set off for my return trip. She escorted me to the plank which crossed the river, walking in front of me and watching out for dry spots among the puddles for me so at least I wouldn't get the heels of my pumps dirty ...

I forgot to tell you the reason I went to that settlement in the first place. First off, I had never been there, and there's a Romani saying that goes: *odoj manuš džal, kaj mek na sas, kaj te dikhel so mek na dikhľa* – a man goes where he's never been to see what he's never seen. Although I myself am a Romani woman, I had really seen something here that I had never seen. And secondly – I came to found a local chapter of the Red Cross. But the Red Cross came back to mind only on the train, after I had pulled myself together again from my experience.

A member of the Red Cross among the high and mighty in Bratislava

I have been a member of the Red Cross since 1948. I joined because I hoped that an organization which took care of healthy people wouldn't leave us to live at Korpáš and would manage to help us get into flats. That was something they didn't do, but they did convince us that they would help if they could. "Remain actively engaged, comrade, and work!" the comrades said in a voice which promised that if I had enough Brownie points for drumming up activity it'd be possible to arrange a flat somehow. "We don't have anyone who'll go around the settlements and look after hygienic conditions!" But what good was looking after hygienic conditions when there were no access roads to the settlements, no wells, and they drank the water from the stream? Things were still manageable in those places where the Roma lived next to villages, but they were unimaginable when they lived downstream from a village and the peasants threw all their garbage, filth, and manure in the stream! It's an absolute miracle that those people didn't die of typhus! But we were enthusiastic in those days, and had a rock-solid faith in our party and our government! We were convinced that the leaders of the party and the government wanted the purest goodness and justice for the entire people, and if that goodness and justice didn't come about as planned, it was only because in our midst there were concealed class enemies who were preventing our leaders from knowing what was going on below. We did what we could – if nothing else, we enthusiastically drummed up activity, at least. My husband Jozef organized a fourteen-day course for the regime's hygienists from the settlements, and I founded Red Cross patrols in the settlements. Local organizations. We organized a regional competition for the patrols, and who do you think won? Our Romani women from Giraltovce! They won first place! They ran to the accident victim, bandaged him, nursed him, gave him artificial respiration, carefully placed him on a stretcher, and carried him into the ambulance – a completely professional job, and they were absolutely illiterate and couldn't even sign their names. The doctor just stared at them like a madman.

In 'fifty-one they held elections to the central committee of the Red Cross, and we received notification that we should elect someone for our region. Secretary Novák – rest his soul – said: "We'll elect Lacko." "What do you mean?" I said, but they elected me all the same. Jozef was in Bratislava at the six-month course for hygienists when that happened. Once when he had come home for a Sunday I said to him: "Listen, Jožu ..." "What now?" "They elected me to the central committee of the Red Cross ..." He kept on eating, not lifting his eyes from the plate, as if I hadn't said a word. "What that means," I went on, "is that I'll have to go to Bratislava once every two months." "And who's going to look after the children for you?" "My mother will take them for a day for two." "I've had it up to here with all this! Are they your children or your mother's?"

I was silent. Suddenly it occurred to me that he was now living in Bratislava, getting his training, and that I could go and see him on business trips. "Then let them send you to Bratislava as quick as they can!" he said, and that was how I got permission to become a member of the Red Cross central committee.

But there was no meeting coming up in Bratislava, as it happened, and I was completely beside myself. How would I get to see him? Yet just then the good Lord ordained that I was delegated to a conference of the committee for the protection of children being held by the Union of Women. I got a delegate's pass for three days, just the right amount of time for me to make the rounds with Jozef of all his relatives in Bratislava, after the meetings. He had two cousins there, one male and one female, and a friend of his – dear, dwarf-sized Lajka. Going somewhere and not visiting your relatives is a great offense. We in particular couldn't afford not to, because if ever we didn't, on the word would go out that we were officials, making ourselves out to be big shots and losing touch with our own families.

At the regional committee we had a small plane, and so I flew to Bratislava by plane. I had become used to dealing with high-ranking comrades and with powerful officials, but I had never been in such exalted company as there was at this conference. I pretended it was nothing out of the ordinary for me. After commissioner Terek presented his paper, a discussion began. They called one of the comrades to the platform, but she wasn't ready yet. From behind the table where the presidium sat I heard: "Then we call on comrade Lacko!" I stepped up to the podium as if in a dream, bowed, and started speaking: "In the keynote paper I heard all about what our regime has done for our children: swimming pools, playgrounds, and health care. But in our parts there are many children who go around completely naked, drinking water from a stream, with lice falling from their hair..." and then I told my story about the woman who was boiling water in a pot so she could delude the starving children at least for a while with the promise of food. My voice was shaking and it took all my strength for me to keep from breaking down in front of the assembly of the high and mighty before me. After I finished, I heard sniffling, people blowing their noses, and sobs, although most of the delegates were men.

Commissioner Terek returned to the floor to bring the discussion to a close. He said: "I assure comrade Lacko that we shall not forget about the Gypsy children." It was six years after the war. Not too much longer and it will be fifty years after the war, and in eastern Slovakia you can still find settlements where the people drink water from a stream and in the early spring wade through puddles of mud to their shanties, slapped together out of sheet metal and boards. The one thing I no longer see today is naked children. They've been civilized to the extent that they cover their prepubescent nakedness with their grimy T-shirts imprinted with blonde women's beckoning faces or grinning tigers' muzzles. I don't want to point fingers, but I don't think the people who are still living this way today are the guilty ones. In those days I enthusiastically believed that the promise of comrade commissar Terek would come true in a year or two at most.

Following the afternoon session everyone went to the Carlton for a luncheon. At that time, it was the most luxurious hotel in Bratislava. I sat down at a free table, trembling with anxiety and nervousness and wondering if I would be able to converse appropriately with whoever sat next to me. All of a sudden a tall, dashing man in evening dress came up to me and said: "Allow me to escort you to the table of the commissar of schools, Mr. Sýkora." I let myself be led away and the man in evening dress – a waiter, as I had ascertained – seated me on the chair like a lady. Commissar Sýkora shook my hand and said: "I didn't think there would would be such an intelligent woman among the Gypsies." "It doesn't take intelligence to understand what I spoke about," I said. "It's enough to go to a Gypsy settlement. Would you believe that in some settlements the Roma still don't know that the war is over?"

At that time I still didn't know how to eat with a knife and fork. I was terribly self-conscious. I watched as the commissar cut his dumplings and followed his example. All the while I kept thinking of the hungry children from that one settlement and imagined how it would be if they could only sit with us and eat!

After the luncheon there were discussions in various committees. Commissar Terek had me summoned and said: "I don't know if you're doing us an injustice, comrade. I have word that they're carrying out disinfections in Gypsy settlements with DDT."

And I told him – may I never get up from this chair again if I'm lying: "Am I hearing this from the highest official in our health care system? What good is dusting the settlements with flea and lice powder when the people don't have any water to wash themselves with? They sleep on the ground and have no clothes to wear! And they'll never get a job anywhere!"

The commissar was taken aback, and he asked: "So what would you propose?" I said: "Just like they have a program for those who were disabled during the war, there should be a program to humanize the conditions in the settlements or to liquidate the settlements. To get the Roma back to living in the villages, in the cities, among other people, to find jobs for them ..." He said he would invite me to every meeting. They never invited me to any meetings. I couldn't even have gone, because I had children and a family.

When the conference was over I went off to find my husband. He was living in a dormitory on the embankment, not far from the office of the commissar of the schools. "So tell me, you, how's your training going?" I asked and he replied: "Don't be afraid,

I'm not running after any women." That was what I wanted to hear.

We took a walk along the embankment, to the National Theater, and took a ride to the Petržalka. We spent the night at his cousin's and the next day we visited his other cousin and his friend Lajka, and in the evening I went home to the children.

At President Gottwald's

There was one more major event awaiting me in 'fifty-one. On the occasion of International Women's Day the Red Cross sent me as part of a delegation to see President Gottwald. There were three women delegates from the Prešov region: Nihil, Adamčik – and Lacko. Me. A booklet called *The Second Women's Visit to the Castle* came out for the occasion, and inside there's a photo of the president with all of us, including me. This is a great historical document! But where is it? The children were probably playing with it ... or it disappeared somewhere as we were moving. We've moved so many times ...

The president received us in the Spanish Hall. Alongside him stood his wife Marta. She was wearing long, green, velvet clothes. Then every delegation chose one person to go say a few words to the president. Adamčik and Nihil said: "You go, little Lacko, you know how to speak better." I went up to the president and broke down in tears. For a black girl from a Gypsy settlement to be so honored! The president shook my hand and said: "Thank you, Gypsy woman!" Then we all made way for him and the photographer arranged us for the picture-taking. Marta Gottwald laughed and said: "Watch out, the lens will crack!" The lens didn't crack, but there was no flash. First their daughter tried to fix the flash, then their son-in-law, Minister Čepička, then Marta Gottwald, then President Gottwald – everyone kept fiddling with it, and no one could fix it until the photographer finally managed to. And then he took our picture.

Then they took us into the adjoining hall. On the tables there was food such as I had never seen before even in my dreams. Like in a fairy tale. Everyone took a small plate and walked around the table trying things to see how they tasted. I was just afraid there might be some fancy food in there like frogs, crayfish, or snails. Then the waiter brought the wine around. "What shall we have?" I asked the women in our group. "You know what, first let's try the white and then the red!" Nihil suggested. But we all drank a glass of the white and already our heads were spinning. It was terribly strong wine!

Then I got up the courage to search out the president. So I could get close to him and tell the folks at home how I walked with my hand on his arm. And that's what actually happened! The president said: "Do you know what, women? I'll walk you through the Castle. Never did a worker use to set foot in this Castle! The Habsburgs ruled here for centuries." He led us round the Castle and in every hall he had a little tobacco pouch on the table so he could fill his pipe.

I was unbelievably happy! What Gypsy woman had ever lived to walk on the arm of the President through the Prague Castle?

Ďodǔ

A beautiful little boy was born to us. We named him after his father Jozef and called him Ďodǔ. And so we had four children. Ďodǔ was truly a marvelous child! He had enormous black eyes and long, curly eyelashes. When he was nine months old, he started walking, and said Papa and Mama. He made all of us terribly happy. But at the age of nine months he developed an upset stomach. I ran with him to the hospital and left him there. I was still breastfeeding him. I used to go and nurse him both when he was in daycare and when he was in the hospital. In the morning before I went to work, and in the afternoon when I was coming home from work. I had to limit the number of trips I made to the settlements and out into the surrounding area at that time. One day I went to see him in the hospital, took him to my breast, and I noticed that his little mouth was very hot. Like an oven. And it was as if his eyes were under a veil. I told the nurse, but she said it was nothing. I began looking for the doctor. No doctor anywhere. Finally I ran into someone in a white coat in the corridor, grabbed him, and made him swear to examine my Ďoďu. I showed him my identification as a member of the executive council of the Red Cross, he looked it over, and he said: "I do autopsies." His name was Plank. "Then get me someone who does live ones!" I shouted. "Who's responsible for the sick children who are alive? Tell me, or I'll report this to the Office of the President! I know Gottwald personally!" He thought I had gone mad, but he found some pediatrician for me. The doctor examined Ďoďu and said that his heart was all right, his lungs were all right, and that he didn't see any reason he should have such a high fever. But so I wouldn't be afraid, he said it would pass. I wanted to put a cold compress on Ďoďu's head like our mother used to do when we were sick as children, but the nurse wouldn't let me. In my training I had acquired a respect for education and authority, and unfortunately I had begun to doubt our healthy faculty of reason and hundreds of years of experience.

There was a staffing shortage in the hospital at the time, so like the other mothers I used to go and help out. I fed little Ďoďu, changed him, and suffered terribly over the fact that they wouldn't give him compresses. The nurse wouldn't allow it. Ďoďu had a fever for two weeks. His brain cells were burning up.

Before we put him in the hospital he had started walking, he was gabbling, repeating various words, reacting to everything around him, smiling at Máňa and Evička, and he always stretched out his little arms toward me and called out "gi! gi!" – give! give! – because he knew that I brought him something every time I came. When they gave him back to us from the hospital, he didn't recognize any of us. He had stopped talking, stopped moving. When I called to him, it was as if he didn't hear, and he just looked straight in front of him, not even turning his little head.

At that time I was working as a cultural official on the regional committee. I said I was worried about my child and that I needed to stay home. They soothed me, saying he would get over it, and I absolutely could not leave my work because society had invested money in my education, that I was the only Gypsy woman in such an important position, that I had a responsibility to our people's democratic regime, and that they didn't have anyone else who would go visit the settlements, and so on, and so on. They immediately arranged for me to be able to leave Ďoďu in daycare, although they normally didn't take sick children. There was an awfully kind director in the daycare and she fell in love with Ďoďu, in spite of the fact that he couldn't walk and he couldn't speak and she had to change him even though he was three years old. When I used to come back late from trips in the field, she took him home to her place, and many times I picked him up from her late at night.

I saw that things with Ďoďu weren't getting better, though the officials were trying

Ilona Lacková bringing her son Ďoďu, to hospital in Prague;
he died aged fourteen, 1955.

to convince me that he would snap out of it. I packed myself up and went with him to the hospital in Košice. They kept him for observation. A month later they sent him back and told me that he had suffered severe meningitis and that he would never speak or talk again. It made me crazy, I didn't believe it, and I went off with him to Prague. I didn't know anyone in Prague, but I had heard that the best children's hospital was in Krč. Somehow I found my way to Krč, but they didn't want to take us there, saying we weren't from Prague and that we had no referral, but when they saw how devastated I was and that I had traveled from such a distance with the child in my arms, they took us. They kept Ďoďu for observation, and three weeks later they told me the same thing as in Košice.

We had Ďoďu at home for seven years. We changed him like a baby. For seven years I washed his diapers. He would sit motionless in the carriage or on the bed and look straight ahead of himself with his large, beautiful eyes with lashes like not even dolls in display cases have. I loved him just as much as the other children and even more, although he didn't nestle up to me, didn't hold me round the neck, and possibly couldn't even tell me apart from the others. In my spirit I held onto the hope that one day a spark of response or feeling would awaken in him. But the physical labor was killing me – the cooking, the laundry, everything a housewife has to do, on top of which were diapers and more diapers, day after day for seven years. Then my co-workers talked me into putting Ďoďu in an institution. I listened to them. They took him in at Špišské Vlachy. Every two weeks we went to see him. I remember when oranges appeared on the market for the first time since the war: I stood in line and brought Ďoďu a kilo. I peeled him an orange and fed it to him in pieces. I hung on his eyes to see if they wouldn't give some sign of how the orange tasted to him. He ate it, but in his expression there was absolutely nothing to see.

Then – I was already taking correspondence courses from the Faculty of Culture and Journalism at Charles University – one day I was in Prague for a consultation. We had just had a lecture about the meaning of art. An employee from the reception desk came in and handed me a telegram. I opened it and broke down in tears. Jozef was calling me home, saying that Ďoďu had died. He was fourteen years old.

Like my own son

Of my own children, four survived – in 'fifty-six another child, Luboš, was born – but I can't tell you how many other children felt like my own! I became especially attached to one boy from Kučín. I don't want to give his name because he's working as a cultural attaché in the diplomatic service, and it wouldn't be nice for him if people found out about his origins.

In Kučín they organized a course for illiterate gypsies and called the regional committee, telling them: send Lacko to help us get the people in. The course was only supposed to be for adults, but we also enrolled ten to twelve-year-old children who still hadn't been to school yet.

Sometimes it happens with people you've never met before that at first sight you feel as close as if you were blood relatives. You don't even have to speak to each other, but you feel very good when you're near each other. That happened to me in Kučín with one twelve-year-old boy. Hardly had I gotten my first look at him when I knew I liked him.

He didn't go to school at all and couldn't read or write. I asked him if he would join the course with me. He nodded his head, took me by the hand, and I led him to the schoolhouse. He let himself be taken for the whole three weeks I was helping out with the course. Every day he waited for me in front of the door of the shanty where he lived, and as soon as he saw me he came running, caught me by the hand, and we went to school. He learned unusually easily. In an hour he would learn what it took others a week. At the end of the two-month course they took him straight into the third grade, and he completed two grades in one year. He left elementary school and went to Prešov to study at the teachers' middle school. That made me enormously happy, but I saw him little because I was always swamped with work. But what do you think happened? The boy secretly began to make friends with our daughter Máňa. They'd go for walks together, to the movies, and my husband and I didn't know anything about it!

One day in town I met his sister, who leaned toward me and said: "Auntie, what do you say about the fact that we'll be relatives?" "What do you mean?" I asked, amazed. "I mean our boy and your Máňa!"

At that time Máňa was fourteen years old, and many Romani girls were already starting a family at that age, but I wanted her to finish at least elementary school. On the other hand, I liked the idea that a boy who was so close to my heart would marry into our family. In my spirit I said: wait, first you have to find out how things are. I would get to know their family and then have a talk with Máňa. I arranged a business trip to Kučín for myself so I could show some documentary films in their cultural center. Of course, his family invited me to their home. After the screening I went to see them. The table was decked out like at an engagement party, the boy was sitting in the corner with his eyes cast down, and I asked: "So, when are you going to going to get married? And do you already have some girl in mind?" He was so embarrassed I was sorry for him. Then he got a hold of himself and said he'd like to marry our Máňa. He still hadn't confessed his love to her because he was bashful. "And what about school?" I said. He said that after he finished middle school he would try to get a job in Prešov and then apply to take correspondence courses at the pedagogical faculty in Košice. I was glad. I liked the fact that the boy knew what he wanted to do, and I believed he would do it. "You know," I said, "who would have thought that when I first took you by the hand to school that you would be my son-in-law!" He just beamed and was also very pleased with the way things had worked out.

I went home and Máňa was dolling herself up at the mirror, as fourteen-year-old girls have a way of doing. "You're not planning a wedding, are you?" I laughed. And then I started asking her about her boyfriend from Kučín. Bull's-eye. She got angry and exploded that she wasn't going to marry any hick from Kučín! That she didn't want him and didn't love him! That brought me to the boiling point, and we started arguing senselessly. "You know you're not getting married until you finish elementary school!" I shouted, although right away I contradicted myself and started singing her the praises of the boy I loved like my own son. Máňa dug in her heels even deeper. From that time on she wouldn't listen to a word about him. He wasn't allowed in her sight, she hid herself from him, and sent messages turning down his invitations. I don't know why. I can't explain it. Because he was so black? I really don't know.

He was unhappy. People said he even cried. He went to Bratislava to forget about Máňa. He graduated from the university there with degrees in mathematics and Russian.

They sent him to Leningrad on an internship, he found himself a Russian girl, and he married her. When he came home he got himself a job with the Foreign Ministry.

One day I was returning home to Prešov from some business trip to Bratislava. It was in the summertime. I was sitting at the airport and walking past me was some young person, brown as an Italian or rather an Indian, perfectly dressed in a light grey suit, white shirt, and silver tie. Everything about him was nice and friendly. In my spirit I said: "What country can he be from?"

"I kiss your hand, Mrs. Lacko!" he said, all of a sudden. Only when I heard his voice did I recognize him! My little ragamuffin from Kučín. "My oh my, boy, is that you? How did you get here?"

He told me what he was doing, what he'd been through, and that he'd gotten married. "But auntie, I can't forget Máňa ... Even now, if she wanted to ... my wife and I don't get along at all ..."

But Máňa was already married and had a little boy named Jiříček. I said: "Get Máňa out of your head! You're married, she's married, leave things the way they are. Whoever you're married to, you live with them. If you'd married Máňa, you wouldn't be who you are today. Everything has happened the way it was supposed to happen." And in saying that I was really reassuring myself, because I was sorry that he wasn't my son-in-law.

When he was still a runny-nosed, uneducated boy, this cultivated diplomat gave me faith that my work in the settlements wasn't wasted. Thanks to him I have realized the truth of the Romani saying *šel manuš, šel naturi* – a hundred people will have a hundred different personalities. One person has a clever head on their shoulders, another will be slow and lazy in his thinking; one person will be scared, another will have the courage to take life by the horns; one person is comfortable, will snuggle in cozily with a stereotype, and in the dungheap of life will feel like a dung beetle rolling his ball of dung around, while someone else will long for the taste of something finer. Even within the Gypsy settlements, where at first glance people all look equally wretched and, in the eyes of the *gadže*, are all "Gypsies," you can find the most varied human types, characters, and various levels of determination embodied in a person. But even the most hardheaded human being, gifted with creative abilities and the desire to realize them, needs an opportunity, hope, encouragement, and teaching. If, in such a backward, wretched settlement, there were found one, two, or three who got the opportunity to develop their humanity and their abilities, then those who were weaker, more comfortable, more hesitant, more helpless, suddenly saw that Roma could do things and would do things. They wanted to catch up and were ashamed to stay behind. They began to try too. As as time went by, there were fewer and fewer such "Gypsies," to whom nothing mattered, who were rotting alive, and who found neither God nor the devil buried in the mud of indifference.

The Kučín settlement where my diplomat grew up had yet another pleasant surprise in store for me. One day I went to see if the literacy course was coming to a close. In Kučín there was a long, wooden fence, and as I was coming in on the bus I saw written all over it in chalk: "Julius Gorol, Julius Gorol, Julius Gorol"! One after another, above and below. Sixty-five-year-old godfather Gorol had learned to write, and he wrote his name all over the fence from sheer joy.

Don't speak to those Gypsy children...

The elementary school in Varhaňovce got a new, energetic director, and he determined that not a single class had a Gypsy child in it, although the field beyond the Gypsy settlement was teeming with hundreds of them. In many settlements the Romani children didn't go to school and, to tell the truth, the teachers were happy because they didn't know what to do with them. The Varhaňovce school director somehow – I don't remember how – arranged things so that one day a whole horde of thirty Gypsy children turned up in the first grade classroom. Not a single one of them spoke a word of Slovak. Of course, the teacher didn't know a word of Romani. She ran out of the classroom, frightened, and she broke down in tears in the director's office, saying she was tendering her resignation, and that after her long years of service she didn't deserve something like this. The truth of the matter is that they put people on the so-called "Gypsy question" either as a punishment or because they weren't good for anything else.

The director, taken aback by the success of his own initiative, called the district committee asking what he should do. And from the district they called the regional committee: "Send Lacko! Urgent!" The secretary of the regional committee himself came to see me: "Go to Varhaňovce immediately." "When does my bus leave?" I asked. "There's no time for a bus, the children are in the classroom, the teacher doesn't know what to do with them, and she wants to quit, so we'll take you there by car."

They released me from my work at the regional committee for a month and sent me to help out in the school in Varhaňovce. I had made my own Gypsy childhood: some alive in a Slovak school. But now I looked at the whole situation from a bird's-eye view, because I had also been able to take on the role of a teacher. The teacher told a child "sit down," and the child stayed standing, because he didn't understand. When something like that happened thirty times an hour, she grew tired and forgot that the child wasn't doing it on purpose but simply because he didn't understand. The child wanted to go to the bathroom and the teacher wouldn't let him go, thinking he wanted to run away from school, the child peed in the classroom, and the teacher scolded him. I taught her the most important Romani words and phrases and she was boundlessly grateful. I also taught the Romani children in Slovak. Then the teacher asked the children how to say this and that in the Gypsy language, and the children were happy to be teaching the teacher. They were terribly proud of that. We made up a fun game of teachers and pupils, the real teacher and pupils switching roles and giving each other grades, awards, and small punishments, class was going splendidly, and every one of us took away something new that we had learned in the game. Many years later, when I was studying at the university by correspondence courses, I found out that Comenius himself had advocated *schola ludus* – learning through play.

But then some responsible officials remarked earnestly that it was inappropriate to cultivate backward habits in the children such as speaking Gypsy. "Gypsy isn't a language at all but a dying mumbo-jumbo, progressive gypsies decided all by themselves to refuse to speak Gypsy, and teaching children Gypsy is a regressive tendency which deviates from the line of the party and the government. Citizens of Gypsy origin will never measure up to standard if they don't abandon their backward way of life and their backward way of speaking!" Thus read the decree. I got a directive to go around to all the Romani families and persuade the parents not to speak Gypsy to the children.

One comrade asked me: "Comrade, how do you say 'kiss me'?" I didn't know what he meant by that, whether I should be offended or laugh. But he had a very serious expression on his face and explained himself, saying: "Imagine, comrade, that a Gypsy mother is caressing her child and says to him 'kiss me,' how do you say that in Gypsy?" " *Čumide man*," I replied. "Well there you go!" he exclaimed victoriously, "you yourself be the judge, which sounds better, our Slovak '*pobozkaj ma*' or your Gypsy '*čumide man*'?" And that was another argument for our children forgetting about their native language.

I had within me a thousand-year-old shyness with "white" people, and we Roma had appropriated a scornful attitude toward our own language, in which not a single public sign was written, in which not a single book had been printed, which was not heard on the stage, on the radio, or in any public tribune, and so I actually did begin trying to persuade Romani parents, saying: "Speak Slovak with your children so they don't have problems in school! They won't get anywhere with Gypsy speech. After all, you want your children to live better than the Gypsies live today. If they don't go to school, they'll never be civilized, they'll never understand what their rights are, and they'll be shunned everywhere just like people shun you, in the courtroom, in public offices... Don't speak Gypsy to your children!" And I laid all this on people's hearts in our beautiful, sweet, ancient tongue. They nodded their heads, in some places the lady of the house quickly made some *haluški* so she could treat me like a guest, in some places I had to drink a toast with a glass of slivovitz – black coffee wasn't the fashion yet in those days – and then we starting talking about the usual topics: what was interesting, horrifying, or comical that had happened somewhere in the region, about our relatives, there were a number of songs, and I even took part in storytelling sessions – and as I was leaving on the last bus to Prešov, I said to myself in my spirit that a way of speaking so given to song and storytelling could never disappear from the earth.

Grocery ration cards

I went to Stropkov to carry out an inspection of the cultural activities in the district. At the regional office they made a reservation in a hotel for me, yet after finishing my work I didn't go to the hotel but into the settlement to see the Roma. There was a large settlement at Stropkov, perhaps fifty shanties. Dirty, naked children, skin and bones, lice-infested, their eyes running with pus, scabies.

My arrival at this settlement was a strange one. I had never been there before and they didn't know me. When from a distance the people saw that a city-dressed person was approaching the settlement, they disappeared so fast it was as if the earth had swallowed them up. The shouting of children's voices was enveloped by the silence among the shanties. During the war, the Hlinka Guards and gendarmes had probably made plenty of visits here, too, to harass the gypsies for their own twisted pleasure. Roma retained their fear of the *gadže* for a long, long time after the war, and just as the *gadže* made no distinctions between Gypsies, so did many Roma see every *gadžo* in the world as a *dilino*, a blockhead, a madman, a tightwad, and a filthy creature who would eat even shit if it didn't stink.

I stood on the edge of the deserted settlement and shouted: "*Aven arde, Romale! Ma daran!*" – come here, people, don't be afraid! Only now did a swarm of children come streaming out and the women stand on the thresholds of the shanties.

166

I set out in the direction of the first shanty. One after another, the women came out to meet me. *"Khatar sal?"* – where are you from? – the usual opening question in the getting-acquainted ceremony, asked by a thin, dark Romani woman who looked more like an Indian. I introduced myself as Mikluš' daughter from Šariš, and the people began opening up to me. "I work at the regional committee and I came to ask if there wasn't anything you needed," I said.

"My, woman, but you're a godsend!" rejoiced the dark Romani woman.

"Don't tell her anything! Don't tell her anything!" another woman shrieked from the doorway of one of the shanties. "They'll take us to the camp, they'll make us into soap!"

"Listen, aren't I just as black as you are? Don't I speak our language? May my children die if I've come to do you harm!" The fact that I'd sworn on my children's lives had an effect.

"If you help us in our trouble," the dark woman said, "heaven will give health and happiness to you and your children and your entire clan! Listen to what they're doing with us! They're not giving us grocery ration cards. We have nothing to live on!" And one mother after another started pushing their emaciated, rickety children in front of me. They crowded, pressed, and thronged, this blended mass of human bodies. If a *gadžo* official found himself in a situation like this, he'd have been scared stiff. If only because he'd grown up in an environment where from the time they were little, people kept their distance from each other. Keeping their distance in spacious flats, in the paved streets of the towns, on the classroom benches, and in office rooms. Roma, from the time they're born, touch each other: when they sleep three or four to a bed, when they press onto a bench around the table, in the crowded rooms of their shanties, one person can't walk around another without touching him. When fifty people take their place on twenty square meters to listen to a *paramisi* – fairy tale, they can't not touch. And when people are discussing matters in a group *pre vatra*, in the public area of the settlement, one woman leans against another and brothers, cousins, friends hold each other round the shoulder – and this touch binds them, gives them strength, security, a feeling of safety. But anyone who doesn't grow up with this can't understand it.

The men made their way to this serious discussion of grocery ration cards, and they explained to me how things were. Only those who were employed got ration cards. The Roma worked for the peasants on the free market – and they were paid under the table, because private entrepreneurs weren't allowed to employ anyone. There were no other job opportunities.

"Listen," I said, "I can't promise you anything, but tomorrow morning at nine o'clock, come to the district committee. The tenth department is responsible for the distribution of goods." They invited me in, wanting to treat me at least to a pancake made of flour and water, but I had to get to the bus.

The next morning I traveled to Stropkov again and went straight to see the head of the district committee. "How come the Gypsy citizens aren't getting grocery ration cards? Are they kulaks or something?"

The head of the committee looked at me, surprised, and directed me to the tenth department. So I went to the tenth department and said to the lady official working there: "How come the Gypsy citizens aren't getting grocery ration cards? The committee head instructed that they receive them even if they aren't employed. This instruction is supposed to affect the kulaks and not citizens who don't keep cows or pigs or chickens or even moths, because in their homes the moths would die of hunger!"

The lady official started making excuses that such a thing wasn't possible, because they had regulations and directives for these things. But in the meantime the committee head called, and I heard what kind of lecture he was giving her over the phone. He was afraid I would file a report with the regional committee.

I said to the official, amicably: "Aren't Gypsies people?" "Sure, but when they come to my office, they're always shoving!" "And because of that their children don't have a right to their milk?" "Our citizens come one at a time, but with them, if one person wants something, then the whole horde comes running!" "And because of that you take their bread from them?" "And then they start speaking their mumbo-jumbo right away, and it looks like they're arguing! And also it's all Cina, Cina, Cina, every other one is named Cina, and then I don't know who I've given a ration card to and who I haven't." "Why don't you go to the settlement to find out?" I asked, spitefully, because I knew very well why: a *gadžo* would never set foot in the settlement. "I'd never come back alive!" the official snorted. "You've got to be afraid of them!"

I couldn't even get angry after I saw her in her little poplin blouse, her hair coiffed, her hands well-tended. A person like that could hardly grasp that someone who went around ragged and barefoot, with dirt under their fingernails and hair like feathers was just as scared of her painted fingernails and high-heeled shoes as she was of their rag-covered nakedness.

I promised the official that I would help her make a list of the families in the settlement, and that for every Cina we would determine their true, *romano nav* – Romani name – which would distinguish them from the rest of the Cinas. She thanked me and was glad.

In the meantime the men from the settlement had come to look for me at the office. There were about ten or fifteen of them. They had put on the best clothes they owned. Their lard-smeared hair was arrested in billowing waves. The head of the cultural department was walking along the corridor. "Where's your banner?" he kidded them. I told him to stop. He rolled his eyes and walked away.

We went down to the settlement to make a list of the adults and children. They started distributing the grocery ration cards the very same day. When the Roma saw me sitting behind an official's desk in an office, they said only: aaah! I was supposed to go back to Prešov that evening, but the people wouldn't let me go. In every shanty there was in the settlement, they had put together a feast from what they had bought with the ration cards. I had to eat at least a mouthful in everyone's house. Then they called me up to the first shanty, where the woman who had first spoken with me lived. They had the largest room. There were so many people you could breathe only with difficulty. She overwhelmed me with a flood of questions: what's going to become of us? What do the *gadže* want to do with us? Why are we black? Where will we find work? How do Roma in other countries live? Why do they curse us, calling us Gypsies ...? I had spoken at many conferences, congresses, to delegates from sixty countries at the international congress of the Red Cross, at training sessions for political workers, and in the highest places I had had to answer questions about why gypsies this, why Gypsies that, but never had I been so helplessly ignorant as then in Stropkov. After we are educated enough to secure our own equality, after we understand what kind of society we live in, and how we should live in it ... I spoke from my heart, but I knew that it was a long and winding road to what I was saying.

Day was breaking, and the people were still asking questions and more questions.

My eyes closed. I could hardly speak anymore.

"Get out of my house!" my host shouted in Romani fashion, which can seem harsh, but no one took any offense from it. "Get out of my house, can't you see that the woman is dying with fatigue?" The people began to disperse and my host fixed up a bed for me. A snow-white duvet cover. Where had she gotten it in the middle of such poverty? And where did all the others go to sleep when they had left me their only bed? Half-asleep, I felt my host putting one more blanket over the duvet and saying: "Our partisan fighter."

Just for fun

There's a Romani saying that goes: *ruv furt lela palal bakres, gadžo furt lela palal Romes* – the wolf never stops chasing the sheep and the *gadžo* never stops hounding the Rom. I had become a member of the Communist Party, a lot of comrades treated me with respect, gave me a hand in my work, did their best to help me out when I couldn't manage with the children and the housework – but my experience showed me that the saying was still true.

One night at home someone knocked on our door. We were still living in the basement apartment. "Who is it?" I asked. "Open up, auntie!" someone said in Romani. On the other side of the door was a group of Roma. I didn't know a single one of them. The womenfolk were all in tears, the men were bruised all over, blood on their shirts. Ragged, barefoot. I immediately invited them in. My husband also got up from the bed. The Roma were from Sobrance. They had come to tell us that the cops had beat them up for no reason. They came to the settlement and started thrashing Roma like there was no tomorrow.

"But why? What did you do?"

No one really knew why. Nothing had been explained to anyone. They beat anyone they got a hold of and then drove off. "That's impossible," I said. "They must have had some reason! If you want me to stand up for you, you've got to tell me the truth!"

"Better make them some tea and give them something to eat!" my husband said. I made *haluški* and tea and then I took some shoes and two men's shirts from the wardrobe and gave them to the group. I said that in today's world a cop didn't have the right to beat anyone, and that they had to go to the doctor the next day to get a medical report written up.

The next day they really did go to the doctor's. He examined them and gave them a medical report sealed in an envelope. They proudly came to see me to show me the envelope. I opened it up, even though I knew that wasn't something you were supposed to do. I read the report and shouted at them: "Look at what that doctor wrote for you!" They stood up and looked on helplessly. Not a single one of them knew how to read. I read it to them myself. I didn't understand all the words, but the report said their bleeding and burst blood vessels, manifesting themselves as bruises, were caused by a vitamin deficiency and that they should supplement their diet with more fruits and vegetables. "Do you understand now why they treat you like dirt? Because you have no education! Because you can't read and write! Do you send your children to school at all?"

And once again my husband told me: "Give them something to eat and make them some tea."

I set out for the regional police headquarters. I knew the chief, and he had seen our theater perform and liked it. His name was Holub. I explained to him what the situation was. "That's impossible!" he said, then he put me in his car and went with me to Sobrance personally. The local police chief's answer to our questions was such that I didn't know whether to laugh or to cry. "If the Gypsies fight among themselves and go around with a busted head it doesn't bother them, but if our boys knock them around a little, the first thing they do is go complain!"

"And why did they knock them around? What did they do that for?"

He said the womenfolk were shouting at each other in Gypsy in town, walking around barefoot, carrying wood in sheets of canvas, and so making a public nuisance of themselves. "And that's why your men beat them up?" I asked. "Well how are we supposed to teach them to wear shoes and not shout all over the place in Gypsy?" "That's what Maria Theresa used to do, have a Gypsy given fifty lashes for speaking Gypsy!" I said, angered. "And did your men at least beat the ones who go around shouting?" "That doesn't matter, one Gypsy's as good as another, one of them shouts one day, tomorrow it'll be a different one. And if one of them is taught a lesson, the rest'll pay attention!" "That's what I used to hear from the Hlinka Guards and from the gendarmes under the wartime Slovak state!" I said. "You're standing up for them! As if you were one of them!" the local police chief looked me over, suspiciously. "And what do you think I am? One of them!" "I thought you were a Bulgarian or something ..." Like many other people, he couldn't make the connection between what I looked like and the way I dressed and acted.

The regional police chief was entirely on my side. He threatened the local chief with dismissal if anything like this ever happened again. The local chief evidently took it to heart, because later I heard from the local Roma that the cops were leaving them alone.

I had traveled from hope to despair and from despair to hope. New laws, slogans, headlines, speeches at meetings, and training sessions promised that we would start to live better and more happily. We believed it would happen right away. But the cases I had to deal with day after day showed that the new, better life was taking hold unbearably slowly. But on the other hand, when I managed to secure someone a building permit, social support payments, or to organize a literacy course in which a few people learned how to read and write, I began to believe once again that everything was changing for the better.

In 1952 we got a flat. A real one. It was on the first floor of an older but well-preserved house. We had a room and a kitchen, and at that time there were six of us living there. Even that flat offered me hope that everything was developing for the better.

A living bridge

One time my path took me to a town on the banks of the Topľa. A lazy, sprawling, eastern Slovak river. On the other side of the river there was a settlement. A hillside and some shanties rocking back and forth. The shouts and laughter of children reached across the river. I resolved to go to the settlement and have a look. I looked for a bridge, and there was none anywhere. A peasant who was walking past me said: "Oh, the bridge is out in Domaš, that's seven kilometers from here."

"And how do the citizens get to the other side?" I asked.

170

"What citizens?" the peasant asked, amazed. I pointed with my arm outstretched to the Gypsy settlement.

"Those are just Gypsies," the peasant said. "And if one of our people wants to get over to that side," he added, "well – you see those two people over there?"

On the bank of the river, a little downstream, there were two people standing. A tall man and a small but hefty woman.

"Go talk to them, they'll have something to tell you ..." and the peasant walked off. I set off in their direction.

"Get up on my back!" the woman was shouting with a typical Romani intonation, which shoots up high and then comes hurtling down. "Come on, I tell you, get up on my back! Don't be afraid!"

"But lady, what's all this about?" the tall man asked skeptically, all confused. By his accent I could tell he was from western Slovakia. He was some kind of tourist, with a camera across his shoulder. I still didn't understand what was going on.

"Don't be afraaaid!" the woman cried out. "The Topľa isn't deep, come on, get on, get on! You'll hang onto me round my neck. Only five crowns!" The woman could have been forty or forty-five years old, maybe fifty. A bedraggled skirt of indeterminate color, all wrung out. "Five crowns, kind sir, so my children can have some bread! May heaven bless you, get up on my back, my husband's dead, one little five-crown piece for bread for my children!" Exactly the same beggar's litany our Romani women used in Šariš. All of a sudden I was embarrassed. I didn't want this tourist fellow to lump me together with a Gypsy beggar woman. I felt like disappearing. At that instant the woman shouted: "Wait a minute, Lackaňa, until I get this young man and his snazzy clothes over to the other side, I'll come get you too!" I started panting for breath and stood rooted to the spot.

The tourist finally consented. He got up on the woman's back, broad as a table top, and she stepped into the river and slowly started wading through to the other side. I had never seen anything like it! The other thing that amazed me was – how did she know me? How did she know my name was Lacko?

The woman had waded up to the middle of the river, the water rising higher and higher on her, up to her waist. "May he have a stroke, the cheapskate," she muttered to herself in Romani, "may his hands wither up, the snazzy-pants, afraid to reach into his money-bag for a fiver!" The gurgling of the river swallowed up her muttered soliloquy: up until the middle of the river where the water covered her ample breasts, when she drowned out the river herself: "Don't squeeze my neck so hard, you snazzy-pants, you'll choke me! And you'll drown like a mouse!"

Once on the other side of the river, the tourist got down. He took out his change purse and paid. The woman stuck the money in her bosom. Five crowns in the old money – that's worth one crown in the new money. The tourist went on his way and the woman waded back toward me. "Come on, Lackaňa, get on, get on!"

"How do you know who I am, woman?"

"Aren't you the partisan fighter Lacko, Mikluš' daughter from Šariš?" she asked, wanting to make sure, but then she answered herself. "Who else would you be, black as shoe polish and dressed like a lady ... you get grocery ration cards for the Roma and keep an eye on the cops so they don't beat us up ... Come on and have a look at where we live!"

"But auntie, you can't carry me on your back!"

171

"May you have a stroke by morning if you don't get up on my back this instant!" she shouted good-naturedly. And then she told me that she had been ferrying people for over a year now, since her husband died. She carried peasants, tourists, saleswomen, teachers, the postman, and even the head of the district committee. Not cops, though, they had a car and drove to Domaš where there was a bridge. The Roma waded through the river by themselves. She was forty years old and still had two small children she had to feed.

"Why don't they build a bridge for you all?" I asked with enlightened umbrage.

"Don't get crazy, Lackaňa, after all I couldn't earn any money if they put up a bridge! Who would I carry over? I have seven children, the hungry little mites!"

I positioned myself on her back and she crossed over to the other side with me. I wanted to give her money for her children. She wouldn't take it from me. From her bosom she took out the five-crown piece the tourist had given her, and she gave it to me. "What are you doing, auntie, are you crazy, you have seven hungry children!"

"Don't you get crazy, Lackaňa, I've only got two hungry children, the rest of them feed themselves, the scoundrels, they've all got their own families! May you be crippled by morning if you don't take that money from me!"

"But what for, auntie?"

"For going around so nicely dressed and bringing honor to the Gypsies!"

It felt like the world went spinning and I will apparently never be capable of describing the sun that lit up inside my head at that moment.

Why there was no cardboard for roofing

Everything happened because there was no cardboard for making roofs with. I went to Svidník. That whole area was devastated by the war. Burnt-out houses, scorched countryside, the blackened stumps of trees. In the town they had started building a new hotel, the Dukla, and they needed workers. In the district they asked me: "Get us some Gypsies, you know how to talk to them, you're a dark one yourself, they trust you." They didn't say: you're a Gypsy woman yourself, they didn't dare, because "Gypsy" was understood to be offensive, as an insult.

I went traveling all over the Valley of Death – that's what people called the whole burnt-out area – and drummed up workers. The peasants didn't go to work on construction projects. They traveled en masse to the Czech lands to wheel and deal. They traded lard and bacon for grocery ration cards and sold the ration cards at home. Mostly to the big landowners – people called them kulaks – because they had no right to grocery ration cards. It was the Roma who went to work on construction projects, and the fact that they had found work there became apparent in the settlements. In many of the settlements in the area you began to see small houses with walls, even *štokovce*, one-story structures, and people went around well-dressed and the children weren't as gaunt as they were elsewhere.

The Dukla Hotel was also built by Roma from Kapišová. One day the Kapišová men came to see me at the regional committee in Prešov, and they said: "Comrade auntie, get us some cardboard for roofing. The water's getting in our houses, the children are sick, and they don't want to give us anything at the district office. We'll pay for it, we don't want something for nothing, we'll earn the money, but there's no cardboard!"

I revved off to the district office to ask for some materials Roma could use to repair their houses. At the construction department they told me there weren't any materials for the settlements because everything was going for Project P – for those who had been hurt by the war.

"You mean to say that Gypsy citizens weren't hurt by the war?" I asked, angered.

"Not according to the guidelines for Project P, because the settlements are on the edge of civilization and so they weren't burned out."

"You mean to say that Gypsy citizens weren't hurt by the war, the way racist laws drove them from the towns into temporary shanties?"

"Under the guidelines in effect for Project P that's not being hurt by the war!" The official had started digging in his papers and was about to read me the guidelines for Project P. I slammed the door and went straight to the secretary of the district committee. He cut me short, saying there simply wasn't any cardboard for the Gypsies' shanties! "What are you racking your brains for, comrade," he cracked, "the gypsies have always known how to take care of themselves."

I slammed the door yet again and decided to take advantage of my official powers. I went straight off to Bratislava to the labor and social affairs commission. They treated me quite beautifully. "You know what, comrade," the director of the labor section suggested to me, "You get your charges work in the Czech lands and we'll give you negotiating authority."

I found out from our Roma that they were recruiting laborers at the coal mines in Most, and that they were willing to offer housing to seasonal workers. At the Bohemia Brown Coal Mining Concern, that is. I traveled off to Most. The Northern Bohemia Brown Coal Mining Concern were all applause! Excellent, we'll take the seasonal workers! We've got these barracks left over from when there were French prisoners of war here, they'll get along beautifully there.

"But these citizens won't go anywhere without their families. Gypsies are used to being together with all their relatives," I said, a little apprehensively. But the coal mine bosses agreed to everything. "Let them come with their great-grandmothers too," they joked, because they had a real labor shortage.

I went from Most back to Bratislava, and the labor and social affairs commission entrusted me with organizing the transfer of the Kapišová Roma to Most. The Prešov regional committee was supposed to cover the transit costs.

Four moving vans come to Kapišová, we loaded up the women, the men, the children, their pots and feather-blankets, and drove to the train station in Prešov. The district committee secretary could have gone crazy over it all. "You're taking our workers from us! Who's going to finish building the hotel?" All of a sudden he was willing to give them the cardboard for their roofs. No wonder he was enraged, he'd lost seventy workers. And I said: "It's too late."

The seventy men and their families went to the Czech lands. Four hundred people in all. When the trucks were going through Svidník, the Roma were waving, shouting, and singing – they were heading for the promised land. Clumps of gaping onlookers stood on the streets and stared at what was going on.

In Prešov we took our seats on the train. We had two cars reserved. We traveled all night. And had another transfer in Prague. Finally we were in Most! Representatives of the coal mines were waiting for us at the train station. They went to install us in our housing. Another transfer, into moving vans, and off we went to Záluž. They plopped us in front of these long, wooden barracks. Every family got one large room, maybe thirty square meters. Every room had a stove and an iron bed, a table and four chairs, and a wardrobe. Our Roma had never dreamed of such luxury! The children went skipping along the floorboards – at home they had only walked on compacted earth – squealing at how it boomed, and the old people groaned with fear that they would fall through to the devils.

The whole afternoon we moved the individual families into their quarters. Toward the end it was too dark to see, but the electricity wasn't working because in those days the current often went out. And all of a sudden the light came on. On the sidewalks, in all the rooms, in the washroom, everywhere. The whole barracks was glowing. Plenty of the Kapišová Roma had never seen an electric light. At that instant it was so quiet you could have heard a fly crawling along the strings of a violin, and then everyone started yelling, squealing, calling to each other, the men threw their hats up to the ceiling, jumping, rolling on the ground, the children jumping up and down, stomping on the floor, and the women hugging each other.

The gentlemen from the coal mines were terribly frightened. They pressed in around me: "What's happened to them? What's wrong?" I explained that most of these dark-skinned citizens had never seen an electric light before, and that they were rejoicing.

The Kapišová Roma stayed in the Most area for three years. All the men worked, even a one-legged, seventy-year-old grandfather – he tended the roses in the park. The people were earning money. The Prešov regional committee sent me on an inspection tour once every three months. Every time, the Kapišová men pulled out their wallets stuffed with hundred-crown notes and boasted: "Looky here, auntie! Looky here!" But then a recruiter from Svidník started coming after them and tempting them home. He made them promises up and down, cardboard for their roofs, materials to repair their shanties. And so one day the whole Kapišová brigade packed up and headed back to Slovakia. They got some help from the district too, the settlement had done well for itself, and some people put up nice little houses with the money they'd saved. But after a while they started coming to see me again: "Ilonka, take us back to Bohemia!" "If you were able to get back here, you can get yourself back to Bohemia!" I said, and didn't worry about it any more after that.

I want to mention one more adventure that happened to me on the train when I was traveling with the Kapišová Roma to Most. I was traveling first class, I needed to get a good sleep. I was awfully tired from organizing everything, and the following day the trip back awaited me. I found a free seat in a compartment, leaned my head against the wall, and started falling asleep. All of a sudden I heard a man's voice: "This Gypsy woman's probably lost her way." I was nicely dressed, in an outfit, and at first I didn't think it had anything to do with me. Then it occurred to me that there was no other Gypsy woman here. I opened my eyes. "Lady," said the gentlement sitting opposite me. "This is first class here. After the conductor comes you'll have to change your seat. You'd better move now so you find a free place."

"And what makes you think I ought to move?" my blood started boiling. I knew why: evidently he'd never seen a Gypsy woman traveling first class before!

"I only wanted to let you know ... excuse me ... if you don't have a ticket to somewhere else ..." he started apologizing.

I pulled out my first-class ticket and showed it to him, then I pulled out my travel orders from the labor commission, my identity card as a member of the central committee of the Red Cross, my working papers from the regional committee ... I stuck everything in from of his face so he could see.

"No, no, no!" he was defending himself, desperately. "I believe you ..."

"You think that a Gypsy woman has to be ragged and dirty and uneducated!" I was awfully tired and didn't have the strength to get a hold of myself. Then I saw how the man was paling with horror over what this Gypsy woman would do to him and whether she wouldn't slit his throat. My rage passed. I put my papers together and back in my purse. "No offense taken," I said, "you're not the only one with that kind of opinion about Gypsies."

Then another gentleman spoke, this time in Czech. He said he remembered the Gypsy tinkers from before the war. They were excellent craftsmen, and their wives wore golden earrings. They murdered them all during the war. Another man, from Slovakia, added that he knew an outstanding lead violinist who had a withered arm and played the violin like a cello, but he played in a way that brought the professors from the Bratislava conservatory to listen to him. Then we fell asleep. In the morning we said good-bye amicably and wished each other a pleasant journey.

Gypsy woman

The thing our Roma are touchiest about is when people call them Gypsy. It's such a humiliating and disgraceful word that it sounds like the worst insult to us. How could it be otherwise, when instead of saying "don't lie," Slovaks say "don't Gypsy." Or "dirty as a Gypsy," "ragged as a Gypsy," "hungry as a Gypsy," "steals like a Gypsy," and "as messy as in a Gypsy Camp!" How then are those Roma who aren't either ragged or dirty and who don't lie and steal not supposed to feel offended when someone calls them a Gypsy?

How did my co-workers at the regional committee look at me as a Gypsy woman? I was the very first Romani woman official, just as sure as Prešov is Prešov. A Gypsy woman official, and as black as I am on top of it all! I tried hard to go around perfectly dressed so that no one could call me "Gypsy woman!" I tried hard to be twice as well-behaved and polite. My co-workers treated me nicely, I can't complain, but all the same when I closed the door, I can't tell you how many times I heard the words "that Gypsy woman!" Maybe they didn't even mean anything bad by it, they just couldn't conceive of what someone felt like when you called them a Gypsy woman instead of Ilona or Lacko. It hurt me. And it hurt me still more when someone wanted to show me respect and said: Ilon, you're so well-behaved or you're so intelligent, it's as if you weren't even a Gypsy! Usually I didn't say anything in reply, but deep down inside I had to grapple with a hatred towards all things white.

There were three of us women working in the office. We dealt with the clients who came in by sides. If some people from the white "side" came in, of course you addressed them formally: good day, please sit down, what do have on your mind, what do you need? If a Rom opened the door, my co-workers let fly with: hey you, what do you want? Why'd you come? People from the black "side" were of course always treated just any old way. A twenty-two-year-old whippersnapper with painted nails would speak that way to the mother of ten children, to the respected mayor of a settlement, or to a renowned lead violinist. It was unheard of for an office worker to offer a Gypsy a chair. The Roma delivered their petitions or complaints standing in the doorway. A white client was automatically invited to sit down. Sometimes this behavior so incensed me that only with difficulty did I manage to keep from insulting my colleagues in the ancient Romani way. Sometimes I wanted to tell them to treat people from the black "side" like human beings. But I didn't know how. I was afraid that I would get inappropriately angry and explode or that I would break out in tears. Then I started to do it by offering a chair to the Roma who came in to see me, and addressing them formally on principle, even if we knew each other, and treating them like members of the aristocracy: "Won't you sit down, what can I do for you?"

My co-workers gradually began to realize that they had to treat Roma differently than they'd been treating them. One of them then started saying Mr. and Mrs. to those from the black "side," and the other just sent all the Roma to me: "Over there, yes, there, that's where your representative is!" She couldn't learn a new way of doing things, just couldn't bring herself to say "Mr." and "Mrs." and doing things the old way felt embarrassing to her.

When a Rom becomes an official

When a Rom becomes an official, it's just like it is with a Czech or a Slovak: some people look for ways to help others, other look for ways to help themselves and their family.

One day a woman came to the regional committee dressed up to the nines. I said to myself: "Is it a Romani woman or not?" She looked like a Romani woman, even though she was lighter than I was. She had a cultured way of doing things, she knocked on the door – and that was something most Roma didn't do then. In poor settlements the way into a shanty was through a piece of sackcloth, not a door – so what were they supposed to knock on? The young woman greeted us in Slovak, but when she looked around and determined that there were just the two of us in the room, she said in Romani: "So you get to be an official but I don't?"

She was younger than I. I said: "Where are you from? Who's your family?" "I'm the daughter of Cina from Stropkov. They call me Zuna." "Why couldn't you be an official? But you have to have some schooling to do that." "I finished fifth grade," she said, "and also a two-year program of studies. I always enjoyed learning, but I had to look after the younger children, you know how it goes!"

I took a trip with her to Stropkov to see the secretary of the local committee. He liked to drink. He was a congenial fellow. I put in a good word for her to get them to give her a job working on the Gypsy question and to give her some kind of a chance to finish her schooling and learn some office duties. "Well, well, well," said the secretary, "we've got a whole flock of Gypsies here and we can't even talk to each other, she can translate for us, at least!"

And so there was one more Romani woman official, Zuna, daughter of Cina from Stropkov. In those days that was a very big deal. The next time I came to Stropkov, she knew how to type. She really was very clever. I was glad. I said to myself: "If only there were more of us like this! I was even more glad that she really did work for Roma lovingly and with fairness.

Naturally, I also met Roma who climbed the ladder in order to grab as much for themselves and their family as they could. There's a saying: *te Rom kamel, kaj les o gadžo te likerel manušeske, mušinel pes ajci šelvarbiš te presikhavel sar koda gadžo* – if a Rom wants a *gadžo* to consider him a human being, it has to be a hundred and twenty times more obvious that there's something to him. Some of our people take this to mean that if their *gadžo* neighbor has one television, one car, and one house, they have to have two televisions, two cars, and two houses or better yet, two palaces. If they distance themselves from Gypsyness – messiness, dirtiness, the defensive wiles of the powerless – that's all right, but often, out of fear that someone will associate them with Gypsies, that kind of people end up distancing themselves from Romaniness. They pass themselves off as Hungarians, they're ashamed of our way of speaking, and they look down on all other Roma. That's why there's a saying: *te pes Rom dochudel pre kajso than sar gadžo, mek goreder dikhel opral pre Romende sar oda gadžo* – if a Rom gets to the same place as a *gadžo*, he disparages other Roma even worse than the *gadžo*.

I met one Romani functionary like that. It was all the same to him who he fleeced, the most important thing was that everyone else display envy of who he was and what he had. I won't give either his name or the name of the settlement he came from. He worked in a highly-placed position on the party district committee. His father had made his fortune before the war. How? Because he was a *degeš* and didn't shun any kind of work. They needed someone in the town who would empty out the cesspools. No *žužo Rom*, clean Rom, would take on that kind of work. It was all the same to this family, though, the four brothers got down on the horses and cart and started emptying out the cesspools. They loaded the human waste into barrels and dumped them into the river. Though they had become enormously rich, the other Roma shunned them, shouting *god'aris*, shit-drinker, at them. But those *degeše* had skins like sheet metal, all that mocking just bounced off of it and they went on getting richer. I don't know what they were up to during the war, maybe they paid off the people from the Hlinka Guards and had a good time, but I can't confirm that because I really don't know. In any case, their son graduated from the high school – naturally, they'd moved from the settlement to the town – and he got on the district committee of the Slovak Communist Party. The Roma from the settlement went to see him like he was one of them. One person would want decent housing and needed a construction permit, one person came asking for social welfare payments, and another one was looking for work. The functionary would tend to lots of matters, but only for those who could grease his palm. After some time he had built, not a house, but a palace. One day I went walking by there and some other people on foot said: "Hey, hey, that's where the gyp lives!" They were amazed and envious, but they still called him a gyp.

One time it happened that a river that had overflowed its banks washed away a couple of shanties in the settlement where he grew up. I came to deal with the situation of the afflicted families. I found out about him, went to see him at the district committee of the Slovak Communist Party, and said to him in our speech: "My boy, will you come with me to the settlement? You're from here, you know the people, we'll consult about what to do and how to do it."

He replied in Slovak, as if he couldn't speak our language at all: "Cooom-rade, you want to go to the settlement? I absolutely refuse to go among all those *degeše*!" "And aren't you one of them? Didn't you grow up among them? Don't you have any relatives there?" He looked at me so much like the devil, that I started to be afraid he would give me the evil eye. I went by myself. On foot, because there was no transportation to the settlement. When I came back, he was waiting for me at the district committee. He asked in his unpleasant, slippery way: "So, cooom-rade, how did you do?"

"You could have come with me, comrade, and you would have seen," I said and didn't speak with him anymore after that. He hated me and lodged a complaint against me, but it didn't stick. On the contrary, his way of operating and his bribe-taking were discovered and he was immediately thrown out of office and also the party. But he started working on a forced-labor crew and made even more money.

That's what some Roma are like. It's too bad. But what can you do? In every society you'll find people who don't deserve to be called human beings.

Laci Petalo

We dealt with the situation of the families whose shanties had been washed away by the river by moving them to Třinec. We were constantly receiving information about places in the Czech lands where there was a labor shortage. The settlement afflicted by the flooding was a large one. They had their own school there, and even – something you absolutely never saw! – their own Gypsy cemetery. The director of the school was a humane person, could speak Romani decently, and was a great help to me. He let the afflicted families sleep in school provisionally. We summoned all the Roma to the school, I read them the terms of seasonal employment in the Třinec steelworks, and not only those who had lost their housing but a host of others as well signed up. Within a week they were in Třinec with their families.

The factory housed them in nice, new dormitories, and they even had a soccer field and a volleyball court there. I went on an inspection tour three months later. The factory was happy with the workers. One young girl had been trained as a crane operator. She had hair black as midnight, long and thick, and she tied it up in a kerchief like a pirate, with the knot over her ear. She operated the crane with the expression of a queen on her face. I asked her: "Little daughter, doesn't it make your head spin?" "Not at all, auntie!" she laughed.

One day the district committee invited me to the town where the settlement was to come and negotiate something important. I went. They said that all the officials would be happy if their gypsies stayed in Třinec for good. That way the settlement would be made significantly smaller, and it would be easier to liquidate. And you would absolve yourselves of any responsibility for the gypsies, I said to myself in my spirit. But even to me, it seemed like a way for the local Roma there to get better flats and better jobs.

I set off for Třinec. At the factory, they told me they were satisfied with our people as laborers, because they took jobs as trench-diggers and cleaning women, as assistant laborers, and no one else wanted to do that kind of work. "We'll take them right away!" said the factory leadership and the Revolutionary Union Movement and the party. "And they'll get flats within six months." The Roma gave their agreement and were joyful and enthusiastic. The next day a meeting was called where all the details were to be negotiated. "Boys," I said, "what to you say to having flats with washrooms within six months?"

"Nooooo!" they said, and it exploded like a hand grenade. "We're going home!" They wouldn't even hear of staying in Třinec. They left the meeting and went back to the settlement, where they built new shanties with the money they had earned. I was devastated and said to myself: "No, never again in my life do I want to have anything to do with Gypsies!"

But all of a sudden a song started to make the rounds among Roma, one that evidently no one remembers today:

Dža tu Laci Petalona,	Go away, Laci Petalo,
dikhes sar roven o Roma,	look at how the Roma are crying,
te len čororen kideha,	you gather them up, the poor ones,
so ča tu len te chal deha?	and what will you give them to eat?

A notice appeared in the newspaper *Red Justice* that Petalo, the Gypsy king, was asking the United Nations for some territory in Africa, where he wanted to establish a Gypsy state. On the basis of this report an enormous panic spread among Roma that they were going to be taken off to Africa. The Roma who had come to the Czech lands to work returned en masse to Slovakia, to the settlements, to their communities, where they felt safer. And so there was nothing for me to do but show understanding for this flight from Třinec and to tell myself: "I have to stick it out. I have to keep going."

An award

Always, whenever I felt I just couldn't go on, at just the right moment I was given some formal recognition, and that roused me to keep working. In 'fifty-five, on the tenth anniversary of the liberation, I was decorated for rebuilding the city of Prešov. My husband didn't know anything about it. He was walking along the street with some officials, when suddenly he heard from the city radio station: "Among those decorated for the rebuilding of the city of Prešov is also our dear comrade, Elena Lacko." Then I had a short speech. Jozef stopped in his tracks and said to the officials: "Wait a minute, wait a minute, that's my wife speaking there!" Then he came over to see me, the officials right behind him: "Come on, show me! Show me!" I heard him shouting even before he got there.

"And what should I show you?" "Your certificate, you! Your award!" They had given us a certificate rolled up in a red case with a star on it. My husband was proud of me, and invited me to the Savoj for coffee.

How did I come to deserve any credit for the rebuilding of Prešov? During the war, Prešov had been bombed to pieces during the carpet bombing. They needed people who would build it back up again. The peasants were busy with getting their farms running again, so they didn't go to work on the construction projects. But our Roma, on the contrary, didn't have jobs. They came to see me from the construction offices: "Look here, you get us some gypsies. If we send our recruiters into the settlements, the Gypsies run away and hide from them, afraid we're going to take them off to some camp. We can't arrange anything with them."

And so I went round the settlements and got up some men for work: Chmiňany, Sabinov, Svinia, Šariš, everywhere we used to go for the fairs and where I knew the Roma. We got at least five hundred people together for doing construction work.

In 1956 I got another award. I was sent to the international congress of the Red Cross as a delegate. The congress was held in the Municipal Hall in Prague, and there were participating delegates from sixty-six countries. Before the congress I got together with several Romani people I knew from Prague. At that time there was a singing and dancing ensemble in Hloubětín, they wrote a welcoming statement for the congress, I read it out, added a few words of my own, and was applauded for it. During the break the secretary of the congress came up to me and said I should speak up in the general discussion, because the delegates would be interested in hearing how the Gypsies lived in our country. Fine. The next day I stood up during the discussion. I spoke of how the Roma today were joining the workforce, the children were starting to go to school, literacy was on the increase, and so on – but! Then I started talking about the situation in the settlements and for the rest of my speech I asked: why is it that even today, under a people's democratic regime, people are living in shanties? Why aren't there wells in the settlements? Why are Gypsy children suffering from malnutrition and trachoma, why do they have scabies and lice? Why are there still Gypsy settlements at all, with no access roads leading to them? And again I heard sobbing in the hall, and when I had finished, I received a big ovation.

The next day the newspapers wrote about my speech. It said: "The most warmly received of all the delegates was citizen of Gypsy origin Elena Lacko. She spoke of the beautiful and joyous life of the gypsies in our people's democratic republic."

What the citizens, Gypsy women, got out of the community meeting on health care

Today, years later, I wonder whether with my title and my function I couldn't have done more for the Roma in the settlements. I don't know. I had a family and children, and we had another child, Luboš, he was the last one. Someone was always wanting something from me, they practically beat down our door, one person wanted me to fill an application for social support for them, another asked me to get him a construction permit, a third to represent him in court, another for me to bring their dead husband back – I couldn't push things aside even in this case, and I tried hard to help her! Then it came about that I no longer had the energy to think clearly and I slid into the routine of a functionary. And even when I got an idea for how to deal with a situation differently than the regulations called for, it often happened that I didn't have the strength to see it through. And so once again I satisfied myself with organizing get-togethers, meetings, and cultural lectures.

One time I put together a get-together of the women in Svíně. There were two settlements in Svíně, one situated up higher and the other one down below. I went into the lower one, it was March, cold, snowing, the children were naked, barefoot, wearing only their little shirts. I went from shanty to shanty, and there was no one anywhere! The men were at work, but where were the womenfolk? I opened all the doors, one by one, looked inside, no one in the house, cold, just those naked children. There was one woman from here, Máňa, I knew well. I went to see her. "Máňa, where are all the womenfolk?"

You could smell the booze on her. "Auntie, the women have all hidden from you in the attic. They're drunk. They're ashamed. They're afraid you'll call them names!"

"Since when have I ever called you names? May you have a stroke, may you be crippled by morning, may you get a crick in your necks, may you all be taken away by typhus! Aren't you sorry for your children? Look at those children, Máňa! Naked, barefoot, in that cold! I came to invite you all to a women's get-together. A woman doctor is going to come here on Saturday and give you all a lecture, aren't you ashamed, you stinking, lice-infested, stupid women? You be at the lecture on Saturday, and if a single one of you is missing, may God punish her, may she kick the bucket!"

"You can count on it, auntie, I'll tell all the women!" Máňa could hardly keep on her feet, she was so drunk. I went away. Was I supposed to go clambering up to the attic after the drunken women? I was shaking with rage and pity. The women were drinking *čuču*, cheap fruit wine. Nothing mattered to them. Did it do any good in that squalor, in that decay, in that bog, to organize a community gathering? But the doctor had been invited, the cultural facility had been rented, and the get-together on health care had been announced ...

On Saturday all the Gypsy women came to the gathering! I was amazed. Not even one of them smelled of alcohol. The doctor spoke on hygiene. It was laughable, hygiene in those shanties! The doctor was using doctor-type words, and still, silence was strictly observed in the hall.

The lecture came to an end and I went with the doctor back to Prešov. On Monday the chair of the local women's association called me up: "Comrade Lacko, do you know what your get-together on health care brought on? The Gypsy women had such a fight that they were tearing each other's hair and an ambulance had to come and take them away afterwards!" I immediately went off to Svíně and found out what had happened. The doctor spoke in Slovak – and our Romani women understood Slovak very poorly. What's more, she was using technical words and I myself had quite a job of it trying to understand what she meant. Never in her life had she been in a Gypsy settlement, and she had no idea what the women's concerns were, how Roma operated, and how to talk to them. The Svíně Romani women were concerned with the same thing as people in other settlements: housing! Shanties in such numbers there was no room to move around in, the overpopulation of the settlement, the mud, the shortage of drinking water. One woman had somehow understood that the doctor was promising her a flat. "The *doktorka* promised *me* a flat!" she bragged to the other women after the lecture. "She promised *you* a flat? She promised *me* a flat!" "You think *you* need a flat? *We're* the ones who need a flat! How many of us are there? Like the hairs on your head – and you've only got ten of them!" The womenfolk had succumbed to a mass psychosis and started arguing. And the argument turned into such a big fight that the *gadže* had to call an ambulance.

And that's how the citizens, the Gypsy women of Svíně, got bruises, a torn ear, and bloody scratches out of the community get-together on health care.

The *bižužo* and the every-other-moon creature

The women's gathering in Šarišský Čierný went better. There were no difficulties whatsoever. At the same time I managed to help out three families by getting them building permits in the village.

I had managed to get an official car for a business trip to Šarišský Čierný. The person in charge of our car fleet was a former partisan fighter and he had seen our play *The Burning Gypsy Camp*, so I had some pull with him. He used to say: "You, Lackaňa, are a poor woman, so I'm going to make a lady out of you and you're going to be driven around in a car!" Whenever it was possible, he reserved me an official car. Of course, normally it wasn't possible and I traveled by train or by bus.

Yet that time a driver took me. I was glad, because the Šarišský Čierný settlement had also been moved away from the town during the war, and you had to go a half hour on foot just to get to the bottom of the hill, and then you had to clamber up the hill to the edge of the forest. The driver stayed waiting for me on the highway and said: "Finish what you have to do quickly, I want to be home early tonight!"

I went clambering up the slope to the settlement, and even before I got there I could see that something was wrong. There was screaming and yelling, and people were running around in front of the shanties. I tried to make my way up there as fast as I could, almost crawling on all fours, grabbing at tufts of grass to keep my feet from sliding down the muddy slope. The children ran up to meet me and told me: *Bižužo! Džungalo!* – Uncleanness! An abomination! Roma are afraid of frogs and snakes, believing they are unclean forces, devils. The children led me into the shanty where the *bižužo* appeared. I saw something that I may never see again until the day I die. A snake! But a snake so enormous that it exists perhaps only in fairy tales. It was coiled on the topmost part of the stove, its head hanging down and inhaling the steam coming from a pot of milk on the stovetop. It was as fat as a Japanese wrestler's arm I had seen not too long before on television. I also started screaming, and I ran out of the shanty and waved to the driver with all my strength to come up the hill. Quickly! quickly! I gestured to him. So he locked the car and crawled up the hill to the settlement. I led him into the shanty and pointed out the spectacle to him. As soon as he saw the snake, he disappeared. "What are we going to do?" I asked.

"You know what," the driver said. "Have them put out the fire. And then we'll smash up the stove." The driver wasn't sorry any more that he had come, because not even he had seen such an enormous snake before.

The women took the burning coals out of the stove and the men smashed it up. In an empty space among the bricks they found a nest with a bunch of little snakes. They crawled out on every side. The people let out a yell and ran to hide. In the wink of an eye the snakes disappeared as if the earth had swallowed them up. No one could persuade the Roma that they weren't an unclean force.

The women were crying that they weren't going to keep on living in this unclean place. The family where the snake appeared moved away to a neighboring settlement to stay with relatives the very same day. The rest of the families started begging me to get them building permits, that they had the money and wanted to build in the village, but the peasants wouldn't let them live there with them. I went to the local committee and told them about the terrible apparition. The driver backed up my words and described a snake still more horrible than the real one.

"You want to leave those poor Gypsy citizens to the tender mercies of an unclean force like that?" I said. "That could boomerang on you, and one fine day an unclean one might visit you as well!" It wasn't exactly the way officials spoke, which was supposed to struggle against backward superstitions and to spread atheism. Nonetheless three families from the settlement got building permits within a week and began to build in the village. The peasants accepted them. I didn't hear of any quarrels that came about. The rest of the people stayed on in the settlement. They didn't have the money to build. They began to reassure themselves by saying that the *bižužo* was an ordinary snake. There was nothing else they could do.

In eastern Slovakia, not only the Roma but also the Slovaks were made ignorant by superstitions. Not far from Prešov is a large Romani settlement – we used to go to the fairs in that village before the war and we and the Roma living there knew each other well. A woman named Taragoš was expecting a child. She worked up until the last minute, illegally, for a peasant in business for himself who had refused to join the collective farm. "May heaven preserve him from all evil," prayed Taragoš, "where will we get potatoes and milk after he joins the collective farm?!" But what do you think happened? In her seventh month, the little Taragoš baby began dancing in her womb. Every child moves, but that creature was doing somersaults, handstands, and they said he even sang on top of that. Taragoš was going not only around the settlement, but also to the village so the womenfolk could touch her belly. The peasants' wives judged that the Gypsy woman Taragoš would give birth to an every-other-moon creature. An every-other-moon creature is a being who's a man for one month and a woman the next month. They say some every-other-moon creatures are hairy, others have bats' wings, and no one has ever seen one, but everyone knows someone who has seen one in the flesh, with his own eyes.

Taragoška's birthing pains came and the peasant women prepared themselves! They surrounded her shanty, every woman with a weapon in her hand – a pitchfork, a log, a scythe, a club – in order to neutralize the creature. They waited and waited, arguing about how they would dispose of the every-other-moon creature, the main thing being not to let it fly away! An hour later the midwife came out: "Don't be scared, women, a beautiful little boy was born." Only after they had put aside their pitchforks and clubs did she come to show them the child. They looked him over from every side to see if he didn't have boar's teeth or webbed wings. They found not the least defect on him and left for home disappointed. They had so looked forward to neutralizing the every-other-moon creature!

Today there's an every-other-moon creature living somewhere in the Czech lands, with a wife named Serina and seven children. He worked in some sideline manufacturing concern, got himself a rubber stamp, and distributed money to Roma. They did well when he was around, but he didn't do so well for himself. He ran up a debt of twenty thousand and went to the clink. Poor Serina! So many children.

We don't want a Gypsy in our village

Getting a building permit for a Rom wasn't a simple matter. According to an edict by the party and the government, the settlements were supposed to be liquidated, and so an order went out forbidding construction in the settlements. The Roma didn't give a damn about that and built illegally – if they had the means. Some of them finished, some of them had to pay a fine of up to fifteen thousand and kept building, but there were cases when the officials sent a bulldozer and rolled it right over their structure as a punishment. In some places they got permission to build in town, but for the most part the villagers didn't want to let any gypsies into the community.

One day I had a meeting in Nižní Slavkov. After the meeting I stopped by the settlement as usual. The Roma lived far from the town on a steep hillside. They were rather wealthy, having made money in the Czech lands, and they wanted to build. But the local committee didn't want to give them building permits. I said: "I'll help anyone who gets a plot of land the permit to build on it."

Not even a week later, there came a knocking at our door at home. The children were already asleep, Jozef was listening to the late-night news on the radio, and I was ironing. I went to open the door. Some Rom. "Don't you remember me? I'm Kotliar from Nižní Slavkov," he said. "I got myself a plot of land and I'd like to get that permit. I want to build."

And my, my, I didn't know it would come so quickly! Once again I had gotten myself mixed up in something. But I wanted to keep my promises, so people wouldn't say I was talking out of my ear. "So! If only you'll really arrange that building permit for me!" said Kotliar, as he was looking me right in the face. "May the death-knell sound for me by morning!" I said. Jozef assured the man: "When this woman gets something into her head, she'll do it if she has to go around the world three times!" We laughed and Kotliar left.

He had bought a plot of land right in the middle of the village from a peasant woman. They didn't want to give him the permit for anything, excusing themselves by saying "they would deal with all the Gypsies together at one time" – but I pointed to the constitution, to the laws, to specific sections in the laws, I used the word "illegal," and finally Kotliar got his building permit.

He fired his own bricks, coming as he did from a family of old hands in the brick trade, got the materials, and started to build. Some time later he came to see me again and said they had ordered him to stop construction because they said he was building of someone else's property. The deed wasn't valid. He begged me to go with him. I went. He had the house almost finished. A one-story house with several rooms, a washroom, a veranda, something just splendid!

"The peasants are frightening me, saying they'll kill me if I come to the village to build," Kotliar said. "By law they have no right to do that!" I said, upset. "Come on, we're going to the local committee." We went. They tried to prove to us that the deed was invalid and that the plot belonged to some relative of the peasant woman who had sold it to Kotliar. I said I wasn't going to talk about it with them, let them tell it to the court. They took it to court, I consulted with our legal experts, Kotliar hired a lawyer to represent him, and he won the case. He finished building the house. From his shanty he moved the bedcovers and a few pieces of furniture, and the whole family went to celebrate the first night in their new house. But the peasants came during the night with their axes and started demolishing Kotliar's windows, doors, and everything else they could. In the morning Kotliar put his things together and left, in horror, for the Czech lands.

I found out about it only a few months later. But what could I do? It was no longer about the law here, but about prejudice and human malice. Some time later I went to Nižní Slavkov on another business trip. Kotliar's house was standing on the village green and falling apart. From the time the peasants broke his windows and doors, Kotliar never showed himself in the village again. He was afraid. I found out his address and wrote him at least to come back and sell the house. He came and sold the house for peanuts. Then he went back to the Czech lands.

You can get along even with dog-eaters

One settlement which every decent Rom avoided became a favorite of mine. The *rikoňara*, dog-eaters, lived there. Before the war we used to go past this settlement to fairs. The people looked wild, dressed in sackcloth, and lived in holes dug out of the earth, roofed with branches in the form of a tent. The branches were covered with turned-over sod. They made their living by going round the villages buying up dogs, eating them, and selling the fat to pharmacies. Sometimes they made *valki*, adobes, unfired bricks, for the peasants.

In the *rikoňara* settlement, not long after the war, something happened that amazed the whole region. They sent one young man all the way to Bratislava to do his military service. He was just as illiterate as the rest of them, black as a sour-cherry tree in the wild – and a countess had fallen in love with him! She told her parents she was going to marry him, and they immediately disowned her. She went with him to the settlement. She was so beautiful that Europe hasn't seen anything like her since. She learned to eat dogs and horses and made *valki* with them. Travelers stopped on the highway and from a distance they watched as with her bare feet she trod the clay earth mixed with weeds, and how from from out of that filth her golden hair shone for the whole world to see. Her parents came for her from Bratislava in a car and wanted her to go off to Italy with them, saying they were old and who would take care of them? She said she wouldn't go with them, but she offered to put them up in a small chalet and to take care of them there. They saw they weren't going to get anywhere with their daughter, disappeared someplace in Brazil or somewhere, and she lived with her *rikoňaro* husband in love until her death.

One day I came on business to the village to which the *rikoňaro* settlement belonged. It was during the harvest and I had to settle a purchase agreement. I got off the bus, the village green was full of people, and the peasants had scythes, pitchforks, and fence-posts in their hands. There was shouting, excitement, and people were upset: "We'll kill them! We'll crush them, the black Pharoahs! The Gypsy scum!" I got frightened. That I, a black Pharoah woman, should appear in front of these enraged peasants and negotiate a purchase order with them? But where was I supposed to run? Some of them knew me, I'd been here several times already on business, but people are capable of doing anything when they're out of their minds. One peasant woman was watching what was going on with detachment, from the passageway to her courtyard. I stepped up to her, asking if she would let me come inside her house. She told me the Gypsies had stolen the fence-posts from the cattle pen, the cows had gotten out, and they had trampled the crop. There were cries of: "After a while they'll come right into our courtyards to steal! We'll teach them a lesson!" The fury grew. The throng of peasants was planning to go out to the settlement.

To this day I don't know how it happened, but all of a sudden I was standing in the peasants' way. They were so surprised that for a moment they fell silent, and I took advantage of that moment to adjure them not to go anywhere. I would go see the Gypsies myself and by evening the fence-posts would be back in place. The madness of the crowd abated, and they abandoned their punitive mission for the time being. The fact that I was from the regional committee also played a part in it.

I set out for the settlement. "Just you wait and see, they'll cook you up there!" I heard behind me. "What kind of a dog do you think I am?" I joked. Laughter. Anytime people laugh, that's good.

The settlement was a good two hundred meters from the highway, with a path beaten out through the orach and the sorrel that led to it. From a distance you could see that the Roma were waiting for the peasants' punitive mission. The men were standing in from of the shanties, axes and clubs in their hands. I approached them, alone, through a meadow of sour grass. But I was never afraid of Roma. I entered the settlement and the men started waving their axes over their heads, one of them so upset that he had foam at his mouth. Later the children told me that it was he who took the fence-posts from the cattle pen. "Ayaaah! Ayaaah!" rang the battle cry. "Kill them! Beat them! Ayaaah to the peasants!"

"For heaven's sake, boy," I said, although he couldn't have been much younger than I, "I kiss your dear heart, don't bring misfortune upon us! All the peasants are ready with their clubs and their pitchforks and their guns and revolvers" – which of course they didn't have! – "think of your children! Do you want them to grow up orphans?"

That sentence had its effect. The arms holding the fence-posts and the axes came down. Only this furious man with foam at his mouth was so upset that he had to take out his rage on something, and because he had nothing to do so on, he swung with his ax at the calf of his own leg. A piece of flesh came off and the blood flowed in a stream. Perhaps in his lunacy he didn't even feel the pain. He just stood there, taking deep breaths. At the same time the womenfolk started shrieking. I can't stand the sight of blood, so I told them to bind up his leg, and I headed for the village to get help. In those days no one had a car yet, so I asked a peasant to come for the unfortunate man with a rack wagon and some horses. He did it and took the Rom with his calf chopped off to the hospital. Then together with the women we took the fence-posts and carried them back where they belonged. Then we dug up the horse skulls, dog bones, and the worst of the trash over which swarms of flies were hovering.

I don't know why that settlement became a favorite of mine. Maybe because everyone looked down on the *rikoňara*, while they were people like anyone else. When I went there a second time, again I dug up the bones and trash with the women, but when I came a third time, unexpectedly, I saw that they were digging up the trash by themselves. There is good in every person and a longing for beauty, but it's necessary to wake it up and constantly to give that person hope that it makes sense to try to realize his human, creative striving.

One day I came to see the *rikoňara* at a time when the first television sets were coming out. In the village, one or two peasants had a television and the rest of them went over to their houses to watch and envied them. In the Gypsy settlements a television was a rarity, because for the most part they didn't have any electricity hookup there.

I was walking from the highway through the meadow to the settlement and I couldn't believe my eyes! There were television antennas sticking up out of the earth-dwellings! How did they get an electricity hookup out here? We would have had to know about it at the regional committee. Or maybe there were television sets that ran on batteries? At that time people didn't even dream about transistors. I went into the first shanty, looked around, and no television set! "People, what do you have the antenna here for?" I asked.

"You're a fine one!" said Holub, who lived there. "And only the *gadže* have antennas and not us? Let them see how we can afford it too!"

But what do you think happened in a few years? The local national committee refused to run an electrical hookup to the settlement, saying it was too far from the highway, that there was no money, that the settlement was going to be liquidated, and all kinds of things. People were still lighting their homes with *ududi*, little lamps made out of potatoes. But in the meantime humanity had thought up transistors. And while the peasants were watching their old television sets, the dog-eaters bought themselves modern, beautiful, portable transitor sets, record players, and radios. They put them in their window frames and let them caterwaul away so the whole world could see what they had. Unfortunately, there aren't any transistor washing machines, and they'd be more necessary there than televisions.

Not long ago I stopped in front of a bookstore in Prešov. A man and a woman were standing in front of me. Dressed like they were poor, but clean. The woman was wearing a men's jacket and suit. Even from behind I could tell that they were Roma. It was payday, when the Roma from the surrounding villages come to Prešov to shop.

The man and woman were looking at the window display with interest. "Look, *kalemardi*," said the man – *kalemardi* means, literally, a woman condemned to be black – "there's a book in there about us!"

I could tell by their accent that these were people from the *rikoňaro* settlement, Marienka the songstress and her knock-kneed husband Štefan. A book about us? What was that supposed to mean? A book about Roma? That they would put out a book about Roma? All of a sudden I caught sight of some Bedouin or Berber woman on the cover, and the title of the book was: *Travels through Africa*, or something like that. "Get out your money and go buy it, we'll show the people at home that they also write books about Roma!" The woman pulled down her outer skirt and in the top of her underskirt, in a little corner of it, she had her money wrapped up. I said: "Štefan, Marienka, it's about Africa, it's not about us!"

"Hey, Lackaňa!" they said, and we greeted one another, welcoming each other – and all of a sudden I was completely out of sorts and unhappy that I had taken their illusion from them. Neither one of them knew how to read. But if they had brought home a book about Africa and claimed it was about Roma, the younger ones, who knew how to read, would have made fun of them.

"Well there you go, Lackaňa, and I was so happy they were putting out a book about us too!" said Štefan, disappointed.

Two cases of murder

I had to deal with a murder case in my work on two occasions. The first murder happened in Čemerný. Two families had agreed that their children would live together. There was an engagement feast and a wedding *tel jekh thuv*, under one smoke, as they say, and the young people started to live together. But he – his name was Miľo – was insanely jealous. His wife wasn't allowed to speak with anyone, she wasn't allowed to look at anyone, and she wasn't allowed to smile at anyone. But what good is it for a young woman to spend the whole day at home and stare at the wall? In Čemerný it was one shanty on top of another, a lot of people, happy, she couldn't resist, and she went out *pre vatra*, to the public area, and chatted with the other young women. And then he grilled her for hours and hours at home, asking where she had been, who she'd talked with, why, called her a bitch, and beat her. At first she loved him, he was a beautiful

187

person, and she didn't have thoughts for anyone else, but after a while she couldn't bear that kind of life any more and she ran away to her mother's. Her mother didn't want to get into an argument with his family and sent her home after a few days.

He didn't ask her anything and said: "Tomorrow we're going to the peasant's place to dig potatoes." The Roma in Čemerný made their living as day laborers working for the peasant farmers, smashing the stones in the road. It was a poor settlement. They made a little money for themselves only after they opened up a quarry in Huncovce.

The next day they both set off for the fields. They worked all day and all evening before the time came to go home, when Miľo said: "Sit on the boundary marker for a little while, we'll have a rest." She sat down and he pulled out a razor. He wanted to slit her throat. She defended herself, swearing on the child that was going to be born that she hadn't even looked at another man, but he was like a madman and slit her throat. He returned to the settlement with his face and his neck all scratched up, disheveled, and beside himself. "Where did you leave your wife?" people asked. "I slit her throat." They went to the field and there they found her.

He got twelve years. It happened just before the war. He did six years and after the war they let him out with the political prisoners by mistake. He went home to Čemerný and married again. After a while the officials discovered their mistake and locked him up again so he could serve the rest of his sentence.

One day a young woman showed up at my house, one child in her arms and another hanging onto her skirt, and she begged me for the love of God to write a petition for clemency for her husband. "Why did they lock him up?" I asked. She broke down in tears and told me the whole of Miľo's story. "Did you know he murdered his first wife?" I asked, appalled. "And aren't you afraid to live with a murderer?"

She said that he was awfully sweet to her and that when they were together he'd never hit her even once. Again she implored me to write her husband a petition for clemency. She had nothing to live off of, there was no work, her parents didn't want to support her, holding it against her that she had married a murderer. There were a lot of small children among his relatives, so she didn't want to be a burden to them.

I didn't know what to do. On the one hand I was supposed to stick up for someone who had murdered his wife, but on the other hand who now took beautiful care of his new wife, with whom he had two children. I told that little woman that I would look up the court records, study them, and then let her know. I read the court records through and for a week I was crying out in my sleep with horror. I said I wasn't going to ask for clemency for a person like that! But my husband said: "That's what he was like ten years ago, maybe now he's completely different." I consulted with all of my relatives. Some of them tried to dissuade me, saying: "Don't write the petition, word will get out about you that you're standing up for a murderer and that he paid you off with God knows what!" Others told me: "Write the petition, a person can't suffer for the rest of his life for something he did. And besides, he's got two children." My husband's cousin, who'd married into Miľo's family in Čemerný, came to see me and she also put in a word for Miľo. Said he'd become a completely different person. So I wrote the application for the rest of his sentence to be commuted, and sent it all the way to the Interior Ministry in Prague. Miľo was released.

When he came back, his relatives put together a big feast for me and invited me to Čemerný. I saw him there for the first time. He was good-looking, with big, soft eyes. No one would have said he'd murder anyone. They put the food and the drinks on the table, but I couldn't eat a mouthful. I took Miľo off to the side and told him: "Mister, I had no desire to write that petition at all!"

"I'm not surprised," he said. "But you don't know what I went through afterwards. Night after night it appeared to me all over again, before my eyes. Today I can't understand how I could ever have done something like that. A *bižužo*, an unclean one, must have overpowered me, I can't explain it any other way."

"All right, that's enough about that," I said. "But treat your new wife like a human being!"

They've been living together all this time and there hasn't been any word of anything bad about them. On the contrary, they've done well for themselves, because he works in the quarry in Huncovce, and people say about her that her bedcovers are as white as snow, that she's clean, and that she knows how to look after her husband.

There was one other case of murder that I dealt with. In Solivar there was a fair. The fairs started up again after the war, and until the atheism crusade started up, it was almost like it was before the war with the fairs. Roma from the whole surrounding area gathered there. In those days even the Roma from Skrabský came to Solivar. There was also one young man who came, alone, without a wife, without any brothers. It's not for nothing that they say: "Don't ever go anywhere by yourself, they'll kill you!"

In the evening people were drinking in the pub, the guys drank quite a bit, one said this, another said that, and all of a sudden there was an argument. The one from Skrabský got mixed up in the argument. Then he realized he was there all by himself, without his relatives, with no one to back him up and no one to stand up for him, and so he high-tailed it out of the pub and headed off through the forest for home. But those drunks set off after him and killed him in a fight.

The man who'd been killed was survived by a young wife and three small children. What must it have been like for her, her husband leaving the house in the afternoon alive and then the next day they bring him to her on a cart, dead? She went mad. Her relatives came to see me at the regional committee to arrange social support payments for her. I got her the payments, but what good was it when she was going crazy? They came to see me a second time and begged me to come talk some sense into her. I made the trip to Skrabský; it isn't far from Prešov. They took me to her. She was a beautiful young woman around twenty years old. Her eyes were burning as she said: "Auntie, everyone's lying. They're saying my husband's dead, but he isn't! They're jealous of me because he was so good-looking and kind!" I stood there stunned, not knowing what I should say in reply. "If you don't believe me, come with me into the forest, I'll show you he isn't dead!" She was delirious. I found out from the other Roma that she went round the forest gathering up the piles of firewood that other families were putting together, shouting that it was her firewood and that her husband was chopping it for her. Some people were sorry for her and overlooked it all, others got upset that she was taking their wood, and were fed up with her craziness. I felt terribly sorry for her, but I knew I wouldn't be doing her a favor by lying to her. I told her: "Girl, you've got to take life as it is. Your husband is dead. He doesn't go to chop you any firewood, it's the Roma who are putting up those piles, and you can't take it from them. You've got to get a hold of yourself. You have three children and if you go completely off your rocker they'll stick you in the madhouse, and what's going to happen to your children?" She cried like the rain, sobbing for heaven to protect her. Then she said: "Auntie, write me an application for heaven to return him to me!" I'd had a couple of courses in atheism behind me already, and in my examinations in Marxism-Leninism I'd answered that religion was the opium of the people. But I wasn't at an examination in Marxism-Leninism here. I cried with her, stroking her hair. And then I said: "Girl, can you read and write?" "No, I can't." "That's too bad, because the kind of application you want to to write has to be written by the petitioner herself!" "And would that help then?" she asked, hopefully. "You'll have to try it and see."

We talked for a good while longer and finally she promised me not to take people's piles of firewood. I left. After some time I found out that she'd gotten married again.

*P*išota

Sometimes I made the rounds of the settlements with my husband. He for the health-care section, I for the cultural one. One day we came to Sobrance. We went from shanty to shanty determining hygienic conditions. From the point of view of admissible norms not even one shanty was inhabitable, but where were you going to get housing for sixty families and ten or twelve children? And so in our report we only drew attention to the most alarming cases, and otherwise, as usual, we filled out the applications for social support payments, for construction permits, tried to persuade those who were sick with tuberculosis to come to the hospital for treatment, and the like.

All of a sudden a young woman came running up to us from behind: "Ilonka, come and eat!" I said thank you, that I wasn't hungry. Partly because I really wasn't, and mostly because I knew how picky Jožka was and that he didn't eat in Romani strangers' houses and didn't want me to either.

"Oh, Ilonka!" the woman sighed with such disappointment that I said: "I'll come, I'll come, just as soon as I finish writing this." Jozef was registering his own clients somewhere at the other end of the settlement. Besides, he didn't have to know I was going to eat. The woman stood next to me waiting patiently, and I could feel how urgently she wanted me to taste her food. I turned to her and she laughed: "I made you some *pišota*, I know how much you like them!"

Pišota are my favorite food, little pies filled with boiled potatoes and onion! "I've poured melted butter over them!" said the young woman, joyfully. I finished my writing and we hurried to her shanty. "I've sprinkled them with curd cheese!" she declared, happily. "Don't be afraid, I'm a *žuži Romňi*!" Literally that means a clean woman, but the deeper meaning is that the person in question doesn't eat horses, or dogs, or any other unclean food, and so the guest doesn't need to be shy of the food in her house. "I'm a *žuži Romňi*!" she repeated several times on the short trip to her shanty, so I wouldn't by chance change my mind and at the last moment refuse to eat her *pišota*.

We arrived at her shanty, it was summer and she'd had the table brought outside, and on the table was an enormous serving bowl full of *pišota*. But what do you think there was inside that bowl? Her two-year-old son was sitting drenched in waves of butter and curd cheese, stuffing *pišota* into his little mouth with both hands. We both froze. My mouth had been watering the whole way, thinking I would soon be eating *pišota*, and I swallowed on an empty stomach. It was a dish that took a lot of work to make, and I myself never had enough time to make it. The young mother cried out, dashed to the table, and pulled the little boy out of the bowl. Butter was running down his little legs and tears down her face. She patted him on the rear, the child laughed, and she begged me terribly to forgive her. There was nothing to forgive. On the contrary. If I had eaten the *pišota*, I would have long ago ceased to remember the momentary enjoyment I took in them. But the sight of that naked little boy in the bowl full of *pišota*, made with love, is something I will never forget as long as I live.

I get boundless pleasure from thinking back on my "official" years, making visits to the settlements. I used to come home late in the evening, tired, wishing I could just fall into bed, but then my second shift started: the housework. Sometimes I said to myself: does it do any good? Is it worth it? But usually just then someone knocked on

From left to right: Ilona Lacková with her husband Jozef
and her youngest sister Vilma in the early 1970s.

the door: "Ilonka, help me ... Ilonka, can't you ... If you don't help us, there's no one left for us to turn to!" But they also came to invite me to a feast for the success of an application I'd filed for them, for the fact that they'd run an electrical line out to their settlement, and for my being able to find them the jobs where they were making money. They were happy and smiling, and they said: "Our Ilonka!" And I was glad. Because a person experiences true happiness when he makes someone else happy.

To Ústí nad Labem and my studies at the university

Nane barvalo oda, kas hin,
aľe oda, so džanel

Wealth belongs not to one who has things
but to one who has knowledge

To Ústí nad Labem

There was an administrative reorganization in 1960. They abolished the Prešov region. I was transferred to the District House of Culture in Košice. I was supposed to work among the Roma: I organized courses for cooking, sewing, and handymen's clubs. My co-workers were nice to me and I liked it there a lot, but what good was that? Commuting from Prešov to Košice every day – that was no good. Four children at home and the youngest one, Luboš, was four years old. The fifth one, Ďoďu, was in the institution. We went to see him almost every Sunday. Jozef said: "You're not going to commute to Koviše, you're going to stay home! Let the children finally know that they have a mother!" I asked around about work in Prešov, but I wasn't able to get anything. I wanted to work maybe as a manual laborer; they offered me a job as an assistant in a print shop for one crown fifty an hour. It wasn't worth it. Jozef was making a good thousand five hundred. In 'sixty that wasn't bad money when you added the state social support payments for children, but then Jozef drank. There was a lot of drinking in Prešov. A guy who didn't drink wasn't considered a real man. What's more, Jozef kept the company of big shots and officials and he wanted to show them what an ordinary Gypsy could afford, so he always treated the whole gang. People used to say of him that he was open-handed, generous, hospitable – while at home we went hungry. My mother used to say: "Don't be angry, little girl, but I'm not going to lend you any more money. What for? So the money drowns in drink?" She didn't leave us hungry, she'd invite us over and feed us – and it was terribly embarrassing for me.

We lived in a two-room flat with six people. When we moved there from the dark underworld of the basement, we felt like we were in paradise, but there was progress, with stories in the paper about how society was giving everyone opportunities, and once in a while a Romani family would procure a nice flat or would get a flat from the state and our two-room paradise no longer seemed to us like a paradise.

I was going through a bad time: my husband drinking, no money, no work, a small flat, what was I supposed to do? I cried or I sang. When Jozef came home drunk and started raising hell, I started singing and that calmed him down a little. He liked to listen to me. Or sometimes it happened the other way around, him ordering me to sing, and I would have to sing, even if I felt like crying instead.

People from our settlement in Šariš were moving to Ústí nad Labem. They traveled home to visit their relatives and sang the praises of Bohemia.

And so one day I packed up Máňa and Luboš – Milan was already doing his military service – and I left for Ústí nad Labem. I left Evička with my sister Maruša. I didn't even leave Jozef a message. Let him look for us if he cared about us!

I had never been in Ústí. We arrived there in the afternoon, about three o'clock. We got off the train, I with a small suitcase in one hand and holding onto little Luboš with the other, while Máňa, a young miss of fifteen, walked alongside us. I was looking around the station in case I might see a Rom I could ask about people from Šariš. There was no one at the train station. But hardly had we gone outside when I started hearing people say: "Auntie, what brings you here?" A young man straight from Šariš! He immediately invited us home to his place and we spent a couple of nights at their place. They supported us. That went without saying: *Rom Romeske te merel na dela* – a Rom won't leave another Rom to die. Those poor people had only one small room and there were twelve of them living there, with the three of us as well! We slept on the floor and there was barely room even on the floor. Word got out among the Roma that we had no place to live, so a Romani woman from Čemerný came for us. We each knew about the other but we didn't know each other personally. She told me: "You'll live at my place until you find something better." She had a room and a kitchen, a husband, and eight children. There were five of us sleeping on one bed: the three of us and also her two small children.

The very first day after I came to Ústí I went to the municipal "national committee." I presented them with my references from the Prešov district committee and also from the District House of Culture in Košice, and presented them with all my membership cards – and they just stood there gaping at me. They instantly offered me a position in the park of culture and recreation. So I could work on people's creative ensembles. I couldn't have wished for anything better. They put Luboš in a school for me and found Máňa a job as a waitress. She didn't have any job training, but she was a great beauty and knew how to conduct herself – and in those days they didn't pay as much attention to your training as now. Especially if they were short-handed.

Jozef's brother Jano also lived in Ústí, but I didn't go see him, in order that he wouldn't find out we were there and write Jozef. But you won't keep any secrets among Roma. One day Jano came to get us, saying it was shameful for relatives not to live with each other, and he immediately moved us into his place. We lived at Jano's place for two months. They had a room and a kitchen, he slept with his wife in the kitchen, and my children and I in the room with his six children.

I was hearing from our Roma how things looked at home in Prešov. Jozef had his pride and pretended he wasn't interested in me. At work they were sorry for him because his wife ran off. He was a favorite of theirs. He did his work excellently and won praise everywhere. He joked with everyone when necessary and knew how to sympathize, but he didn't have any sympathy for his own family. No one knew what our home life was like. I didn't use to go and complain about him, because I didn't want people to say about us: "You'll never make bacon out of a wolf! You can't reeducate a Gypsy." Every day I gave him a clean, ironed shirt, so everyone could see how well-dressed a Gypsy could be.

Our Maruša had a message sent to me that Evička was crying and wanted to go to her mother. I sent her a telegram that I would come for my girl but that she should say nothing to Jozef. I arrived at my sister's place and didn't even show myself at home. I was shaking all over, afraid that Jozef would come to thrash me.

He came. He didn't thrash me. He was utterly sorrowful, and he said: "Girl, why did you leave?" He knew I had left because of his drinking. I found myself feeling sorry for him, seeing him softened like this. He tried to persuade me to stay. "And where will I get work? Where are we going to get money? I have a marvelous job there and they've promised us a flat." He left and I stayed at Maruša's for the night.

The next day when he was at work I stopped in at home for some things. Naturally he suspected I would go home, and he showed up in the doorway. Again he tried to persuade me to stay. He promised to stop drinking. But how many times had he promised me that already? "I'm going back to Ústí," I said. He saw that he wasn't going to get anywhere with me by playing mister nice guy, so there was nothing left for him to do but beat me. He beat me so badly I could hardly stand up on my feet, but none of it did him any good. I gathered up my suitcase and Evička, and off we went.

A few days later he came to see us in Ústí. He had left his position in the hygiene office and come. In less than three months we got a beautiful flat in a new building, with a room, a kitchen, a washroom, and central heating. We had never lived in such a marvelous flat before!

Jozef got a position in the regional hygiene office. His job was to measure air quality. He went around the factories and noted how much dust had accumulated in the control areas. There was a somewhat older official with him, a woman who didn't say a single word the whole day long. And Jozef was a social kind of person, he liked talking with people. He said: "Girl, get me some other job, I'll wither up and die if I stay here."

Part of my duties was delivering lectures. I used to go lecture at factories where there were concentrations of Romani workers. One time a reclamation cooperative asked me to come and lecture. Afterwards – I don't know what got into me – I asked the foreman if a job for my husband might not be found there.

"That's outstanding," he said, when I had sung all of Jozef's praises thoroughly, "we really need a master worker right now." I became frightened, because Jozef had never done that kind of work before in his life, but I didn't want the foreman to think I was talking out of my rear, so I said: "Hey, that's just what my husband really wants to do!"

The next day Jozef came to the reclamation cooperative before he had even quit his job at the hygiene office. The foreman put some plans and a leveling rod into his hand and said: "Hurry up, Lacko, measure that off so the people can get to work!" Lacko turned as pale as a corpse but gave no other outward sign. He unfolded the plans, squatted down on his haunches next to them, and stared and stared. He didn't know what reclamation was, but he knew the water supply systems because he'd passed a test on that. When they were looking for the source of some contamination, a broken pipe, he had to know how to deal with it. That knowledge helped him. Whatever else you can say about Lacko, there's no denying he was enormously intelligent. He talked with the foreman about the plans in a low-key way, asked questions about this and that in a low-key way – and in two hours everyone was working!

Jozef took great pleasure in the reclamation work. He was making decent money. I was also enjoying my job. Milan got married near Ústí. He had been in Jílový near Děčín for his military service and became acquainted there with Olina – she's from a terrific family of Roma from Solivar – Máňa was won over by a two-meter-tall Czech, an electrician, and they got married. We had a nice flat in Ústí. There were so many things binding us to Ústí, and yet Jozef was constantly feeling the tug of Prešov.

One day a man from Prešov came to our place and said: "Well, I'm here to look at the flat!" "What flat?" "Well, you placed an ad, didn't you?" Only after I talked to him some more did I find out that Jozef had placed an ad to exchange flats: "will exchange two-room, Ústí, top category, for Prešov." I wanted to throw the man out. "I'm not moving anywhere!" I said. But Jozef said he would move to Prešov by himself. There was nothing I could do but go with him. And so we were back in Prešov. We got a three-room flat and there were four of us: Jozef, me, Evička, and Luboš. Máňa stayed with her husband in Ústí, and Milan with his wife Olina in Jílový near Děčín.

The black Czechs

It was too bad! I liked it in Ústí. I had an interesting job. One day the director called me up and said: "Organize a lecture about Cuba." I called the Cuban embassy asking them to send someone. They promised that they would. I had posters made up and booked a large room in the House of Culture. And then I said to myself: "Well, what if nobody comes? Is that poor guy going to drag himself all the way from Cuba to Ústí nad Labem and find the room empty?" I was sorry for him in advance and determined that the Roma would have to rescue him. I made the rounds of the families in Ústí, Trmce, and Bínov, telling them how in Cuba the people were dark like Roma and that one of them was going to come show up here, so they should certainly come. He would be something like their king or mayor, in short, a *chibalo*, a leader. And I still had no inkling that the ambassador himself was going to come and lecture!

The Roma started coming an hour before the beginning of the lecture. When the lecturer arrived, the hall was completely full. There were some three hundred Roma and twenty or twenty-five Czechs. It was the actual ambassador himself lecturing, and he was a black man. The Roma were enthralled that there could be someone even blacker than they. His color stood out all the more because a pale, blonde woman was translating for him. They showed some slides of Cuba and won huge applause. After the lecture I invited the ambassador behind the park of culture to the Savoy for dinner. He asked me: "Tell me, what kind of black Czechs are these you have living here in Ústí? They're almost like the people in our country, in Cuba!" I told him that they were Roma and that I was also a Rom, and that made him so happy he clapped his hands. And I told myself: "If Jožka were here now, he'd sure give it to me!"

But nothing happened, we said goodbye, and I gave him my address – and a few days later I got an official letter from the Cuban embassy that they were offering me a two-week stay in Cuba. For free! It was a wonder I didn't faint! I wrote back that my husband wouldn't let me go by myself. Instantly there came another letter in which they invited my husband as well. But Jozef said he wasn't going, and that he wouldn't let me go by myself. What could I do?

In 1952 I was awarded a trip to Moscow. He didn't let me go then, either. But I've been in Hungary, Romania, and Poland. I organized excursions of Roma to Hungary and Romania. We rented a bus. But how those people behaved on the bus! Like little children! Jokes, cracks, the whole trip we laughed, sang, danced, and fell down with the movement of the bus. A little ways across the border we came to Arad. It was hot and muggy and suddenly we saw a wide, shallow river. We asked the driver to stop, and all of us, just as we were in our clothes, threw ourselves into the water. It used to be that a Rom wouldn't strip down to his swimsuit even if they were going to execute him. And a Romani woman? That would have been absolutely out of the question! In my younger days the womenfolk didn't even wear short sleeves, because it was a shameful thing to expose your arms. We swam in our clothes, squirted water at each other, yelped, sang, and danced in the shoals. Cars stopped on the highway and people got out to stare at the circus. We spent the night in Arad, took a sightseeing tour of the town the next day, went shopping, and went home. It was marvelous, and to this day everyone thinks back to what a great time we had in Romania.

The first Gypsy woman at Charles University

When I was still working in the park of culture in Ústí nad Labem, my supervisor called me into his office and said: "Comrade Lacko, what if your were to further your education?"

I was scared of what I had done. Had someone complained about me that I had lectured badly? I gave lectures for the Socialist Academy, mostly about Roma – and also for Roma. Had I said something nonsensical somewhere? I started off by defending myself and ticking off all the training courses I had completed.

"I don't mean you should go to another training course," said my supervisor, "but you should go to the university to set an example for your young people."

"What in the world could I begin to study at the age of forty-three?" This man possibly didn't even know what he was saying, and he couldn't mean it seriously. But he started trying to convince me, started explaining it to me in terms of the party, and I listened and listened, while in my spirit I was telling myself: "At my age, I'm not going to let myself be ordered around anymore," and I left with the thought that I wasn't going to apply to any university.

I came home and said to Jozef: "You want to hear something funny?" And then I told him about my supervisor's suggestion. I hoped he would get angry and forbid me to go to any more schooling. But instead he said to me: "Girl, that wouldn't be such a bad thing. Study law. Lots of Roma come to you wanting your advice, and at least this way you could advise them in accordance with the legal code."

I didn't sleep the whole night, thinking about what I should do. I had tried to persuade so many of our people to go to school, leading some of them by the hand straight to the campus, to the high school. In my lectures I expounded on how important it was for us Roma to have our own intelligentsia ... I thought it all over: the children are grown,

Ilona Lacková after passing her final examination at Charles University, Prague.

Milan's on his own, it's only Luboš who needs me still, but Maňka and Eva will do backup for me when necessary. And so the next day I went to tell my supervisor that I had just decided to go on to my post-secondary studies. I didn't dare try for law. It felt too difficult for me to learn so many laws and statutes by heart. Besides that, I had always been tempted to write, writing articles for the newspapers when time permitted, and so I applied to Charles University's Faculty of Culture and Journalism.

There were sixty of us who came to the admission interview. They were all younger than I was. They all had their high school diploma, except for me, but at my workplace they asked the Ministry of Schools to make an exception. They took half of the sixty applicants. I was looking forward to being one of those they didn't take. I was still afraid of the university. But a letter came saying I had been accepted into the program.

When the dean spoke at the opening ceremonies for the new academic year, he said in the conclusion to his speech: "Students, there is a Gypsy woman among you. This is perhaps the first time in history that a Gypsy woman had stood on the grounds of our famed university." There were a couple of Romani boys at that time who had gotten a university education – Gusta Karik, the lawyer, Janek Cibula, the doctor, three or four teachers – but I think I was really the first woman. Then the dean continued: "I appeal to you students to help your Gypsy fellow student in a comradely fashion. She is the mother of five children" (Ďoďu was still alive then, he was in the institute) "and she has not had the opportunity to complete a high school education. I would be glad if our department could boast of having had the first woman citizen of Gypsy origin to successfully complete her studies."

I wanted to thank the dean, but as soon as I stood up, I broke down in tears. He waved to me, seeing how I was wiping my eyes.

I have to say that my fellow students were an outstanding bunch. They helped me willingly whenever I needed it.

Hey you, Mommy, buy her a ring!

I had finished two years of study. I had passed all the exams. But then I had to interrupt my studies. We moved to Prešov, and what do you think happened? Though Jozef had gotten a good position, they took him back at the district hygiene office, he fell seriously ill and was at home for almost a year. And I didn't get a job. I was used to working as an official, in the cultural sphere, with Roma, I enjoyed my work, and I don't want to brag, but people praised me. I wanted to keep working in culture, and I used to tell myself: "Now, when on top of everything else you're studying at the faculty of culture and journalism by correspondence, they'll grab at me everywhere with all ten fingers." But they didn't take me anywhere! At the district office they even told me that as a Gypsy woman I couldn't work with Gypsies because I'd hold them back. I couldn't believe my ears. I came home in tears.

At first we tried to get by on Jozef's sick pay. He was getting a thousand five hundred. Though there were only three of us, Jozef, Luboš, and me, because Eva had also gotten married, it was no good. "We're going to go sell at the fairs," said Jozef. I laughed, taking it as a joke. "We'll apply for the permit, buy some glass beads, and make bracelets, toys, and little dog figurines at home. I can't go to work, but making bracelets won't harm my health any."

199

"You can't be serious!" I said, angrily. "People know me everywhere as a cultural inspector, and now I'm supposed to go traveling around the fairs? I used to go make them think about cultural affairs, and now I'm supposed to call out at them: 'Hey you, Mommy, buy that child a ring! Look at what beautiful ones we have, with hearts, with four-leaf clovers for luck, buy her a ring!'"

"There, you see how good you are at it?" Jozef laughed. "I'll go apply for the permit tomorrow. We've got to make a living somehow."

So we started making bracelets, rings, and little dog and cat figurines, and we went around the fairs to sell them. By train. We traveled a long way, as far as Stará Lubovňa, where the people didn't know me as an inspector from the regional office. I would have fallen through the floor with shame if the people I knew saw me like that. I had become too high and mighty and forgotten the saying *manuš dživel sar pes del* – a person lives as best he can. We usually hit the road in the evening, arriving late at night and sleeping at the train station, then selling from morning til evening and coming back to Prešov in the evening. I spent the whole day on my feet, and with my varicose veins, my legs swelled up. I called out: "Hey you, Mommy, come buy that little girl a ring! Come on up, little one, take your pick, look, this one's got a heart, or would you like this one with the glass beads? Make your child happy, Mommy!" And among the rings and bracelets I had an open textbook of Marxism-Leninism, and I studied about how "freedom is necessity recognized" and "the material foundation is primary, the cultural superstructure secondary," and that justified my fairground activities. I comforted myself with the thought that I was acting in harmony with the philosophy of Marxism-Leninism.

Hawking at the fairs was hard work and what's more, after we took out for taxes, we had hardly enough left for a bare subsistence. We quit doing that after a year. Fortunately Jozef got better and started earning money again. After a year-long break I continued my studies at the university. I told myself: "Now I'll finally have more time! No rings, bracelets, no traveling to who knows where like Stará Lubovňa, just Luboš at home – now I'll be able to do some serious studying!" But what do you think happened? Eva got divorced and foisted her two children on me, Evička and Petra. Evička was two years old and Petra fourteen months. I had them with me for six years. I used to tell myself: there, you see, you foisted your own children on your mother and now you're raising their children! There's no escaping your responsibilities.

Eva got married at the age of sixteen. Some man named Šmíkal, a Czech, had won her over. He had no father and was an illegitimate child, raised by his grandmother. He wasn't a bad person, but he lacked any sense of responsibility. He'd work somewhere for a while, then stop enjoying it, so he'd pick up his guitar and disappear. For fourteen days he'd wander, roam about, no one knew where. In his identity papers he had one stamp after another, the way he changed his employment so often. Though he was a trained mechanic, he worked at unskilled jobs, loading potatoes at the train station, because they took one look at his papers in the personnel department and then they wouldn't take him on. We forbade Eva from going out with him and used to lock up her clothes, but unfortunately there was this loose woman who lived in our building and she lent her her own clothes. Eva became pregnant, they got married, and had one child after another, three in a row, every nine months. When they got divorced, she kept the little one, Ivetka, four months old, and I raised Petra and Evička. Fortunately Eva got married again and has a very nice husband, brought him another two children into the world and took Petra and Evička back after six years.

My examinations

Once a month I traveled to Prague either for consultations or to take examinations. I had to pass the examinations on the first try, because the trip to Prague and back cost a hundred crowns, even with a discounted fare, and so for financial reasons I couldn't afford to fail and throw another hundred into a retake. With three children I didn't have as much time for studying as I needed. I couldn't move an inch without little Petřík following right behind me. He was on me like a tail, holding onto my skirt, and when I excused myself to go to the bathroom, he stood on the other side of the door and called out: "Come on out already, Grandma!" He wouldn't fall asleep unless I was holding him in my arms. He snuggled up on my lap and leaned his head against me while I studied. If I ever laid him down on the bed, look out! He shouted so the whole building could hear. And so, in fact, I studied for all my examinations with Petřík in my arms.

I went to my examination in political economy. Straight from the train station to the faculty, the train was late, all my fellow students were standing in the hallway, and almost all of them had already been examined. Four of them failed. "Elen, do you know all the material?" they asked me. "He's an awful brute! He let four people flunk, everyone's getting C's, not a single A!" My head spun and it went dark before my eyes. "You'd better not go in there today! Maybe he'll be in a better mood next time. I pulled out too, and I'll go during the second examination period!" said one fellow student, trying to convince me. But I never considered doing that.

It was my turn. My fellow students waited to see how I would do, even those who had already completed the exam. It was terribly nice of them. We were examined by this tall, thin docent. And as kind fate decreed, my question was "the gross income of an enterprise." That was just the question I had been preparing for! I said everything and got only a little bit confused because I was nervous. He said: "You're right between an

Ilona Lacková's Master's diploma, 1991.

A and a B, so I'll ask you one more question." And he asked me how a collective farm contributed to state income. And I, who had helped arrange bulk purchases from collective farms for so many years in my work at the regional committee, was all of a sudden unable to remember a thing. Obviously, the answer is "in kind!" But that's not what I said. "I would give you an A," said the docent, "but such fundamental ignorance! Will you be satisfied with a good grade, or do you want another question?"

"That's excellent, excellent! Just give me the C!" I cried out. So he put down a C. Outside, my curious, impatient fellow students asked: "So out with it, Elen, did you pass?" I showed them my card, because I couldn't speak at all. They were so happy for me they threw their caps up to the ceiling.

There was one old virgin who lectured us on the history of culture and journalism. She didn't have an attractive appearance. A couple of times she looked at me with such an unpleasant, rancorous expression that I said to myself, why? Never in my life had I considered myself beautiful, but the truth is that every woman has a time in her life when she is beautiful: for some it's long, for others it's short, some are most attractive at the age of fifteen or sixteen, others maybe when they're forty – and I was one of those others. I liked myself, although at that time I was already a grandmother nine times over. That gives a person a certain kind of feeling. My fellow students gravitated toward me.

One day they were standing in the hallway and cracking jokes with me and I didn't even notice how that professor was walking past. We didn't say hello to her. Only when she had gone past did someone say: "Boy, is that one going to give us a hard time during examinations or what?" The professor turned sharply and came back toward us. She pierced me through with a look and then she called me over to the side. "How many children do you have?" she asked. I told her how many. "And you want to go to college? You're wasting your time and money on traveling to Prague for nothing. I would advise you to forget it!" And she marched off. I was completely crushed, but then I got a hold of myself and said to myself: it's just spite!

At the end of the year I took my examination with her. I was afraid she would take revenge on me. But I have to admit that she gave me easy questions: the 1918 cultural law, the people's library, and cultural administration on the district level. After all, I had dealt with cultural on the district level for ten years! I knew it from experience. I passed the examination with an excellent grade.

When I graduated, all our professors shook our hands and congratulated us. That thin female professor came up to me and said: "I bow deeply before you." Literally, just like that. She looked hard and unkind, but her heart was as good as bread. I broke down in tears. When she saw that I was crying, she stroked my hair.

And so I graduated from Charles University's Faculty of Culture and Journalism, the grandmother of nine children. When I returned home with my diploma, I was enormously happy that I had done all right in the great examination of life.

Last stop: Lemešany

Lemešany was my last stop before retirement. We had stopped selling at the fairs, I had finished college, and was left with empty hands. I couldn't find a job in Prešov. For me to go to work as a manual laborer, at the age of fifty, with my brand new college diploma, that was something I didn't feel like doing! It seems to me that in the last few years hatred toward "Gypsies" has grown. Or fear. The *gadže* want to keep us under their watchful eye and won't allow us to deal with our problems by ourselves. While they used to send me around the settlements, saying: "You're one of them, you can deal with them better!" – now all of a sudden they wouldn't even take me as a teacher's aide at a summer camp for our children out of fear that I might speak Gypsy with them, or that I might reinforce the Romaniness within them. Finally I got mad and wrote a letter to the newspaper *Red Justice*. They looked into my case and instantly arranged for a job for me in the House of Culture in Lemešany. Though it wasn't working with Roma, I took it; what else was there for me to do? I was there part-time as a cultural worker and part-time as a librarian.

The cultural section had its office at the national committee right next door to where the chairman had his office. When I walked through the village with the chairman, people called out: "Where'd you get such a suntanned secretary?"

"She was in Italy for her vacation," the chairman laughed. But the people recognized that I was a Gypsy woman, and again I felt those mistrustful looks at my back.

Then I started announcing various events on the local radio station, reading items about cultural activities, and the like. I did the best job I could. Then I played a song. One day we were celebrating the chairman's name day, there was drinking, I had two or three glasses, and I started to sing. The chairman liked it and made me sing on the local radio station. The next day people were stopping me and telling me: "You've got a nice voice, little lady! Dear me, what a voice, whenever are you going to sing something for us again?" And all of a sudden they started inviting me to weddings to sing there! The things I've lived to see! And so I went to the villagers' weddings and sang. If I hadn't gone, there would have been trouble! We got to know each other better, they started trusting me with their problems, with their worries, coming for advice what to do with their husband when he drinks, and where their child should go to school, and never in my life did I think that in my old age I would be giving advice to *gadže*, me, a black Gypsy woman!

I wasn't unhappy there, but as soon as my working years were over, I asked to retire. I didn't retire because I didn't want to work any more, on the contrary, so I could keep working. So I could do the things I enjoy doing and that I've longed to do all my life. So I could write.

I had been lucky that I found the work I did enjoyable. I even enjoyed it when I didn't enjoy it, because I told myself: there's got to be something you can learn from this! *God'aver manuš džanel te sikhl'ol savorestar* – a wise person can learn from everything, and so try at least to learn something and know something. And thank heaven, in every job that life has foisted upon me, I've had the opportunity to learn and to find out something new.

Postscript

Lačho lav sar maro
A good word is like bread

I've been retired for fifteen years

I have a beautiful flat at the end of the housing estate, one with three rooms. I live on the sixth floor and in front of my windows is wide open space, sky and a grassy hillside. I retired mostly so I could write. Roma have always respected the word. *O lav tut šaj anel pro lačho drom, aľe o lav tut šaj marel paj o drom tele* – words can carry you to a good road, but words can also lead you astray. *God'aver lav mol buter sar love* – a wise word is worth more than money. *Lačho lav sar maro* – a good word is like bread. When I think about my life I only wish that I could sift it all and couch it in good and wise words, and that my experience could be useful to others. My grandmother always said: "Child, if I could give you my life experience!" She was sorry that couldn't happen, because she knew that *sako mušinel peskero te predživel* – everyone must live their life themselves. On the other hand, if a person didn't have the experience of others to lean on and make him think, his life would be a much more painful one.

But everything is different than how we imagine it and how we wish it, and that's how it turned out with my writing as well. Though I began living by myself, because my last son, Luboš, got married and finally got a flat, I was almost never alone. My flat was always full of grandchildren, and Roma didn't stop coming to see me: Ilonka, give me some advice, Ilonka, write me an application, Ilonka, come to court with me as my lay attorney, and even the Slovak women who are my neighbors have gotten used to pouring out their hearts to me, so I resolved to escape into a job. A seasonal worker, in my retirement. To be honest, another reason for this decision was: "Mama, lend me money, Grandma, lend me money!" What was I supposed to do? So I began working for the Dopleta cooperative. I travel around the villages and take orders for colorized photographs from people. In our parts in eastern Slovakia, colorized photographs are the fashion. People send photos of their weddings, sons in the army, daughters' graduations, and children, to be enlarged. At the university they gave us lectures on kitsch. Maybe those colorized photographs are kitsch, but they make people here happy. And maybe there's worse kitsch than colorized photographs ... I'll earn a little money for my retirement. How can I not give to my children when they need something? My grandsons and granddaughters are already getting married, and my great-grandchildren are being born – how is it possible for me to come to a wedding or a christening with

Ilona Lacková, 1984, collecting photographs for colorizing and enlarging.

empty hands? Evička, Eva's oldest girl, who lived with us for six years, married a man in Azerbaijan named Shakh Abbas. They have two children together. We bought them a car, a Volga, so his relatives wouldn't talk. They're all doctors.

I have good children, it would be blasphemy if I complained about them, but what mother in the world can say her children don't make worries for her? The unluckiest one is probably Luboš, my youngest. And at the same time, he has such a good heart! And how talented he is! He drives around in a freight truck, and he had it all worked out that he was going to go to Turkey and Kuwait as a driver, but his wife wouldn't let him go. He married a Slovak woman with five children, much older than he is. They have a son together, just adorable. Her children come to see me as if I were their real grandmother. But oh, the trials Luboš had to go through before that!

When he was still in the army, he came home one day on leave, and walking home from the train station he saw a girl crying on the street. She was crying terribly, the poor one, sobbing, staggering, her knees giving way beneath her. Luboš stepped up to her, wanting to help her somehow, and saw that it was someone he knew. He'd danced with her a couple of times at a party. A Slovak woman. A very beautiful girl. She was going to agricultural school.

Luboš kept asking her questions about what had happened to her, and she confided everything to him. She was in her fourth month from some boy who'd left her. She was afraid to say anything at home. But a social worker came to their house to inspect the environment the child would be born into. And that was how the girl's mother found out that her daughter was expecting a baby. She grabbed a chair and thrashed her daughter with the chair. Then she threw her out on the sidewalk. Luboš met her in that

206

condition. He brought her to our place. He didn't tell me what and how, asking only if she could live with us.

"Do you want to marry her?" I asked. What else would a mother think when her son brings a girl into the family? He said he did. He went back to the army and left the girl with us. We put her up as our daughter-in-law-to-be. I asked her if she wouldn't mind having a Gypsy for a husband. She claimed that she wouldn't. Then we threw them a big wedding and the girl asked only that I not invite her mother for anything in the world. If you don't want her there, you don't want her there, it's your affair – so I didn't invite her mother. Luboš came back from the army and they stayed with us. She gave birth to a little girl. A little white one. And still we didn't know it wasn't his. Though Luboš is very dark, since he takes after me, we told ourselves the child might take after its mother.

But one day the girl met up with the young man who got her pregnant. She looked well, since we decked her out like a princess. She was truly marvelous, and we were sorry to spoil her beauty with ordinary clothing. We didn't want people to reproach us for having a beautiful daughter-in-law and couldn't dress her right. We dolled the little girl up even more. Well, and then the father of the child said, let her get divorced, he'd marry her. She asked for a divorce. Left Luboš. But that lazy bum didn't marry her after all. She lives by herself, working in the garment factory, and would like to come back to Luboš – but what kind of an idiot does she think he is? All he got out of it was one bitter life experience. Unfortunately, he didn't learn much from it. Because what he's going through now isn't much better.

I've always been drawn to the Vlach Roma

Whenever I've written anything, it has always been about Roma. The Slovaks and the Czechs don't know us at all and look at us with unbridled prejudice, but I've become convinced that if they get just a little bit of the truth, many of them are willing to look at a Gypsy like a Rom, like a human being. I can't tell you how many times my first play, *The Burning Gypsy Camp*, showed that! *Ňiko na prindžarel avreskero jilo* – no one sees into anyone else's heart. If he did, people would be kinder to each other, more considerate of each other, and they'd be able to forgive. All you have to do is say the word *jilo*, heart, to a Rom, and he'll become all sentimental. A Rom carries the best part of himself in his heart. Sometimes it's very deep, in the shadows, but the seed of goodness, love, and harmony with the universe is there. All you have to do is let it sprout. But the problem is that even love comes in all kinds of forms, and even goodness can take different shapes, so the herb that grows out of one person's heart can seem exotic to someone else, or frighten him, or he won't know what it's good for. And I've always been drawn to the exotic, wanting to search out something familiar in the unfamiliar.

To be truthful about it, even Roma can discriminate against others. Roma are people, and like all people, even Roma suffer from prejudice toward the unfamiliar. But few Czechs and Slovaks know that not all Roma are the same, that we're divided into different groups something like the Czechs, Poles, Bulgarians, Serbs, and Croatians, every group for itself, with its own customs and rituals, its dialect, its family professions, in short, its way of life. Each group knows the others only from a distance, from other people's tales, from legends that distort the truth, from superstitions and prejudices. I don't want to exaggerate, it's not about being enemies, God forbid, because all the Roma in the whole world, whatever group they belong to, know and at the right moment can use the curse *sem Roma sam!* – well, we're Roma! A curse which will put him in a brotherly mood toward any Rom, and admonishes him to show respect and to offer aid. But unless it's absolutely necessary, the members of one group live for themselves only and avoid Roma from the other groups.

For us, for the so-called Slovak Roma, the Vlachs were *aver*, different. My ancestors – and few *gadže* know this – had started to settle on the edges of Slovak villages, supplying the peasants with their blacksmith's goods, weaving baskets and wicker containers for them, and going to play at their weddings and gatherings. The Vlachs moved through the area, perhaps originally on foot, later in carts, trading in horses, others making their living as feather-cleaners, their womenfolk telling fortunes and, to tell the truth, stealing as well. They could get away with it – one day they were here and the next day they were already over the mountains. Sometimes we were enraged at them, because the *gadže*, for whom a Gypsy is a Gypsy, took out their anger on us for everything the Vlachs had done to them. Our Roma didn't like them – as the saying goes, *čorel sar Vlachos*, he steals like a Vlach Rom – but on the other hand, in our souls we secretly admired them: *šukar sar Vlachos*, as beautiful as a Vlach, *džal peskere dromeha sar Vlachos*, he goes his own way, like a Vlach.

I was drawn to the exotic, and that's why I was drawn to the Vlachs. Maybe this longing for the exotic was awakened or at least strengthened in me by the romantic novellas I read so voraciously as a girl. The Vlach Roma used to come to our area when there were market-fairs. The peasants used to lock their courtyard gates before them, saying they stole, and our grandmother said to us: "Don't go after them, they'll grab you up and we'll never see you again!" While the market-fair lasted, the Vlachs spread out with their horses and carts on the meadow by the water. They traveled in carts with canvas drawn tight over them. And whenever I could, I ran after them to see if these mysterious "Gypsies" ate, drank, and cooked anything like people did! And to see what they did among themselves when others' eyes weren't watching. I stood gaping from the edge of the meadow so long they invited me closer, though at other times they kept strangers out. I couldn't get enough of watching the way their women cooked. First the woman swept the earth and unfolded a sparkling white towel on top of it. Then she rolled out the dough for *haluški* on top of it. Meanwhile her water would be heating up in a kettle. The kettle was hung on a *trajfuskos*, a low, three-legged stand. When the water was boiling, she draped the dough over her left arm and with her right hand tore off pieces, dropping them in the water. Her hand just flickered, and I could have watched her all day.

One day a Vlach Romani woman came to our house with a child that'd just been born. She was carrying him in an apron, completely naked. She had heard that my mother helped people. She remained standing by the door. Mama went and tore Papa's old undershirts into diapers. Then she gave the woman half of an old blanket so she could wrap the child up.

From that time on, the Vlach Roma allowed me to travel with them in their carts. I didn't have anything against their "stealing" me, as my grandmother used to say. And so one time I deliberately let myself be forgotten in their cart. Night fell and we traveled on and on, with me snuggled in a corner in the back. But suddenly the leader said: "Oh, oh, Mikluš' girl! They'll be looking for you at home!" And he ordered one of the men to take me back. Like it or not, I had to change over to his cart, and he drove the horses back to Šariš. He had such a skinny old nag that I was afraid it'd collapse at any moment. But we got there all right, and the Vlach asked my parents for forgiveness for bringing me back so late. Though my mother was strict, for some reason she didn't get angry that time. And even as a child I sensed that the things people said about the Vlachs weren't true. And it almost disappointed me, because if they had stolen me I could have traveled the world with them.

The Vlachs always had a lot of gold. They were nomadic, so they couldn't put their money into real estate, into houses or furniture, or into maintaining a property. Gold is easily transported and at the same time, valuable. So they kept their property in the form of gold. Their women wore gold chains, gold earrings, the men rings – and they all had gold teeth made. Many times they had their beautiful, white, healthy teeth pulled out and gold ones put in.

In 'fifty-nine an order forbidding nomadism came out. In a word, it was outlawed. For many Vlachs, it was absolutely devastating. Not only were they used to the nomadic lifestyle, but their way of making a living was also based on moving around the area. How were feather-cleaners or those who collected old paper, rags, or scrap iron supposed to make their living staying in one place? They had to travel around the area, and the people were glad the service came all the way to their house.

When nomadism was outlawed, many Vlachs tried to get permits for collecting old raw materials. It was very difficult, because at the time an opposing trend was under way to put an end to and forbid all private enterprise.

Once in the days when my husband and I were both working as officials, some Vlachs came to our apartment. A husband and wife. I remember it as if it were today, Jozef sitting on the couch and me standing at the stove cooking. They wanted a permit for collecting old raw materials. While the husband was explaining to Jozef why they had come, he wife came up to me from behind and hung a heavy gold chain on my neck. Jozef started shouting: "Forget about that! You've got some nerve! You want them to lock me up?!" Jozef was an honest man and also, he was afraid. Never in his life had he let himself be bribed. It meant a lot to him that people considered him a swell. He grabbed the gold chain and forced it back on the Vlach woman, into her hand. And he got them the collection permit, all the same.

Although I have recognized many times over in my life that the Vlachs are completely normal people, I still projected my romantic love stories onto their supposedly mysterious ways. I've written some of them out in Slovak. They have many pages. So far I haven't gone to any publisher with them. I've rewritten them many times. Or I had them rewritten and paid five crowns a page for that. That's another reason I had to supplement my retirement income – to pay the rewriter. Sometimes I feel sorry that these romantic stories still haven't come out. I'm convinced that lots of Roma and *gadže* would like them. On the other hand, life – and some of my close friends whom I respect – remind me that I should write more about the real life of Roma, and not in Slovak but in Romani. I've been trying hard to do more and more of this lately.

Chundruľa

I probably couldn't write about real life any other way than in Romani. Not because I couldn't do it in Slovak, but because if scenes from the settlements, from Romani home life, juicy curses and marvelous blessings come to mind, it is Romani words that ring in my ears; and I would have to look hard to find their Slovak counterparts. On the other hand, if I want to give someone some ideological training and teach them about culture, it isn't Romani but Slovak that comes from my pen. After all, it was my job to spread the political teachings blessed by the mouths of the highest party and government figures! But a mode of expression for such teachings still hasn't found its way into Romani, because that language was and is considered a kind of gibberish that lacks the basis for further development. For a person, for a Rom, it is sometimes very difficult to orient oneself in everything ... I'd like to write in Romani, very much so, but who would make it available to the public? Even my own children tell me: "What good does that do you, please, Mama, where do you think you'll get with that Gypsy-speak?" And at the same time I can feel what a beautiful language Romani is, and how rich and beautiful it could become if we looked after it a little. Not long ago I was ashamed to be reminded of that by an American man.

How did it happen? Back before World War I, my grandmother's cousin moved to America. We lost contact with them, knowing only that they lived in Chicago. They had children, grandchildren, and great-grandchildren there. One of those grandchildren or even great-grandchildren came to Czechoslovakia. Somehow he managed to find us, and he asked me to make the rounds of our relatives with him. At least the main ones, because to go around and see all of them – that would have taken us more than a year. This person knew only English and Romani. No Slovak. And he spoke such marvelous Romani that all of our hearts melted with happiness, and at the same time we were ashamed that we no longer knew how to speak our language so beautifully.

One day I went with him to Chmiňany, which is where my grandmother had the most relatives. It was a beautiful summer day, and I said: "What if we went mushroom-picking?" – *avas hubenge*? I used the Slovak word for mushrooms. He said: "What are *hubi*?" I realized that it was a Slovak word and thought over what the right Romani expression would be. I remember that Grandma called mushrooms something other than *hubi*, but what was it? "*Chundruľa*!" said the American. Just as Grandma used to say it! I don't know how and for what reason we replaced *chundruľa* with *hubi*. And a Rom from the other end of the world had to come here to remind me that my language isn't so impoverished, and that it makes sense to cultivate it.

In the last few years, I've been trying to write in Romani. I told myself: I'm no longer going to think about whether it will be published or not, but at least I'll have a clear conscience knowing that I said what I wanted and in the way that I wanted to say it. But there was one thing I lived to see: one of my short stories, *Sar o Filipos peske rodňa maro – How Phillip Earned the Money for His Bread –* was published in a bilingual version in the Prešov cultural review. The play *Žužika*, which I wrote in Romani, was broadcast on the radio, and though it was in my good friend Milena's Czech translation, it won a prize in the Prix Bohemia nationwide radio contest. I've written three one-act plays from life in Romani, one of which was staged by Roma from Bílovce near Nový Jičín, who invited me to the premiere of their amateur production, which made me enormously happy.

I don't know what else I'll live to see in my life. We'll see how my health holds up. My gall bladder, varicose veins, and my heart bother me. But I won't give up. I'm not going to let some illnesses tell me what to do! Now, when I can't run around as much as I used to, at least I have more time to think things over, to evaluate my life, and to consider what's right and what's not.

Still, I think that I was born under a lucky star – *uľiľom tel bachtaľi čercheň*. If I could be born all over again, I'd like to be born again as a Romani woman, to live the way I've lived, and to do what I've done. I hope that before I die I'll manage to do some more good for the Roma and for people in general. I'd like to write a good word about the truth of the Romani heart, and I believe that I'll live to see the day when that heart will win a good word from the rest of the world.

1986

Ilona Lacková signing copies of her book of Romani fairytales, 1994, Prešov.

Ilona Lacková on the road in search of clients, 1984.

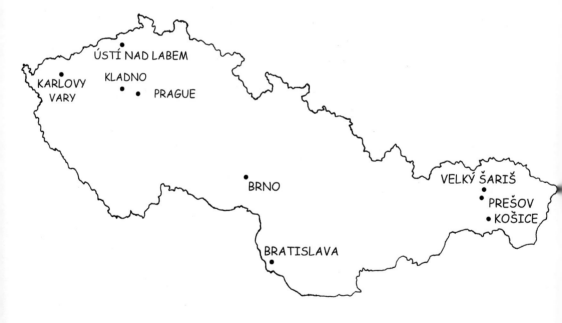

Map by Milena Hübschmanová showing the various towns where Ilona Lacková has liv
over the years. The map correspon
to the present-day Czech Republic and Slovak Republ

Glossary of Romani words and meanings

amare Roma — our Roma; Roma usually draw the border between "our" and "other, foreign" (*aver*) between the various subethnic Romani groups such as the Vlach Roma, the Slovak Roma, and the like. As necessary, it can also be drawn between the inhabitants of one settlement and those of other settlements, between *žuže Roma (qv.)*, clean Roma, and *degeše* (qv.), and so on. See also *Rom*.

aver — other, different, another; in the phrase *aver Roma* (other Roma), these are Roma who do not observe the same customs and speak a different dialect.

barvale Roma — rich Roma; among the settled Slovak Roma, the rich ones were mostly urban musicians and pig traders; *feder Roma*.

bašaviben — the way Romani musicians make their living, by playing; a traditional Romani entertainment, at which there is music, singing, and dancing; music in general.

bijav — a wedding, a wedding feast.

bižužo — unclean, an unclean force; a taboo expression for the devil or an evil spirt; sometimes used of snakes, of which it is believed that they are the incarnation of an evil force.

bľaškaris — the owner of a *bľaški* game (qv.)

bľaški — a gambling game which consists of the drawing of tin cards; qv. *bľaškavis*.

bodvana — a trough, a washtub.

bokhaľi vatra — a hungry settlement; a settlement of poor Roma.

bori — a daughter-in-law; the entire family uses this expression to refer to a girl whom one of the sons has brought into the family.

cikán (Cikán) — a Czech or Slovak term, the different forms of which are used in various European languages to refer to Roma *(qv. Rom)*. When the Roma first appeared in the Byzantine Empire at the beginning of this millenium and also in central Europe two centuries later, it was unknown who they were and where they came from. In several countries they were mistakenly identified with the Asia Minor sect of *athingani*, from which came the name *Zigeuner* (in German), *cygan* (in various Slavic languages), *Tsigane* (in French), and the like. Due to a persistent lack of mutual understanding between the majority societies of Europe and the Romani ethnic minority, the appellative *cikán* gradually acquired a negative connotation. For this reason, Roma distance themselves from this offensive term and prefer their ethnic name, Rom. During the preceding period of assimilationist policy in Czechoslovakia, the ethnonym *Rom* was considered a symbol of efforts to emancipate this ethnic group and was therefore not allowed to be used – except for the short period of the Prague Spring, when the first representative organization of Roma was created, the Union of Gypsies-Roma (*Svaz Cikánů-Romů*). This organization was forcibly disbanded in 1973. Communist ideology decreed that Roma were a social group whose ethnic identity was to become extinct as soon as possible, and in accordance with this doctrine Roma were designated "citizens of Gypsy origin."

ciral — curd cheese; *haluški ciraleha* Slovak dumplings served with curd cheese; *ačhel pro purano ciral* — literally, to stay on old curd cheese (to be left on the shelf).

čačipen — truth, right, justice, reality, experience.

čeranki — an exchange; *pre čeranki* – by exchange, a marriage by exchange: when two or more siblings from one family take siblings from another family as their wives or husbands. A very frequent custom among Roma.

čhaj (čhaja) — a girl (girls); a daughter; an unmarried girl, a young miss.

čhajori — a young Romani girl, a little girl.

čhavo — a Romani boy, a son.

čhibalo — the spokesperson, mayor (of a Romani settlement), a Romani mayor who gives away the betrothed at a wedding ceremony.

čhonoro — little moon.

degeš (degeše) — a Rom (Roma) who feeds on unclean food – horse or dog meat – who do unclean work, such as emptying cesspools, but also the production of unbaked bricks. Roma who consider themselves *žuže Roma* (qv.) hold *degeše* in contempt, do not have relations with them, and in their homes would not take a morsel of food into their mouths. Figuratively, the word *degeš* is used as an insult meaning an untidy, unclean, ragged, crude, or uncultured person.

denašel — to escape; to escape with one's chosen against the parents' will.

dilino — a fool; stupid, a madman, deranged.

džungalo — ugly; a taboo word for an unclean force, for a snake.

farahún — a slang word in Slovak for a Pharoah, by which villages pejoratively referred to Roma; in accordance with one of many mistaken, until recently widespread hypotheses, the Roma came from Egypt.

feder Roma — better Roma; Roma who in addition to being *žuže* (qv.) managed to acquire better housing and win greater social prestige. See also *amare Roma* and *barvale Roma*.

gadžo, gadži, gadže — non-Rom, non-Romani woman, non-Roma; a term which originally referred to every non-Rom, used in the social context of the Slovak village more or less as a synonym for a peasant (farmer).

god'aris — a person who cleans out cesspools, used figuratively as an insult.

gomboda — noodles, a traditional food.

haluški — a basic, traditional Romani food; prepared similarly to Slovak *haluški*, but different in flavor; the varieties of *haluški* dishes are based partly on different methods of preparing and cooking the dough, and partly on different flavorings. *Kikimen haluški* are prepared solely from grated raw potatoes; the dough holds together thanks to long and laborious kneading.

chundrul (chundrul'a) — mushroom (mushrooms).

indraľori — a small, red ribbon (thread) tied around a child's wrist to protect him or her from the evil eye and the influence of evil forces.

jag — fire; also figuratively to mean a skin disease.

jagalo paňi — fire water – water used to cure the evil eye; nine cinders are thrown into the water, and the number of cinders that sink to the bottom indicates how badly the person (usually a child) has been afflicted by the evil eye. The fire water is then used to wipe the wrist, forehead, chest, and finally is thrown onto a dog or cat, or against the hinges of a door, which is meant to convey the curse out of the house. In some places the water is also cast into the four corners of the room.

jepašgod — a half-shirt – a white shirt front with no back, worn by poor musicians under a black jacket when they went to play at a wedding or at a party.

jilo — heart, feeling; a word that evokes the feeling of group identity.

kalemardo — punished by blackness – a very dark complexion.

keriben — magic; an enchanted object, usually a strip of clothing, buried under the hearth, covered up in the stove, or secretly sewn into the lining of the coat of a person who is to have a spell cast on him; see also *kotor*.

kikimen haluški qv. *haluški*

kirno — rotten qv. *kirňavka*.

kirňavka (kirňavki) — potato (potatoes) which have been left in the field over the winter. In the early spring when there was nothing to eat, Roma gathered them and made flatcakes or *haluški* from them. See also kirno and *haluški*.

kirvo (kirvi, kirvipen) — godfather (godmother, godparenthood); the relationship of godparent to godchild is one of the basic relationships in a traditional Romani community, and it obligates the godparents to give mutual aid their whole life long.

kotor — a piece, a period of time, a payment; a strip of clothing from a person who is to have a spell cast on him. See also *keriben*.

kham, khamoro — sun, little sun.

kher — a house, flat, or room.

kuchňa — a kitchen; *kerel kuchňi* — Girls playing at cooking.

ladž; pre ladž — shame, disgrace; disgraceful. One who is disgraceful experiences public contempt expressed through mockery, insulting snatches of song, and the vocal condemnation of his transgression – every person's behavior is regulated by the avoidance of being shameful.

langoš — a fried, leavened flatcake.

lavutaris (lavutara) — musician (musicians).

lavutariko vatra — a settlement where most of the inhabitants make their living as musicians. Musicians' settlements had greater prestige than others.

l'imalo — Snot-nosed – a sniveling fellow.

mangavel — to court a girl; *mangavipen* - Courtship, engagement, after which a girl and boy usually begin to live together as man and wife.

marikl'i — a flatcake, usually just from flour and water, baked dry on a stovetop.

more! — a familiar form of address to a Romani man; Slovak villagers used this word to refer mockingly to Roma in general.

mulo (mule) — a dead person (dead people); the spirit of a dead person, which returns to earth and usually unleashes horror on the living. Belief in *mule* is widespread among all the Roma in the world.

ochmančaka — hoffman's tincture; an object of drug abuse in eastern Slovakia.

papin — a goose; considered a symbol of beauty because of its whiteness. Light-skinned Romani girls often had the nickname Papin, Papiňori (Little Goose).

papuči — a word of Persian origin (*pá-póš*, foot covering); instead of shoes, poor Roma wore a rag sewn together and stuffed with hay or straw.

paramisi (paramisa) — a fairy tale (fairy tales), qv. *vitejziko paramisi.*

parind — a piece of sackcloth, serving both as clothing as as a blanket.

pat'iv — honor, respect, courtesy, propriety.

piraňi, pirano — (female, male) sweetheart; the relationship between two sweethearts was a purely platonic love.

pišot (pišota) — pie(s) or turnover(s), usually filled with potatoes and onions, sprinkled with curd cheese and coated with melted butter.

phumbale jakha — infected eyes, conjunctivitis, sometimes trachoma, or some other eye disease.

pre čeranki qv. *čeranki*

pre ladž qv. *ladž*

prephaglo čhavoro — literally a "child broken in two;" an infant with muscle cramps from being carried badly.

pre vatra qv. *vatra*

pro purano ciral qv. *ciral*

rajkane Roma — high-class Roma; mostly urban musicians who played in coffeehouses and wine bars. They tended to be wealthy and often treated other Roma with condescension.

rakl'i (rakl'ija) — a non-Romani girl (girls).

raklo (rakle) — a non-Romani boy (boys).

Rom — an ethnonym or ethnic name by which Roma call themselves, and which they brought from their ancient homeland in India in barely altered phonetic form; qv. *cikán, gadžo*.

romano nav — romani name, a nickname by which a person is know among other Roma. It sometimes happened that even a person's closest relatives did not know the name entered in the birth registry (the so-called *gadžikano nav, gadžo* name).

rikoňaris — a Rom who makes his living from or feeds on dogs.

romipen — literally, Romaniness, Romani tradition, culture.

šinga — horns; (Christmas) baked goods in the form of rolls.

štokovcos — a multi-story house.

te denašel qv. *denašel*

tel e fala — by the wall; sitting by the wall of a shanty either on the ground or in squatting position was a typical leisure activity of Romani women. They usually kept vigilant watch over the doings of the settlement in the meantime – and thus every act of every individual was under constant, public scrutiny.

tel jekh thuv — under one smoke – used in the event of an engagement party and wedding taking place simultaneously.

te mangavel qv. *mangavel*

trajfuskos — a three-legged iron stand for cooking over an open fire.

udud — a small lantern made from a potato; fat, usually suet, is put inside the potato, and a small stick wound with a piece of rag serves as the wick.

úri — from the Hungarian word *úr*, nobleman; a term for a city official.

valka (valki) — unbaked bricks, produced from clay mixed with chaff; after being well kneaded, the material is dried in the sun in molds. Formerly the most frequent construction material in Slovak villages.

varošis — market-town.

vatra — a settlement; the common social area in the settlement; see also *lavutariko vatra, bokhaľi vatra*.

vičinel andro kher — to invite inside (literally, into the flat, into the house).

vitejziko paramisi — a heroic tale; a story lasting several hours, the central figure of which is the unassailable hero, usually a Rom. Hero tales were an enormous favorite.

zajda — a kerchief made from a folded blanket, in which Romani women carried their blacksmith husbands' wares, the foodstuffs for which they exchanged them, and various and sundry things. The corners of the blanket were tied in front, over the chest.

žužipen — both bodily and ritual cleanliness; qv. *žuže Roma*.

žuže Roma — clean Roma, Roma who observe cleanliness – Roma who do not eat unclean foods such as horse or dog meat, and who do not do "unclean jobs." Qv., *feder Roma, degeš,* and *žužipen.*

Guide to pronunciation

The reader may find the following notes helpful when pronouncing Slovak and Romani personal and place names found in the text. This guide is not, however, intended to present a complete overview of pronunciation in Slovak or in the eastern Slovak dialect of Romani used in this book.

Slovak words are stressed on the first syllable.

Vowels are pronounced as written in Slovak, whether stressed or unstressed Vowels with the ' mark are held longer, but their quality does not change. Slovak vowels may carry that mark wether stressed or unstressed:

a
pronounced like the *a* in *father*.

e
like the *e* in *bet* but more open.

i, y
like the *i* in *sit* but more closed.

o
like the *o* in *hot*, the lips rounded and protruded.

u
like the *u* in *book*, the lips again rounded and protruded.

The ´ mark over a vowel indicates that it is held for a longer time than without such a mark: *á* versus *a*.

Consonants are pronounced as in English, with the following exceptions:

c
is pronounced like the *ts* in *boats*.

č
is prounced like the *ch* in *cheese*.

ch
has no equivalent in English. It is a voiceless fricative pronounced by arching the tongue up to the soft palate and forcing air between the two. A similar sound is sometimes transliterated from Russian and other Slavic languages as *kh*.

g
is always pronounced like the *g* in *good*, never like the *g* in *general*.

j
is pronounced like the *y* in *yet*.

k, p, and *t*, aspirated in stressed English syllables, are always unaspirated in Slovak.

221

ľ

is pronounced like the *ly* in *all you* (unlike the unmarked *l*, which is pronounced as in English).

ň

is pronounced like the *n* in *onion*.

r

is trilled, as in many European languages.

š

is pronounced like the *sh* in *sheep*.

ť

is pronounced like the *ty* in *get you*.

ž

is pronounced like the *z* in *seizure*.

The above rules also apply to the eastern Slovak dialect of Romani used in this book, except that words in that dialect are stressed on the penultimate syllable and the vowel in that syllable held slightly longer. In addition, the ´ mark is not used to indicate a long vowel, as in Slovak since Romani vowels are lengthened only in the penultimate syllable of words and not elsewhere. Aspirated consonants are followed by *h*: e.g., *kh, ph, th, čh*, etc. The reader interested in learning more about this dialect of Romani may wish to consult the grammatical overview contained in *Romsko-český a česko-romský kapesní slovník* (Milena Hübschmannová *et al*, Prague: Státní pedagogický nakladatelství, 1991), pp. 611-651.

List of illustrations

The Interface Collection

Interface: a programme

The Gypsy Research Centre at the Université René Descartes, Paris, has been developing cooperation with the European Commission and the Council of Europe since the early 1980s. The Centre's task is to undertake studies and expert work at European level; a significant proportion of its work consists in ensuring the systematic implementation of measures geared towards improving the living conditions of Gypsy communities, especially through the types of action with which it is particularly involved, such as research, training, information, documentation, publication, coordination etc., and in fields which are also areas of research for its own teams: sociology, history, linguistics, social and cultural anthropology...

In order to effectively pursue this work of reflection and of action we have developed a strategy to facilitate the pooling of ideas and initiatives from individuals representing a range of different approaches, to enable all of us to cooperate in an organised, consistent fashion. The working framework we have developed over the years is characterised both by a solidity which lends effective support to activities, and by a flexibility conferring openness and adaptability. This approach, driven by an underlying philosophy outlined in a number of publications, notably the *Interface* newsletter, has become the foundation of our programme of reference.

Interface: a set of teams

A number of international teams play a key role within the programme framework, namely through their work in developing documentation, information, coordination, study and research. With the support of the European Commission, and in connection with the implementation of the Resolution on School Provision for Gypsy and Traveller Children adopted in 1989 by the Ministers of Education of the European Union, working groups on history, language and culture – *the Research Group on European Gypsy History, the Research and Action Group on Romani Linguistics,* and *the European Working Group on Gypsy and Traveller Education* – have already been established, as has a working group developing a Gypsy encyclopaedia. Additional support provided by the Council of Europe enables us to extend some of our work to cover the whole of Europe.

Interface: a network

- these Groups, comprising experienced specialists, are tackling a number of tasks: establishing contact networks linking persons involved in research, developing documentary databases relevant to their fields of interest, working as expert groups advising/collaborating with other teams, organising the production and distribution of teaching materials relevant to their fields;

- these productions, prepared by teams representing a number of different states, are the result of truly international collaboration; the composition of these teams means that they are in a position to be well acquainted with the needs and sensitivities of very different places and to have access to national, and local, achievements of quality which it is important to publicise;

- in order to decentralise activities and to allocate them more equitably, a network of publishers in different states has been formed, to ensure both local input and international distribution.

Interface: a Collection

A Collection was seen as the best response to the pressing demand for teaching materials, recognised and approved by the Ministers of Education in the above-mentioned Resolution adopted at European level, and also in the hope of rectifying the overall dearth of quality materials and in so doing to validate and affirm Gypsy history, language and culture.

Published texts carry the *Interface* label of the Gypsy Research Centre.

• they are conceived as being complementary with each other and with action being undertaken at European level, so as to produce a structured information base: such coherence is important for the general reader, and essential in the pedagogical context;

• they are, for the most part, previously unpublished works, which address essential themes which have been insufficiently explored to date, and because they do so in an original fashion;

• their quality is assured by the fact that all are written by, or in close consultation with, experienced specialists;

• although contributions come from specialists, the Collection is not aimed at specialists: it must be accessible/comprehensible to secondary level students, and by teachers of primary level pupils for classroom use. The authors write clear, well-structured texts, with bibliographical references given as an appendix for readers wishing to undertake a more in-depth study;

• although contributions come from specialists, the Collection is not aimed at any particular target group: in an intercultural approach to education, and given the content of each contribution, every student, and every teacher, should have access to Gypsy/Traveller-related information, and may have occasion to use it in the classroom. The texts on offer, the work of expert contributors, may embody new approaches to the topics covered (history, linguistics etc.) and as such be relevant not only to teachers, teacher trainers, pupils, students and researchers, but also social workers, administrators and policy makers;

• contributions may be accompanied by practical teaching aids or other didactic tools; these tools and materials are prepared by teams in the field, experienced teachers and participants in pilot projects. Their output is very illustrative of *Interface* programme dynamics : an association of diverse partners in a context of action-research, producing coordinated, complementary work, with a scope as broad as Europe, yet adapted to the local cultural and linguistic context;

• format is standardised for maximum reader-friendliness and ease of handling;

• the *Interface* collection is international in scope: most titles are published in a number of languages, to render them accessible to the broadest possible public.

A number of topics have been proposed, of which the following are currently being pursued:

> • *European Gypsy history*
> • *Life stories*
> • *Romani linguistics*
> • *Rukun*
> • *Reference works*

Jean-Pierre Liégeois
Director, Interface Collection

Titles in the Interface Collection: a reminder

*The **Interface** Collection is developed by the Gypsy Research Centre at the University René Descartes, Paris, with the support of the European Commission and of the Council of Europe.*

1 • Marcel Kurtiàde
- *Širpustik amare čhibǎqiri (*Livre de l'élève)   CRDP - ISBN : 2-86565-074-X
- Livre du maître disponible en : Albanais, Anglais, Français, Polonais, Roumain, Hongrois, Slovaque et espagnol.
  (Un numéro ISBN est attribué à chaque langue).

2 • Antonio Gómez Alfaro
- *La Gran redada de Gitanos*   PG - ISBN: 84-87347-09-6
- *The Great Gypsy Round-up*   PG - ISBN: 84-87347-12-6
- *La Grande rafle des Gitans*   CRDP - ISBN : 2-86565-083-9
- *La grande retata dei Gitani*   ANICIA/CSZ: 88-900078-2-6
- *Marea prigonire a Rromilor*   EA - ISBN: 973-9216-35-8
- *Die große Razzia gegen die Gitanos*   PA - ISBN: 3-88402-199-0
- *Velký proticikánský zátah*   VUP - ISBN: 80-7067-917-4

3 • Donald Kenrick
- *Gypsies: from India to the Mediterranean*   CRDP - ISBN : 2-86565-082-0
- *Los Gitanos: de la India al Mediterráneo*   PG - ISBN: 84-87347-13-4
- *Les Tsiganes de l'Inde à la Méditerranée*   CRDP - ISBN : 2-86565-081-2
- *Zingari: dall'India al Mediterraneo*   ANICIA/CSZ: 88-900078-1-8
- *Τσιγγάνοι : από τις Ινδίες σιη Μεσόγειο*   EK - ISBN: 960-03-1834-4
- *Циганите : от Индия до Средиземно море*   LIT - ISBN: 954-8537-56-7
- *Rromii: din India la Mediterana*   EA - ISBN: 973-9216-36-6
- *Sinti und Roma: Von Indien bis zum Mittelmeer*   PA - ISBN: 3-88402-201-6
- *Ciganos: da Índia ao Mediterrâneo*   SE - ISBN: 972-8339-15-1

4 • Elisa Mª Lopes da Costa
- *Os Ciganos: Fontes bibliográficas em Portugal*   PG - ISBN: 84-87347-11-8

5 • Marielle Danbakli
- *Textes des institutions internationales concernant les Tsiganes*   CRDP - ISBN : 2-86565-098-7
- *On Gypsies: Texts issued by International Institutions*   CRDP - ISBN : 2-86565-099-5
- *Текстове на международните институции за циганите*   LIT - ISBN: 954-8537-53-2

6 • Bernard Leblon
- *Gitans et flamenco*   CRDP - ISBN : 2-86565-107-X
- *Gypsies and Flamenco*   UHP - ISBN: 0 900 45859-3
- *Gitani e flamenco*   ANICIA/CSZ: 88-900078-8-5
- *Gitanos und Flamenco*   PA - ISBN: 3-88402-198-2

7 • David Mayall
- *English Gypsies and State Policies*   UHP - ISBN: 0 900 458 64 X

8 • D. Kenrick, G. Puxon
- *Gypsies under the Swastika*   UHP - ISBN: 0 900 458 65 8

- *Gitanos bajo la Cruz Gamada*   PG - ISBN: 84-87347-16-9
- *Les Tsiganes sous l'oppression nazie*   CRDP - ISBN : 2-86565-172-X
- *Хитлеризмът и циганите*   LIT - ISBN: 954-8537-57-5
- *Os Ciganos sob o domínio da suástica*   SE - ISBN: 972-8339-16-X

9 • Giorgio Viaggio
- *Storia degli Zingari in Italia*   ANICIA/CSZ: 88-900078-9-3

10 • D. Kenrick, G. Puxon
- *Bibaxtale Berśa*   PG - ISBN: 84-87347-15-0

11 • Jean-Pierre Liégeois
- *Minorité et scolarité : le parcours tsigane*   CRDP - ISBN : 2-86565-192-4
- *School Provision for Ethnic Minorities:*
  The Gypsy Paradigm   UHP - ISBN: 0 900 458 88 7
- *Minoría y Escolaridad: el Paradigma Gitano*   PG - ISBN: 84-87347-17-7
- *Die schulische Betreuung ethnischer Minderheiten:*
  Das Beispiel der Sinti und Roma   PA - ISBN: 3-88402-200-8

12 • K. Fings, H. Heuß, F. Sparing
- *Von der "Rassenforschung" zu den Lagern*
  Sinti und Roma unter dem Nazi-Regime - 1   ISBN: 3-88402-188-5
- *De la "science raciale" aux camps*
  Les Tsiganes dans la Seconde Guerre mondiale - 1   CRDP - ISBN : 2-86565-186-X
- *From "Race Science" to the Camps*
  The Gypsies during the Second World War - 1   UHP - ISBN: 0 900 458 78 X
- *Dalla "ricerca razziale" ai campi nazisti*
  Gli Zingari nella Seconda Guerra mondiale - 1   ANICIA/CSZ: 88-900078-3-4
- *De la "ştiinţa" rasială la lagărele de exterminare*
  Rromii în perioada regimului nazist - 1   EA - ISBN: 973-9216-68-4
- *De la "ciencia de las razas" a los campos de*
  exterminio Sinti y Romá bajo el Régimen Nazi - 1   PG - ISBN: 84-87347-20-7

13 • Joint authorship
- *In the shadow of the Swastika*
  The Gypsies during the Second World War - 2   UHP - ISBN: 0 900 458 85 2

14 • G. Donzello, B. M. Karpati
- *Un ragazzo zingaro nella mia classe*   ANICIA/CSZ: 88-900078-4-2

15 • A. Gómez Alfaro, E. M. Lopes da Costa, S. Sillers Floate
- *Deportaciones de Gitanos*   PG - ISBN: 84-87347-18-5
- *Ciganos e degredos*   SE - ISBN: 972-8339-24-0

16 • I. Lacková
- *A false dawn.*
  My life as a Gypsy woman in Slovakia   UHP - ISBN: 1-902806-00-X
- *Je suis née sous une bonne étoile…*
  Ma vie de femme tsigane en Slovaquie   HA - ISBN : 2-7384-8756-4

17 • Жан-Пиер Лиежоа
- *Роми, Цигани, Чергари*   LIT - ISBN : 954-8537-63-X

20 • Ouvrage collectif, Joint authorship

- *Europa se burla del Racismo Antología*
  internacional de humor antirracista   PG - ISBN : 84-87347-23-1
- *L'Europe se moque du racisme, Anthologie internationale d'humour antiraciste*
- *Europa pfeift auf den Rassismus, Internationale Anthologie des antirassistischen Humors*
- *Europe mocks Racism, International Anthology of Anti-Racist Humour*
- *L'Europa si beffa del Razzismo, Antologia internazionale di umorismo antirazzista*

The Rukun Series :

- *O Rukun ʒal and-i skòla*   Groupe de recherche et d'action en linguistique romani
                                      Research and Action Group on Romani Linguistics
                                                      RB - ISBN : 2-9507850-1-8
- *Kaj si o Rukun amaro ?*   Idem

                                                      RB - ISBN : 2-9507850-2-6

I bari lavenqi pustik e Rukunesqiri   Idem
- English: *Spot's Big Book of Words* / Français: *Le grand livre des mots de Spot*
                                                      RB - ISBN : 2-9507850-3-4
- Castellano: *El gran libro de las palavras de Rukún*
  Português: *O grande livro das palavras de Rukún*   PG - ISBN : 84-87347-22-3

All orders, whether direct or through a bookshop, should be addressed directly to the relevant publisher. Generally speaking, the publishers will be able to offer discounts for bulk purchase by associations, administrative bodies, schools etc. Inter-publisher agreements should make all titles easily obtainable : for example the English version of *From India to the Mediterranean* can be ordered from UHP, customers in Spain should contact their local supplier, PG, for copies of *Širpustik amare čhibǎqiri*, etc.

Publishers' Addresses:

• **ANICIA** (avec le *Centro Studi Zingari*)
Via San Francesco a Ripa, 62
I - 00153 Roma

• **CRDP** —
Centre Régional de Documentation
Pédagogique Midi-Pyrénées
3 rue Roquelaine
F - 31069 Toulouse Cedex

• **CSZ** — Centro Studi Zingari
(avec *Anicia*)
Via dei Barbieri, 22
I - 00186 Roma

• **EA** — Editura Alternative
Casa Presei, Corp. A, Et. 6
Piaţa Presei Libere, 1
RO - 71341 Bucureşti 1

• **EK** — Editions Kastaniotis /
ΕΚΔΟΣΕΙΣ ΚΑΣΤΑΝΙΩΤΗ
11, Zalogou
GR - 106 78 Athènes

• **HA** — Editions L'Harmattan
5-7, rue de l'Ecole Polytechnique
F - 75005 Paris

• **LIT** — Maison d'Edition Litavra /
за Литавра
BG - 1000 Sofia

• **PA** — Edition Parabolis
Schliemannstraße 23
D - 10437 Berlin

• **PG** — Editorial Presencia Gitana
Valderrodrigo, 76 y 78
E - 28039 Madrid

• **SE** — Entreculturas / Secretariado
Coordenador
dos Programas de Educação Multicultural
Trav. das Terras de Sant'Ana, 15 - 1°
PT - 1250 Lisboa

• **UHP** — University of Hertfordshire Press
College Lane - Hatfield
UK - Hertfordshire AL10 9AB

• **VUP** — Univerzita Palackého v
Olomouci - Vydavatelství
Palacky University Press
Křížkovského 8
CZ - 771 47 Olomouc

• *distribution de certains Rukun / for some
Rukun titles:*
RB — Rromani Baxt
22, rue du Port
F - 63000 Clermont-Ferrand

• *distribution en Irlande / distribution in
Ireland :*
Pavee Point Travellers Centre
46 North Great Charles Street
IRL - Dublin 1